495
F 7

D0593082

DISCARD
DISCARD

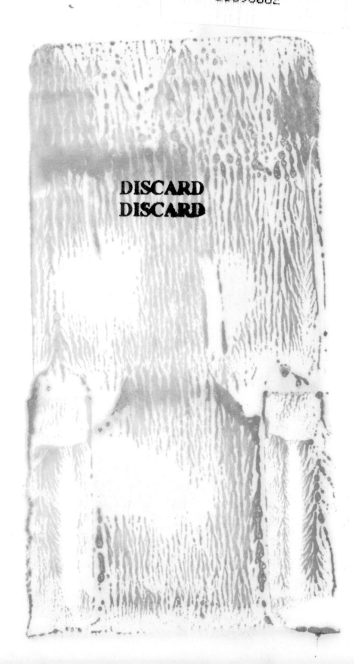

$ 4.95

WHAT WAS NATURALISM?

By the same author

Incident at Harper's Ferry

The Casebook of Ezra Pound
(with William Van O'Connor)

What Was
NATURALISM?

Materials for an Answer

Edited by **EDWARD STONE**
Ohio University

APPLETON-CENTURY-CROFTS, INC.

New York

Copyright © 1959 by
APPLETON-CENTURY-CROFTS, INC.

*All rights reserved. This book, or parts
thereof, must not be reproduced in any
form without permission of the publisher.*

627–6

LIBRARY OF CONGRESS CARD NUMBER: 59–8084

PRINTED IN THE UNITED STATES OF AMERICA

E–84913

To

MARJ

and

THE THREE

FIERY-EYED SNUFFIES

PREFACE

TRYING TO UNDERSTAND the state of mind of a particular period of literature is always an engaging pursuit, though it frequently proves as baffling as it is rewarding. Attempting to perceive a single cluster of ideas as it emerges in the writings of earlier generations and as it structures and flavors the literature of a later time usually proves less baffling though no less rewarding. The selections included here under the title *What Was Naturalism?: Materials for an Answer* encircle a significant pattern of ideas and reveal some of the uses of these ideas in American literature.

Scholars seldom agree wholeheartedly in the answers they give to questions concerning the mental climate of an age or the significant ideas that undulate through it. In the case of Naturalism, any answers to such questions are complicated by the fact that literary critics and historians have used the term *"naturalism"* to describe both an artistic *technique* as well as intellectual *content*. Professor Robert E. Spiller's warning of "the pitfalls into which this word leads its victims" is thus still a timely one. In spite of these complexities that underline a need for caution, there remains the perennially challenging adventure of defining terms in accord with historical fact and logical clarity.

Although there is now some agreement concerning the theoretical works that are most directly responsible for the literature of Naturalism, these works are largely inaccessible today. Modern college students are, accordingly, forced to rely on editorial assurance that certain foreign theories, presented to them either in paraphrase or in some key term, inspired certain achievements in American literature. This is regrettable. Granted that the prose of theorists, foreign or domestic, can be tirelessly voluminous and stylistically forbidding, surely it once burned with brightness and won applause, even though most of it now lies ashen and neglected in the 10-to-25¢ bins of second-hand bookstores. Is there no living spark left in these discarded works, works whose perspectives have so thoroughly permeated our thinking that their original dimensions of men, moments, and ideas are now sunk below our sight?

The present volume attempts to raise the basic question and to provide the basic documents for informed, though by no means final, answers to Naturalism in theory and practice. Its First Part is an anthology of important selections from most of the foreign theorists acknowledged at one time or another to have influenced the literature of Naturalism. These writers represent practically every facet of nineteenth-century thought. Although their multivolumed wisdom has had to be abridged, selections are provided from their most influential works. Here, then, it is hoped, is offered the gist, not only of a book, but of a mind. Part II is an anthology of the recognized or disputed examples of Naturalism in American literature. Here again, in an effort at a mean between snatches and saturation, two or more works by each writer are provided in several cases. Questions in Part III lead the student to a synthesis and correlation. A thorough study of the documents in Part I will make it possible for him to attempt his own definition of Naturalism, and then to apply this definition to the poems, stories, and novels in Part II. Although the selections and apparatus of these first three parts are designed to be largely self-sufficient, Part IV leads the interested student beyond the materials presented by suggesting parallel topics for investigation. These topics begin where those of Part III leave off. Finally, accompanying Part IV and facilitating such further research as it suggests, there is a useful general bibliography of the subject of Naturalism.

The uses of this book, then, are two. One is in courses in American Civilization or in the definition of ideas. The other is in the theory and writing of the research paper. As a text of controlled research materials, this book provides another way out of the growing difficulty and undesirability of assigning to hundreds of students hundreds of topics for compositions based largely on sources available only in the college or university library. At the same time it fosters intellectual independence and integrity on the part of students by teaching them to rely on *primary* rather than on *secondary* source materials. In order to simulate ideal library-research procedures, the examples cited here have been taken mostly from the original American editions of foreign source books and native literature. Page references to the original work are given in the text of articles. Topics are included not only for the usual end-product—the long, documented "Term Paper"—but also for many short research exercises. Throughout the selections, key terms as well as structural and comparative questions are raised. These terms and questions urge the student to acquire the necessary groundwork for the writing of short and long papers.

One final word: It would be helpful if the instructor, on the basis of his own experience, could make his students aware at the outset both of the possibilities and the limitations of this kind of undertaking. He might say to them in effect: "We will have to resign ourselves in advance to the realization that—unlike the paleontologist reconstructing with one bone the entire skeleton of a prehistoric animal—it will never be possible for us to reassemble the mind of a buried generation. Even when we know whether such-and-such a novelist walked or dashed to his desk, was mutilated in a long war or never heard of one, believed that God was a thunder in the sky or a shout in the street, and was inspired by the Virgin or the Dynamo—even then we shall be no better qualified to say with certainty what connection there was between these facts and the novels he wrote. But unless we at least look in the expected places, we are not likely to learn anything at all about him. One of the places in which to look is among the correspondences between the theories of one generation and the literature of the next. These can generally be meaningful. How far the ripples extend from the dropped pebble of an idea may be hard to determine; but that some pebble was dropped and that ripples move outward, there is no doubt."

ACKNOWLEDGMENTS

Many people, it is pleasing to record, contributed to the making of this book: Miss Katharine Beville, of the Alderman Library of the University of Virginia; Mr. Thomas A. Bledsoe, of Cambridge, Mass.; Professor Sculley Bradley, of the University of Pennsylvania; Mr. Harold J. Dies, of Brooklyn, N.Y.; Professor Robert Elias, of Cornell University; Dr. Donald C. Gallup, of the Yale University Library; Professor Stanley Grean, of Ohio University; Professor Luther S. Mansfield, of Williams College; Miss Miriam Minor, of New York City; Professor B. R. McElderry, Jr., of the University of Southern California; Professor Walter F. Naumann, of the Ohio State University; Miss Ann C. Parshall, of the Princeton University Library; Mrs. Jean Pizzo, of Harper & Brothers; Professor Lyon N. Richardson, of Western Reserve University; Mrs. Ann Roe, of Ohio University; Professor Robert W. Stallman, of the University of Connecticut;

Professor Wallace Stegner, of Stanford University; Mrs. Janet Tudor, of Ohio University; and Mrs. Neda Westlake, of the University of Pennsylvania Library. Since most of them had only a hazy notion of what they were aiding and abetting, I testify to their innocence of any of the book's faults. Yet if, as Stephen Crane's little Easterner insists, every sin is the result of a collaboration, so is every textbook.

To several people I owe unusual debts. Mr. William B. Goodman, of New York City, shared with me the original, vital "shock of recognition" about Naturalism. Miss Catherine Nelson, of the Ohio University Library, was my right (bibliographical) hand. And Appleton-Century-Crofts, Inc. enabled me to reintroduce into student society many fine old members of an even older family—their own.

Ohio University   E. S.

CONTENTS

COVER: *Bandit's Roost*, Mulberry Street, New York City (*c.* 1888). Photograph by Jacob A. Riis. The Jacob A. Riis Collection, Museum of the City of New York. Print by Rolf Petersen.

Part I

INDIVIDUAL THEORISTS

❧ THOMAS R. MALTHUS

An Essay on the Principle
of Population

[Rev. Thomas R. Malthus], *An Essay on the Principle of Population, etc.*, London, 1798.

. . . THE POWER OF POPULATION is indefinitely greater than the power in the earth to produce subsistence for man. [13]

Population, when unchecked, increases in a geometrical ratio. Subsistence increases only in an arithmetical ratio. A slight acquaintance with numbers will show the immensity of the first power in comparison with the second.

By that law of our nature which makes food necessary to the life of man, the effects of these two unequal powers must be kept equal.

This implies a strong and constantly operating check on population from the difficulty of subsistence. This difficulty must fall somewhere; and must necessarily be severely felt by a large portion of mankind.

Through the animal and vegetable kingdoms, nature has scattered the seeds [14] of life abroad with the most profuse and liberal hand. She has been comparatively sparing in the room, and the nourishment necessary to rear them. The germs of existence contained in this spot of earth, with ample food, and ample room to expand in, would fill millions of worlds in the course of a few thousand years. Necessity, that imperious all pervading law of nature, restrains them within the prescribed bounds. The race of plants and the race of animals shrink under this great restrictive law. And the race of man cannot, by any efforts of reason, escape from it. Among plants and animals its effects are waste of seed, sickness, and premature death. Among mankind, misery and vice. The former, misery, is an absolutely necessary consequence of it. Vice is a highly probable consequence, and we therefore see it [15] abundantly prevail; but it ought not, perhaps, to be called an absolutely necessary consequence. The ordeal of virtue is to resist all temptation to evil. . . .

3

I see no way by which man can escape from the weight of this law which pervades all animated nature. No fancied equality, no agrarian regulations in their utmost extent, could remove the pressure of it even for a single century. And it appears, therefore, to be decisive against the possible existence of [16] a society, all the members of which should live in ease, happiness, and comparative leisure; and feel no anxiety about providing the means of subsistence for themselves and families.

Consequently, if the premises are just, the argument is conclusive against the perfectibility of the mass of mankind. . . . [17]

Taking the population of the world at any number, a thousand millions for instance, the human species would increase in the ratio of— 1, 2, 4, 8, 16, 32 . . . and subsistence as—1, 2, 3, 4, 5, 6. . . . In two centuries and a quarter, the population would be to the means of [25] subsistence as 512 to 10: in three centuries as 4096 to 13; and in two thousand years the difference would be almost incalculable, though the produce in that time would have increased to an immense extent.

No limits whatever are placed to the productions of the earth; they may increase forever and be greater than any assignable quantity; yet still the power of population being a power of a superior order, the increase of the human species can only be kept commensurate to the increase of the means of subsistence, by the constant operation of the strong law of necessity acting as a check upon the greater power.

The effects of this check remain now to be considered. [26]

Among plants and animals the view of the subject is simple. They are all impelled by a powerful instinct to the increase of their species; and this instinct is interrupted by no reasoning, or doubts about providing for their offspring. Whenever therefore there is liberty, the power of increase is exerted; and the superabundant effects are repressed afterwards by want of room and nourishment, which is common to animals and plants; and among animals, by becoming the prey of others.

The effects of this check on man are more complicated. Impelled to the increase of his species by an equally powerful instinct, reason interrupts his career, and asks him whether he may not bring beings into the world for whom he can not provide the means of subsistence. . . . [27] Yet in all societies, even those that are most vicious, the tendency to a virtuous attachment is so strong, that there is a constant effort towards an increase of population. This constant effort as constantly tends to subject the lower classes of the society to distress, and to prevent any great permanent amelioration of their condition.

The way in which these effects are produced seems to be this. We will suppose the means of subsistence in any country just equal to the easy support of its inhabitants. The constant effort towards population, which is found to act even in the most vicious societies, increases the number of people before the means of subsistence are [29] increased. The food therefore which before supported seven millions must now be divided among seven millions and a half or eight millions. The poor consequently must live much worse; and many of them be reduced to severe distress. The number of labourers also being above the proportion of the work in the market, the price of labour must tend toward a decrease; while the price of provisions would at the same time tend to rise. The labourer herefore must work harder to earn the same as he did before. During this season of distress, the discouragements to marriage and the difficulty of rearing a family are so great that population is at a stand [still]. In the meantime the cheapness of labour, the plenty of labourers, and the necessity of an increased industry amongst them encourage cultivators to employ more labour upon their land; to turn up fresh soil; and to [30] manure and improve more completely what is already in tillage; till ultimately the means of subsistence become in the same proportion to the population as at the period from which we set out. The situation of the labourer being then again tolerably comfortable, the restraints to population are in some degree loosened; and the same retrograde and progressive movements with respect to happiness are repeated. . . . [31]

It is undoubtedly a most disheartening reflection that the great obstacle in the way to any extraordinary improvement in society is of a nature that we can never hope to overcome. . . . [Yet enough] remains to be done for mankind to animate us to the most unremitted exertion. But [we must] proceed [with] a thorough knowledge and accurate comprehension of the nature, extent, and magnitude of the difficulties we have to encounter. . . . [347]

In all our attempts . . . to 'find out the Almighty to perfection,' it seems absolutely necessary that we should reason from nature up to nature's God, and not presume to reason from God to nature. . . . [350] Infinite power is so vast and incomprehensible an idea, that the mind of man must necessarily be bewildered in the contemplation of it.

With the crude and puerile conceptions which we sometimes form of this attribute of the Deity, we might imagine that God could call into being myriads and myriads of existences, all free from pain and imperfection, all eminent in goodness and wisdom, all capable of the highest enjoyments, and unnumbered as the points throughout infinite space. But when from these vain and extravagant dreams of fancy we turn our eyes to the book of nature, where alone we can read God as he is, we see a [351] constant succession of sentient beings rising apparently from so many specks of matter, going through a long and sometimes painful process in this world, but many of them attaining ere the termination of it such high qualities and powers as seem to indicate their fitness for some superior state. Ought we not then . . . to conclude that even to the Great Creator, Almighty as he is, a certain process may be necessary, a certain time (or at least what appears to us as time) may be requisite in order to form beings with those exalted qualities of mind which will fit them for his high purposes? [352]

A state of trial seems to imply a previously formed existence that does not agree with the appearance of man in infancy, and indicates something like suspicion and want of foreknowledge inconsistent with those ideas which we wish to cherish of the Supreme Being. I should be inclined therefore . . . to consider the world and this life as the mighty process of God, not for the trial, but for the creation and formation of mind; a process necessary to awaken inert, chaotic matter into spirit; to sublimate the dust of the earth into soul; to elicit an ethereal spark from the clod of clay. . . . [353]

The savage would slumber forever under his tree unless he were roused from his torpor by the cravings of hunger or the pinchings of cold; and the exertions that he makes to avoid these evils by procuring food and building himself a covering are the exercises which form and keep in motion his faculties, which otherwise would sink into listless inactivity. From all that experience has taught us concerning the structure of the human mind, if those stimulants to exertion which arise from the wants of the body were removed [357] from the mass of mankind, we have much more reason to think that they would be sunk to the level of brutes from a deficiency of excitements than that they would be raised to the rank of philosophers by the possession of leisure. In those countries where nature is the most redundant in spontaneous produce, the inhabitants will not be found the most remarkable for acuteness of intellect. Necessity has been with great truth called the mother of invention. . . . [358]

[To] urge man to further the gracious designs of Providence by the full cultivation of the earth, it has been ordained that population should increase much faster than food. This general law . . . undoubtedly produces much partial evil; but a little [361] reflection may perhaps satisfy us that it produces a great overbalance of good. . . . [362]

The infinite variety of the forms and operations of nature, besides tending immediately to awaken and improve the mind by the variety of impressions that it creates, opens other fertile sources of improvement, by offering so wide and extensive a field for investigation and research. Uniform, undiversified perfection could not possess the same awakening powers. When we endeavour then to contemplate the system of the universe; when we think of the stars as the suns of other systems, scattered throughout infinite space; when we reflect that we [378] do not probably see a millionth part of those bright orbs that are beaming light and life to unnumbered worlds; when our minds, unable to grasp the immeasurable conception, sink, lost and confounded, in admiration at the mighty incomprehensible power of the Creator; let us not querulously complain that all climates are not equally genial; that perpetual spring does not reign throughout the year; that all God's creatures do not possess the same advantages; that clouds and tempests sometimes darken the natural world, and vice and misery, the moral world; and that all the works of the creation are not formed with equal perfection. Both reason and experience seem to indicate to us that the infinite variety of nature . . . is admirably adapted to further the high purpose of the creation, and to produce the greatest possible quantity of good. . . . [379]

If a revelation from heaven . . . were to dispel the mist that now hangs over metaphysical subjects, were to explain . . . the mode in which the Supreme Being operates in the works of the creation and the whole plan and scheme of the Universe, such an accession of knowledge, so obtained, instead of giving additional vigour and activity to the human mind, would, in all probability, tend to repress future exertion and to damp the soaring wings of intellect.

For this reason I have never considered the doubts and difficulties that [384] involve some parts of the sacred writings as any argument against their divine original. The Supreme Being might undoubtedly have accompanied his revelations to man by such a succession of miracles, and of such a nature as would have produced universal over-powering conviction, and have put an end at once to all hesitation and discussion. But weak as our reason is to comprehend the plans of the Great Creator, it is yet sufficiently strong to see the most strik-ing objections to such a revelation. . . . A[n] overpowering convic-tion of this kind, instead of tending to the improvement and moral amelioration of man, would act like the touch of a torpedo on all in-tellectual exertion, and [385] would almost put an end to the existence of virtue. If the scriptural denunciations of eternal punishment were brought home with . . . certainty to every man's mind . . . , this one vast and gloomy idea would take such full possession of the hu-man faculties as to leave no room for any other conceptions: the ex-ternal actions of men would be all nearly alike: virtuous conduct would be no indication of virtuous disposition: vice and virtue would be blended together in one common mass. . . . Under such a dis-pensation it is difficult to conceive how human beings could be formed to [386] a detestation of moral evil and a love and admiration of God and of moral excellence. [387]

When we reflect on the temptations to which man must necessarily be exposed in this world, from the structure of his frame and the op-eration of the laws of nature, and the consequent moral certainty that many vessels will come out of this mighty creative furnace in wrong shapes, it is perfectly impossible to conceive that any of these [388] creatures of God's hand can be condemned to eternal suf-fering. Could we once admit such an idea, all our natural conceptions of goodness and justice would be completely overthrown and we could no longer look up to God as a merciful and righteous Being. But the doctrine of life and immortality which was brought to light by the gospel, the doctrine that the end of righteousness is everlasting life but that the wages of sin are death, is in every respect just and merciful and worthy of the Great Creator. Nothing can appear more consonant to our reason than that those beings which come out of the creative process of the world in lovely and beautiful forms should be crowned with immortality, while those which come out mis-shapen . . . [389] should perish and be condemned to mix again with their original clay. Eternal condemnation of this kind may be con-sidered as a species of eternal punishment; and it is not [surprising] that it should be represented sometimes under images of suffering. But life and death, salvation and destruction, are more frequently opposed to each other in the New Testament than happiness and

misery. The Supreme Being [cannot be thought of] as pursuing the
creatures that had offended him with eternal hate and torture instead of merely condemning to their original insensibility those beings that, by the operation of general laws, had not been formed with
qualities suited to a purer state of happiness. [390]

Life is, generally speaking, a blessed independent of a future
state. . . . The partial pain, therefore, that is inflicted by the Supreme Creator while he is forming numberless beings to a capacity
of the highest enjoyments is but as the dust of the balance in comparison of the happiness that is communicated; and we have every
reason to think that there is no more evil in the world than what is
absolutely necessary as one of the ingredients in the mighty process. . . . [391]

[T]he infringement [on] the general laws of nature by a divine
revelation will appear in the light of the immediate hand of God mix-
ing new ingredients in the mighty mass, suited to the particular state
of the process and calculated to give rise to a new and powerful train
of impressions tending to purify, exalt, and improve the human mind.
The miracles that accompanied these revelations, when they had
once excited the attention of mankind . . . had answered the purpose of the Creator, and these communications of the divine will
were afterwards left to make their way [392] by their own intrinsic
excellence, and by operating as moral motives, gradually to influence and improve, and not to overpower and stagnate the faculties
of man. . . . [393]

The idea that the impressions and excitements of this world are
the instruments with which the Supreme Being forms matter into
mind and that the necessity of constant exertion to avoid evil and to
pursue good is the principal spring of these impressions and excitements seems to smooth many of the difficulties that occur in a contemplation of human life, and appears to me to give a satisfactory reason
for the existence of natural and moral evil; and consequently for that
part of both——and it certainly is not a very small part——which
arises from the principle of population. [394]

Evil exists in the world, not to create despair, but activity. We are
not patiently to submit to it, but to exert ourselves to avoid it. It is
not only the interest but the duty of every individual to use his utmost
efforts to remove evil from himself and from as large a circle as he
can influence; [395] and the more he exercises himself in this duty,
the more wisely he directs his efforts and the more successful these

efforts are, the more he will probably improve and exalt his own mind
and the more completely does he appear to fulfil the will of his Creator. [396]

𝕰 SIR CHARLES LYELL

Principles of Geology

Sir Charles Lyell, *Principles of Geology* [1830–1832], New
and Entirely Revised Edition [9th], New York, D. Appleton &
Co., 1854.

RECENT ORIGIN OF MAN

. . . SINCE THE EOCENE PERIOD there have been several great changes
in the land quadrupeds inhabiting Europe, probably not less than
five complete revolutions, during which there has been no step whatever made in advance, no elevation in the scale of being; so that had
man been created at the commencement of the Eocene era, he would
not have constituted a greater innovation on the state of the animal
creation previously established than now, when we believe him to
have begun to exist at the close of the Pleiocene. . . . From the earliest period at which plants and animals can be proved to have existed,
there has been a continual change going on in the position of land
and sea, accompanied by great fluctuations of climate. To these ever-
varying geographical and climatal conditions the state of the animate
world has been unceasingly adapted. No satisfactory proof has yet
been discovered of the gradual passage of the earth from a chaotic
to a more habitable state, nor of any law of progressive development
governing the extinction and renovation of species, and causing the
fauna and flora to pass from an embryonic to a more perfect condition, from a simple to a more complex organization. . . . [146]

If, then, the popular theory of the successive development of the
animal and the vegetable world, from the simplest to the most perfect
forms, rests on a very insecure foundation, it may be asked whether

the recent origin of man lends any support to the same doctrine, or how far the influence of man may be considered as such a deviation from the analogy of the order of things previously established, as to weaken our confidence in the uniformity of the course of nature.

Antecedently to investigation, we might reasonably have anticipated that the vestiges of man would have been traced back at least as far as those modern strata in which all the testacea and a certain number of the mammalia are of existing species, for of all the mammalia the human species is the most cosmopolite, and perhaps more capable than any other of surviving considerable vicissitudes in climate, and in the physical geography of the globe.

No inhabitant of the land exposes himself to so many dangers on the waters as man . . . and there is no animal, therefore, whose skeleton is so liable to become imbedded in lacustrine or submarine deposits. . . . [147]

But so far as our interpretation of physical movements has yet gone, we have every reason to infer that the human race is extremely modern . . . and we may, therefore, ask whether his creation can be considered as one step in a supposed progressive system, by which the organic world has advanced slowly from a more simple to a more complex and perfect state? If we concede . . . that the sponge, the cephalopod, the fish, the reptile, the bird, and the mammifer have followed each other in regular chronological order, the creation of each class being separated from the other by vast intervals of time, should we be able to recogize, in man's entrance upon the earth, the last term of one and the same series of progressive developments?

In reply to this question, it should first be observed that the superiority of man depends not on those faculties and attributes which he shares in common with the inferior animals, but on his reason, by which he is distinguished from them. When it is said that the human race is of far higher dignity than were any pre-existing beings on the earth, it is the intellectual and moral attributes only of our race, not the animal, which are considered; and it is by no means clear that the organization of man is such as would confer a decided pre-eminence upon him, if, in place of his reasoning powers, he was merely provided with such instincts as are possessed by the lower animals.

If this be admitted, it would by no means follow, even if there had been sufficient geological evidence in favour of the theory of progressive development, that the creation of man was the last link in the same chain. For the sudden passage from an irrational to a rational animal is a phenomenon of a distinct kind from the passage from the more simple to the more perfect forms of animal organization and instinct. To pretend that such a step, or rather leap, can be part of a regular series of changes in the animal world is to strain analogy beyond all reasonabe bounds.

Introduction of man, to what extent a change in the system.— But setting aside the question of progressive development, another and a far more difficult one may arise out of the admission that man is comparatively of modern origin. . . . [148] If such an innovation could take place after the earth had been exclusively inhabited for thousands of ages by inferior animals, why should not other changes as extraordinary and unprecedented happen from time to time? . . . What security have we that they may not arise hereafter? . . .

Now these objections would be unanswerable if adduced against one . . . disposed to indulge in the philosophical reveries of some Egyptian and Greek sects who represented all the changes both of the moral and material world as repeated at distant intervals, so as to follow each other in their former connection of place and time. For they compared the course of events on our globe to astronomical cycles; and . . . they taught that on earth, as well as in the heavens, the same identical phenomena recurred again and again in a perpetual vicissitude. The same individual men were doomed to be reborn, and to perform the same actions as before; the same arts were to be invented, and the same cities built and destroyed. . . .

The geologist, however, may condemn these tenets as absurd without running into the opposite extreme and denying that the order of nature has from the earliest periods been uniform in the same sense in which we believe it to be uniform at present, and expect it to remain so in future. We have no reason to suppose that when man first became master of a small part of the globe, a greater change took place in its physical condition than is now experienced when districts, never before inhabited, become successively occupied by new settlers. . . . [149] In reasoning on the state of the globe immediately before our species was called into existence, we must be guided by the same rules of induction as when we speculate on the state of America in the interval that elapsed between the introduction of man into Asia, the supposed cradle of our race, and the arrival of the first adventurers on the shores of the New World. In that interval, we imagine the state of things to have gone on according to the order now observed in regions unoccupied by man. Even now, the waters of lakes, seas, and the great ocean, which teem with life, may be said to have no immediate relation to the human race—to be portions of the terrestrial system of which man has never taken, nor ever can take, possession; so that the greater part of the inhabited surface of the planet may remain still as insensible to our presence as before any isle or continent was appointed to be our residence. . . . The course of nature remains evidently unchanged; and in like manner we may suppose the general condition of the globe immediately before and after the period when our species first began to exist to have been the same, with the exception only of man's presence.

The modifications in the system of which man is the instrument do not perhaps constitute so great a deviation from previous analogy as we usually imagine; we often, for example, form an exaggerated estimate of the extent of our power in extirpating some of the inferior animals and causing others to multiply. . . . [150] The larger beasts of prey in particular give way before us; but other quadrupeds of smaller size, and innumerable birds, insects, and plants which are inimical to our interests increase in spite of us, some attacking our food, others our raiment and persons, and others interfering with our agricultural and horticultural labours. We behold the rich harvest which we have raised by the sweat of our brow devoured by myriads of insects, and are . . . incapable of arresting their depredations. . . . We are often misled . . . by our knowledge of the wide distinction between the instincts of animals and the reasoning power of man, and we are apt hastily to infer that the effects of a rational and irrational species, considered merely as *physical agents*, will differ almost as much as the faculties by which their actions are directed.

It is not, however, intended that a real departure from the antecedent course of physical events cannot be traced in the introduction of man. If that latitude of action which enables the brutes to accommodate themselves in some measure to accidental circumstances could be imagined to have been at any former period so great that the operations of instinct were as much diversified as are those of human reason, it might, perhaps, be contended that the agency of man did not constitute an anomalous deviation from the previously established order of things. It might then have been said that the earth's becoming at a particular period the residence of human beings was an era in the moral, not in the physical, world—that our study and contemplation of the earth and the laws which govern its animate productions ought no more to be considered in the light of a disturbance or deviation from the system than the discovery of the satellites of Jupiter should be regarded as a physical event effecting those heavenly bodies. Their influence in advancing the progress of science among men, and in aiding navigation and commerce was accompanied by no reciprocal action [151] of the human mind upon the economy of nature in those distant planets; and so the earth might be conceived to have become at a certain period a place of moral discipline and intellectual improvement to man, without the slightest derangement of a previously existing order of change in its animate and inanimate productions.

The distinctness, however, of the human from all other species . . . is real; for we stand in a relation to contemporary species of animals and plants widely different from that which other irrational animals can ever be supposed to have held to each other. We modify their instincts, relative numbers, and geographical distribution, in a manner superior in degree, and in some respects very different in kind, from that in which any other species can affect the rest. Besides, the progressive movement of each successive generation of men causes the human species to differ more from itself in power at two distant periods than any one species of the higher order of animals differs from another. The establishment, therefore, by geological evidence, of the first intervention of such a peculiar and unprecedented agency long after other parts of the animate and inanimate world existed affords ground for concluding that the experience during thousands of ages of all the events which may happen on this globe would not enable a philosopher to speculate with confidence concerning future contingencies.

If, then, an intelligent being, after observing the order of events for an indefinite series of ages, had witnessed at last so wonderful an innovation as this, to what extent would his belief in the regularity of the system be weakened? Would he cease to assume that there was permanency in the laws of nature? . . . [It] may be answered that, had he previously presumed to dogmatise respecting the absolute uniformity of the order of nature, he would undoubtedly be checked by witnessing this new and unexpected event, and would form a more just estimate of the limited range of his own knowledge and the unbounded extent of the scheme of the universe. But he would soon perceive that no one of the fixed and constant laws of the animate or inanimate world was subverted by human agency, and that the modifications now introduced for the first time were the accompaniments of new and extraordinary circumstances, and those not of a *physical* but a *moral* nature. The deviation permitted would also appear to be as slight as was consistent with the accomplishment of the new moral ends proposed, and to be in a great degree temporary in its nature, so that, whenever the power of the new agent was withheld, even for a brief period, a relapse would take place to the ancient state of things; the domesticated animal, for example, recovering in a few generations its wild instinct, and the garden-flower and fruit-tree reverting to the likeness of the parent stock.

Now, if it would be reasonable to draw such inferences with respect to the future, we cannot but apply the same rules of induction to the [152] past. We have no right to anticipate any modifications in the results of existing causes in time to come which are not conformable to analogy, unless they be produced by the progressive development of human power, or perhaps by some other new relations which may hereafter spring up between the moral and material worlds. In the same manner, when we speculate on the vicissitudes of the animate and inanimate creation in former ages, we ought not to look for any anomalous results, unless where man has interfered, or unless clear indications appear of some other *moral* source of temporary derangement. . . . [153]

CONCLUDING REMARKS

It has been argued that, as the different states of the earth's surface and the different species by which it has been inhabited have all had their origin, and many of them their termination, so the entire series may have commenced at a certain period. It has also been urged that, as we admit the creation of man to have occurred at a comparatively [798] modern epoch—as we concede the astonishing fact of the first introduction of a moral and intellectual being—so also we may conceive the first creation of the planet itself.

I am far from denying the weight of this reasoning from analogy; but, although it may strengthen our conviction that the present system of change has not gone on from eternity, it cannot warrant us in presuming that we shall be permitted to behold the signs of the earth's origin, or the evidences of the first introduction into it of organic beings. We aspire in vain to assign limits to the works of creation in *space*, whether we examine the starry heavens or that world of minute animalcules which is revealed to us by the microscope.

We are prepared, therefore, to find that in *time* also the confines of the universe lie beyond the reach of mortal ken. But in whatever direction we pursue our researches, . . . we discover everywhere the clear proofs of a Creative Intelligence, and of His foresight, wisdom, and power.

As geologists, we learn that it is not only the present condition of the globe which has been suited to the accommodation of myriads of living creatures, but that many former states also have been adapted to the organization and habits of prior races of beings. The disposition of the seas, continents, and islands, and the climates, have varied; the species likewise have been changed; and yet they have all been so modelled, on types analogous to those of existing plants and animals, as to indicate throughout a perfect harmony of design and unity of purpose. To assume that the evidence of the beginning or end of so vast a scheme lies within the reach of our philosophical inquiries, or even of our speculations, appears to be inconsistent with a just estimate of the relations which subsist between the finite powers of man and the attributes of an Infinite and Eternal Being. [799]

✿ KARL MARX and FREDERICK ENGEL

Manifesto of the Communist Party

Karl Marx and Frederick Engels, *Manifesto of the Communist Party,* authorized English Translation, Edited and Annotated by Frederick Engels. Second Edition, New York, National Executive Committee of the Socialist Labor Party, 1898.*

THE "MANIFESTO" being our joint production, I consider myself bound to state that the fundamental proposition which forms its nucleus belongs to Marx. That proposition is: that in every historical epoch, the prevailing mode of economic production and exchange, and the social organization necessarily following from it, form the

* *The Manifesto* was first published in German in London in 1848; first published in English in 1850; first published in English in the U.S.A. in 1872. (Engels, Preface to above.)

basis upon which is built up, and from which alone can be explained, the political and intellectual history of that epoch; that consequently the whole history of mankind (since the dissolution of primitive tribal society, holding land in common ownership) [7] has been a history of class struggles, contests between exploiting and exploited, ruling and oppressed classes; that the history of these class struggles forms a series of evolution in which, now-a-days, a stage has been reached where the exploited and oppressed class—the proletariat—cannot attain its emancipation from the sway of the exploiting and ruling class—the bourgeoisie—without, at the same time, and once and for all, emancipating society at large from all exploitation, oppression, class-distinctions and class struggles.

This proposition which, in my opinion, is destined to do for history what Darwin's theory has done for biology, we, both of us, had been gradually approaching for some years before 1845. [8]

✿ KARL MARX

A Contribution to the Critique of Political Economy

Karl Marx, *A Contribution to the Critique of Political Economy*, Chicago, Charles H. Kerr, 1904.*

. . . THE FIRST WORK undertaken for the solution of the question that troubled me was a critical revision of Hegel's "Philosophy of Law"; the introduction to that work appeared in the "Deutsch-Franzosische Jahrbucher," published in Paris in 1844. I was led by my studies to the conclusion that legal relations as well as forms of state could neither be understood by themselves, nor explained by the so-called general progress of the human mind, but that they are rooted in the material conditions of life, which are summed up by Hegel after the

---

* Originally published in German in Berlin in 1859. The edition used here is the first English translation (from the second German edition of 1904).

fashion of the English and French of the eighteenth century under
the name "Civic society"; the anatomy of that civic society is to be
sought in political economy. The study of the latter which I had taken
in Paris, I continued at Brussels whither I emigrated on account of
an order of expulsion issued by Mr. Guizot. The general conclusion at
which I arrived and which, once reached, continued to serve as the
leading thread in my studies, may be summed up as follows: In the
social production which men carry on they enter into definite relations that are indispensable and independent of their will; these relations of production correspond to a definite stage of development
of their material powers of production. The sum total of these relations of production constitutes the economic structure of society—
the real foundation, on which rise legal and political superstructures
and to which correspond definite forms of social consciousness. The
mode of production in material life determines the general character
of the social, political and spiritual processes of life. It is not the consciousness of men that determines their existence, but on the contrary, their social existence determines . . . [11] their consciousness.
At a certain stage of their development, the material forces of production in society come in conflict with the existing relations of
production, or—what is but a legal expression for the same thing—
with the property relations within which they had been at work before. From forms of development of the forces of production these
relations turn into their fetters. Then comes the period of social revo-
lution. With the change of the economic foundation the entire immense superstructure is more or less rapidly transformed. In considering such transformations the distinction should always be made
between the material transformation of the economic conditions of
production which can be determined with the precision of natural
science, and the legal, political, religious, aesthetic or philosophic—
in short ideological forms in which men become conscious of this
conflict and fight it out. Just as our opinion of an individual is not
based on what he thinks of himself, so can we not judge of such a
period of transformation by its own consciousness; on the contrary
this consciousness must rather be explained from the contradictions
of material life, from the existing conflict between the social forces
of production and the relations of production. No social order ever
disappears before all the productive forces, for which there is room
in it, have been developed; and new higher relations of production
never appear before the material conditions of their existence have

matured in the womb of the old society. Therefore, mankind always takes up only such problems as it can solve; since, looking at the matter more closely, we will always [12] find that the problem itself arises only when the material conditions necessary for its solution already exist or are at least in the process of formation. In broad outlines we can designate the Asiatic, the ancient, the feudal, and the modern bourgeois methods of production as so many epochs in the progress of the economic formation of society. The bourgeois relations of production are the last antagonistic [*sic*], not in the sense of individual antagonism, but of one arising from conditions surrounding the life of individuals in society; at the same time the productive forces developing in the womb of bourgeois society create the material conditions for the solution of that antagonism. This social formation constitutes, therefore, the closing chapter of the prehistoric stage of human society. . . . [13]

London, January, 1859

❧ KARL MARX

Capital

Karl Marx, *Capital: A Critical Analysis of Capitalist Production* (translated from the third German edition by Samuel Moore and Edward Aveling and edited by Frederick Engels), London, Swan Sonnenschein, Lowrey, & Co., 1887; 2 vols.*

AUTHOR'S PREFACE TO THE FIRST EDITION, 1867

INTRINSICALLY, it is not a question of the higher or lower degree of development of the social antagonisms that result from the natural laws of capitalist production. It is a question of these laws themselves, of these tendencies working with iron necessity towards inevitable results. The country that is more developed industrially only

* The first German editions appeared in 1867 and 1873.

shows to the less developed, the image of its own future. . . . [I, xvii]

Here individuals are dealt with only in so far as they are the personifications of economic categories, embodiments of particular class-relations and class-interests. My stand-point, from which the evolution of the economic formation of society is viewed as a process of natural history, can less than any other make the individual responsible for relations whose creature he socially remains, however much he may subjectively raise himself above them. [I, xix]

AUTHOR'S PREFACE TO THE SECOND EDITION, 1873

In so far as Political Economy remains within [the bourgeois] horizon, in so far, *i.e.*, as the capitalist regime is looked upon as the absolutely final form of social production, instead of as a passing historical phase of its evolution, Political Economy can remain a science only so long as the class-struggle is latent or manifests itself only in isolated and sporadic phenomena. [I, xxii]

[Marx quotes at length from a "striking" and "generous" Russian article on his work dated 1872]: "The one thing which is of moment to Marx is to find the law of the phenomena with whose investigation he is concerned; and not only is that law of moment to him, which governs these phenomena, in so far as they have a definite form and mutual connection within a given historical period. Of still greater moment to him is the law of their variation, of their development, *i.e.*, of their transition from one form into another, from one series of connections into a different one. This law once discovered, he investigates in detail the effects in which it manifests itself in social life. Consequently, Marx only troubles himself about one thing; to show, by rigid scientific investigation, the necessity of successive determinate orders of social conditions, and to establish, as impartially as possible, the facts that serve him for fundamental starting points. For this it is quite enough, if he proves, at the same time, both the necessity of the present order of things, and the necessity of another order into which the first must inevitably pass over; and this all the same, whether men believe or do not [I, xxvii] believe it, whether they are conscious or unconscious of it. Marx treats the social movement as a process of natural history, governed by laws not only independent of human will, consciousness and intelligence, but rather, on the contrary, determining that will, consciousness, and intelligence. . . .

If in the history of civilisation the conscious element plays a part so subordinate, then it is self-evident that a critical inquiry whose subject-matter is civilisation can, less than anything else, have for its basis any form of, or any result of, consciousness. That is to say, that not the idea, but the material phenomenon alone can serve as its starting-point. Such an inquiry will confine itself to the confrontation and the comparison of a fact, not with ideas, but with another fact. For this inquiry, the one thing of moment is, that both facts be investigated as accurately as possible, and that they actually form, each with respect to the other, different momenta of an evolution; but most important of all is the rigid analysis of the series of successions, of the sequences and concatenations in which the different stages of such an evolution present themselves. But it will be said, the general laws of economic life are one and the same, no matter whether they are applied to the present or the past. This Marx directly denies. According to him, such abstract laws do not exist. On the contrary, in his opinion every historical period has laws of its own. . . . As soon as society has outlived a given period of development, and is passing over from one given stage to another, it begins to be subject also to other laws. In a word, economic life offers us a phenomenon analagous to the history of evolution in other branches of biology. The old economists misunderstood the nature of economic laws when they likened them to the laws of physics and [I,xxviii] chemistry. A more thorough analysis of phenomena shows that social organisms differ among themselves as fundamentally as plants or animals. Nay, one and the same phenomenon falls under quite different laws in consequence of the different structure of those organisms as a whole, of the variations of their individual organs, of the different conditions in which those organs function, &c. Marx, *e.g.*, denies that the law of population is the same at all times and in all places. He asserts, on the contrary, that every stage of development has its own law of population. . . . With the varying degree of development of productive power, social conditions and the laws governing them vary too. Whilst Marx sets himself the task of following and explaining from this point of view the economic system established by the sway of capital, he is only formulating, in a strictly scientific manner, the aim that every accurate investigation into economic life must have. The scientific value of such an inquiry lies in the disclosing of the special laws that regulate the origin, existence, development, and death of a given social organism and its replacement by another and

higher one. And it is this value that, in point of fact, Marx's book
has." [I, xxix]

THE SECRET OF PRIMITIVE ACCUMULATION

[P]rimitive accumulation plays in Political Economy about the
same part as original sin in theology. Adam bit the apple, and thereupon sin fell on the human race. Its origin is supposed to be explained
when it is told as an anecdote of the past. In times long gone by there
were two sorts of people: one, the diligent, intelligent, and above all,
frugal elite; the other, lazy rascals, spending their substance, and
more, in riotous living. The legend of theological original sin tells us
certainly how man came to be condemned to eat his bread in the
sweat of his brow; but the history of economic original sin reveals to
us that there are people to whom this is by no means [II, 736] essential.
Never mind! Thus it came to pass that the former sort accumulated
wealth, and the latter sort had at last nothing to sell except their own
skins. And from this original sin dates the poverty of the great majority that, despite all its labour, has up to now nothing to sell but
itself, and the wealth of the few that increases constantly although
they have long ceased to work. Such insipid childishness is every day
preached to us in the defence of property. . . . In actual history it
is notorious that conquest, enslavement, robbery, murder, chiefly
force, play the great part. [II, 737]

GENESIS OF THE INDUSTRIALIST CAPITALIST

The different momenta of primitive accumulation distribute [II, 775]
themselves now, more or less in chronological order, particularly over
Spain, Portugal, Holland, France, and England. In England at the
end of the 17th century, they arrive at a systematical combination,
embracing the colonies, the national debt, the modern mode of taxation, and the protectionist system. These methods depend in part
on brute force, e.g., the colonial system. But they all employ the
power of the State, the concentrated and organised force of society,
to hasten, hothouse fashion, the process of transformation of the
feudal mode of production into the capitalist mode, and to shorten
the transition. Force is the midwife of every old society pregnant
with a new one. It is itself an economic power. . . . [II, 776]

Colonial system, public debts, heavy taxes, protection, commer-

cial wars, &c, these children of the true manufacturing period, increase gigantically during the infancy of Modern Industry. The birth
of the latter is heralded by a great slaughter of the innocents. Like
the royal navy, the factories were recruited by means of the press-
gang. Blasé as Sir F. M. Eden is as to the horrors of the expropria-
tion of the agricultural population from the soil . . . he does not
show . . . the same economic insight in respect to the necessity of
child-stealing and child-slavery for the transformation of manufacturing [II, 782] exploitation into factory exploitation, and the establishment of the "true relation" between capital and labour-power.
He says: "It may, perhaps, be worthy of the attention of the public
to consider, whether any manufacture, which, in order to be carried
on successfully, requires that cottages and workhouses should be ran-
sacked for poor children; that they should be employed by turns during the greater part of the night and robbed of that rest, which,
though indispensable to all, is most required by the young; and that
numbers of both sexes, of different ages and dispositions, should be
collected together in such a manner that the contagion of example
cannot but lead to profligacy and debauchery; will add to the sum
of individual or national felicity? . . ." [II, 783]

Tantae molis erat, to establish the "eternal laws of Nature" of the
capitalist mode of production, to complete the process of separation
between labourers and conditions of labour, to transform, at one pole,
the social means of production and subsistence into capital, at the
opposite pole, the mass of the population into wage-labourers, into
"free labouring poor," that artificial product of modern society.
If [II, 785] money . . . "comes into the world with a congenital blood-
stain on one cheek," capital comes dripping from head to foot, from
every pore, with blood and dirt. [II, 786]

☙ CHARLES DARWIN

On the Origin of Species

Charles Darwin, *On the Origin of Species by Means of Natural Selection, or the Preservation of Favoured Races in the Struggle for Life* [1859], New York, D. Appleton & Co., 1860 (except where noted).

OWING TO THIS STRUGGLE for life, any variation, however slight and from whatever cause proceeding, if it be in any degree profitable to an individual of any species, in its infinitely complex relations to other organic beings and to external nature, will tend to the preservation of that individual, and will generally be inherited by its offspring. The offspring, also, will thus have a better chance of surviving, for, of the many individuals of any species which are periodically born, but a small number can survive. I have called this principle, by which each slight variation, if useful, is preserved, by the term of Natural Selection, in order to mark its relation to man's power of selection. . . .* [61]

Slow though the progress of selection may be, if feeble man can do much by his powers of artificial selection, I can see no limit to the amount of change, to the beauty and infinite complexity of the co-adaptations between all organic beings, one with another and with their physical conditions of life, which may be effected in the long course of time by nature's power of selection. . . . [101]

But it may be objected that if all organic beings thus tend to rise in the scale, how is it that throughout the world a multitude of the lowest forms still exist; and how is it that in each great class some forms are far [134] more highly developed than others? . . . Natural Selection includes no necessary and universal law of advancement or development—it only takes advantage of such variations as arise

* In somewhat later editions, Darwin followed this passage by the admission: "But the expression often used by Mr. Herbert Spencer of the Survival of the Fittest, is more accurate, and sometimes is equally convenient." (See the American edition identified as "with additions and corrections from the sixth and last English edition," New York, D. Appleton & Co., 1897; I, 76–77.)

and are beneficial to each creature under its complex relations of life. . . .* [135]

It is interesting to contemplate an entangled bank, clothed with many plants of many kinds, with birds singing on the bushes, with various insects flitting about, and [423] with worms crawling through the damp earth, and to reflect that these elaborately constructed forms, so different from each other, and dependent on each other in so complex a manner, have all been produced by laws acting around us. These laws, taken in the largest sense, being Growth with Reproduction; Inheritance which is almost implied by reproduction; Variability from the indirect and direct action of the external conditions of life, and from use and disuse; a Ratio of Increase so high as to lead to a Struggle for Life, and as a consequence to Natural Selection, entailing Divergence of Character and the Extinction of less-improved forms. Thus, from the war of nature, from famine and death, the most exalted object which we are capable of conceiving, namely the production of the higher animals, directly follows. There is a grandeur in this view of life, with its several powers, having been originally breathed into a few forms or into one; and that, whilst this planet has gone cycling on according to the fixed law of gravity, from so simple a beginning endless forms most beautiful and most wonderful have been, and are being, evolved. [424]

@ CHARLES DARWIN

The Variation of Animals and Plants

Charles Darwin, *The Variation of Animals and Plants Under Domestication*, London, John Murray & Co., 1868; 2 vols.

CONCLUDING REMARKS

DID HE ORDAIN that the crop and tail-feathers of the pigeon should vary in order that the fancier might make his grotesque pouter and fantail breeds? Did He cause the frame and mental qualities of the

* This entire passage was added in the third edition (London, John Murray, 1861).

dog to vary in order that a breed might be formed of indomitable
ferocity, with jaws fitted to pin down the bull for man's brutal sport?
But if we give up the principle in one case,—if we do not admit that
the variations of the primeval dog were intentionally guided in order
that the greyhound, for instance, that perfect image of symmetry
and vigour, might be formed,—no shadow of reason can assigned
for the belief that variations, alike in nature and the result [II, 431] of
the same general laws, which have been the groundwork through
natural selection of the formation of the most perfectly adapted animals in the world, man included, were intentionally and specially
guided. However much we may wish it, we can hardly follow Professor Asa Gray in his belief "that variation has been led along certain beneficial lines," like a stream "along definite and useful lines of
irrigation." If we assume that each particular variation was from the
beginning of all time preordained, the plasticity of organisation,
which leads to many injurious deviations of structure, as well as that
redundant power of reproduction which inevitably leads to a struggle for existence, and, as a consequence, to the natural selection or
survival of the fittest, must appear to us superfluous laws of nature.
On the other hand, an omnipotent and omniscient Creator ordains
everything and foresees everything. Thus we are brought face to
face with a difficulty as insoluble as is that of free will and predestination. [II, 432]

✿ CHARLES DARWIN

The Descent of Man
and
Selection in Relation to Sex

Charles Darwin, *The Descent of Man and Selection in Relation to Sex*, New York, D. Appleton & Co. [1871], 1874; 2 vols.

GENERAL SUMMARY AND CONCLUSION

THE MAIN CONCLUSION here arrived at, and now held by many naturalists . . . is that man is descended from some less highly organized form. The grounds upon which this conclusion rests will never be shaken, for the close similarity between man and the lower animals . . . [II, 368] cannot be disputed. [These facts] have long been known, but, until recently, they told us nothing with respect to the origin of man. Now, when viewed by the light of our knowledge of the whole organic world, their meaning is unmistakable. The great principle of evolution stands up clear and firm, when these groups of facts are considered in connection with others, such as the mutual affinities of the members of the same group, their geographical distribution in the past and present times, and their geological succession. . . . He who is not content to look, like a savage, at the phenomena of Nature as disconnected, cannot any longer believe that man is the work of a separate act of creation. He will be forced to admit that the close resemblance of the embryo of man to that, for instance, of a dog . . . points in the plainest manner to the conclusion that man is the co-descendant with other mammals of a common progenitor.

We have seen that man incessantly presents individual differences in all parts of his body and in his mental faculties. These differences or variations seem to be induced by the same general causes, and to obey the same laws as with the lower animals. In both cases similar laws of inheritance prevail. Man tends to increase at a greater rate than

his means of subsistence; consequently he is occasionally subjected
to a severe struggle for existence, [II,369] and natural selection will
have effected whatever lies within its scope. A succession of strongly
marked variations of a similar nature [is] by no means requisite;
slight fluctuating differences in the individual suffice for the work
of natural selection. We may feel assured that the inherited effects
of the long-continued use or disuse of parts will have done much in
the same direction with natural selection. Modifications formerly of
importance, though no longer of any special use, will be long inherited. When one part is modified, other parts change through the
principle of correlation, of which we have instances in many curious
cases of correlated monstrosities. Something may be attributed to
the direct and definite action of the surrounding conditions of life,
such as abundant food, heat, or moisture; and, lastly, many characters of slight physiological importance, some indeed of considerable
importance, have been gained through sexual selection. . . . [II, 370]

It must not be supposed that the divergence of each race from the
other races and of all the races from a common stock, can be traced
back to any one pair of progenitors. On the contrary, at every stage
in the process of modification, all the individuals which were in any
way better fitted for their conditions of life, though in different degrees, would have survived in greater numbers than the less well-
fitted. The process would have been like that followed by man, when
he does not intentionally select particular individuals, but breeds
from all the superior and neglects the inferior individuals. He thus
slowly but surely modifies his stock and unconsciously forms a new
strain. So with respect to modifications, acquired independently of
selection, and due to variations arising [II, 371] from the nature of the
organism and the action of the surrounding conditions, or from
changed habits of life, no single pair will have been modified in a
much greater degree than the other pairs which inhabit the same
country, for all will have been continually blended through free in-
tercrossing.

By considering the embryological structure of man—the homolo-
gies which he presents with the lower animals—the rudiments which
he retains and the reversions to which he is liable—we can partly
recall in imagination the former condition of our early progenitors;
and can approximately place them in their proper place in the zoo-
logical series. We thus learn that man is descended from a hairy
quadruped, furnished with a tail and pointed ears probably arboreal

in its habits, and an inhabitant of the Old World. This creature, if its whole structure had been examined by a naturalist, would have been classed among the Quadrumana, as surely as the still more ancient progenitor of the Old and New World monkeys. The Quadrumana and all the higher mammals are probably derived from an ancient marsupial animal, and this through a long line of diversified forms, either from some reptile-like or some amphibian-like creature, and this again from some fish-like animal. In the dim obscurity of the past we can see that the early progenitor of all the Vertebrata must have been an aquatic animal, provided with branchiae, with the two sexes united in the same individual, and with the most important organs of the body (such as the brain and heart) imperfectly developed. This animal seems to have been more like the larvae of our existing marine Ascidians than any other known form.

The greatest difficulty which presents itself, when we are driven to the above conclusion on the origin of man, [II, 372] is the high standard of our intellectual powers and moral disposition which he has attained. But every one who admits the principle of evolution must see that the mental powers of the higher animals, which are the same in kind with those of mankind, though so different in degree, are capable of advancement. . . . [Man's] intellect must have been all-important to him, even at a very remote period, enabling him to use language, to make . . . weapons . . . [whereby] in combination with his social habits he long ago became the most dominant of all living creatures. . . . [II, 373] The higher intellectual powers of man, such as those of ratiocination, abstraction, self-consciousness, etc., will have followed from the continued improvement of other mental faculties. . . .

The development of the moral qualities is a more interesting and difficult problem. The foundation lies in the social instincts, including in this term the family ties. These instincts are of a highly-complex nature, and in the case of the lower animals give special tendencies toward certain definite actions; but the more important elements for us are love, and the distinct emotion of sympathy. Animals endowed with the social instincts take pleasure in each other's company, warn one another of danger, defend and aid each other in many ways. These instincts are not extended to all the individuals of the species, but only to those of the same community. As they are highly beneficial to the species they have in all probability been acquired through natural selection.

A moral being is one who is capable of comparing his past and future actions and motives . . . ; and the fact that man is the one being who with certainty can be thus designated makes the greatest of all distinctions between him and the lower animals. But . . . I have endeavored to show that the moral sense follows, firstly, from the enduring and ever-present nature of the social instincts, in which respect man agrees with the lower animals; secondly, from his mental faculties being highly active and his impressions of past events extremely vivid, in which respects he differs from the [II, 374] lower animals. Owing to this condition of mind, man cannot avoid looking backward and comparing the impressions of past events and actions. He also continually looks forward. Hence after some temporary desire or passion has mastered his social instincts, he will reflect and compare the now weakened impression of such past impulses with the ever-present social instinct; and he will then feel that sense of dissatisfaction which all unsatisfied instincts leave behind them. Consequently he resolves to act differently for the future—and this is conscience. Any instinct which is permanently stronger or more enduring than another gives rise to a feeling which we express by saying that it ought to be obeyed. . . .

Social animals are partly impelled by a wish to aid the members of the same community . . . but more commonly to perform certain definite actions. Man is impelled by the same general wish to aid his fellows, but has few or no special instincts. He differs also from the lower animals in being able to express his desires by words, which thus become the guide to the aid required and bestowed. The motive to give aid is likewise somewhat modified in man; it no longer consists solely of a blind instinctive impulse, but is largely influenced by the praise or blame of his fellow-men. Both the appreciation and the bestowal of praise and blame rest on sympathy; and this emotion . . . is one of the most important elements of the social instincts. Sympathy, though gained as an instinct, is also much strengthened by exercise or habit. As all men desire their own happiness praise or blame is bestowed on actions and motives according as they lead to this end; [II, 375] and, as happiness is an essential part of the general good, the greatest-happiness principle indirectly serves as a nearly safe standard of right and wrong. As the reasoning powers advance and experience is gained, the more remote effects of certain lines of conduct on the character of the individual, and on the general good, are perceived; and then the self-regarding virtues, from coming within the scope of public-opinion, receive praise and their opposites receive blame. But with the less civilized nations reason often errs, and many bad customs and base superstitions come within the same scope, and consequently are esteemed as high virtues, and their breach as heavy crimes. . . .

The moral nature of man has reached the highest standard yet attained, partly through the advancement of the reasoning powers and consequently of a just public opinion, but especially through the sympathies being rendered more tender and widely diffused through the effects of habit, example, instruction, and reflection. [II, 376] It is not improbable that virtuous tendencies may through long practice be inherited. With the more civilized races, the conviction of the existence of an all-seeing Deity has had a potent influence on the advance of morality. Ultimately man no longer accepts the praise or blame of his fellows as his chief guide, though few escape this influence, but his habitual convictions controlled by reason afford him the safest rule. His conscience then becomes the supreme judge and monitor. Nevertheless, the first foundation or origin of the moral sense lies in the social instincts, including sympathy; and these instincts no doubt were primarily gained, as in the case of the lower animals, through natural selection.

The belief in God has often been advanced as not only the greatest, but the most complete of all the distinctions between man and the lower animals. It is, however, impossible . . . to maintain that this belief is innate or instinctive in man. On the other hand, a belief in all-pervading spiritual agencies seems to be universal; and apparently follows from a considerable advance in the reasoning powers of man, and from a still greater advance in his faculties of imagination, curiosity, and wonder. I am aware that the assumed instinctive belief in God has been used by many persons as an argument for His existence. But this is a rash judgment, as we should thus be compelled to believe in the existence of many cruel and malignant spirits, possessing only a little more power than man; for the belief in them is far more general than of a beneficent Deity. The idea of a universal and beneficent Creator of the universe does not seem to arise in the mind of man until he has been elevated by a long-continued culture. . . . [II, 377]

I am aware that the conclusions arrived at in this work will be denounced by some as highly irreligious; but he who thus denounces them is bound to show why it is more irreligious to explain the origin of man as a distinct species by descent from some lower form, through the laws of variation and natural selection, than to explain the birth of the individual through the laws of ordinary reproduction. The birth both of the species and of the individual are equally parts of that grand sequence of events which our minds refuse to accept as the result of blind chance. The understanding revolts at such a conclusion, whether or not we are able to believe that every slight variation of structure, the union of each pair in marriage, the dissemination of each seed, and other such events have all been ordained for some special purpose. . . . [II, 378]

Man, like every other animal, has no doubt advanced to his present high condition through a struggle for existence consequent on his rapid multiplication; and if he is to advance still higher, it is to be feared that he must remain subject to a severe [II, 385] struggle. Otherwise he would sink into indolence, and the more highly-gifted men would not be more successful in the battle of life than the less gifted. Hence our natural rate of increase, though leading to many and obvious evils, must not be greatly diminished by any means. There should be open competition for all men; and the most able should not be prevented by laws or customs from succeeding best and rearing the largest number of offspring. Important as the struggle for existence has been and even still is, yet as far as the highest part of man's nature is concerned there are other agencies more important. For the moral qualities are advanced, either directly or indirectly, much more through the effects of habit, the reasoning powers, instruction, religion, etc., than through natural selection; though to this latter agency the social instincts, which afforded the basis for the development of moral sense, may be safely attributed.

The main conclusion arrived at in this work—namely, that man is descended from some lowly organized form—will, I regret to think, be highly distasteful to many. But there can hardly be a doubt that we are descended from barbarians. . . . [II, 386] For my part I would as soon be descended from that heroic little monkey who braved his dreaded enemy in order to save the life of his keeper . . . as from a savage who delights to torture his enemies, offers up bloody sacrifices, . . . and is haunted by the grossest superstitions.

Man may be excused for feeling some pride at having risen, though not through his own exertions, to the very summit of the organic scale; and the fact of his having thus risen, instead of having been aboriginally placed there, may give him hope for a still higher destiny in the distant future. But we are not here concerned with hopes or fears, only with the truth as our reason permits us to discover it. I have given the evidence to the best of my ability; and we must acknowledge, as it seems to me, that man, with all his noble qualities, with sympathy which feels for the most debased, with benevolence which extends not only to other men but to the humblest living creature, with his godlike intellect which has penetrated into the movements and constitution of the solar system—with all these exalted powers man still bears in his bodily frame the indelible stamp of his lowly origin. [II, 387]

☯ HERBERT SPENCER

First Principles

Herbert Spencer, *First Principles* (Of a New System of Philosophy) [1862], New York, D. Appleton & Co., 1864.

SUMMARY AND CONCLUSION

143. IF THESE CONCLUSIONS be accepted—if it be admitted that they inevitably follow from the truth transcending all others in authority— if it be agreed that the phenomena going on everywhere are parts of the general process of Evolution, save where they are parts of the reverse of Dissolution; then it must be inferred that all phenomena receive their complete interpretation, only when recognized as parts of these processes. Regarded from the point of view here reached, each change that takes place is an incident in the course of the ever-complicating distribution of Matter and Motion, except where it is an incident in the course of the reverse distribution; and each such change is fully understood, only when brought under those universal principles of change, to which these transformations necessarily conform. Whence, indeed, it appears to be an unavoidable conclusion, that the limit towards which Science is advancing, must be reached when these formulae are are made all-comprehensive. Manifestly, the

perfection of Science is a state in which all phenomena are seen to be necessary implications of the Persistence of Force. In such a state, the dependence of each phenomenon on the Persistence of Force must be proved either directly or indirectly—either by showing that it is a corollary of the Persistence of Force, or by showing that it is a corollary from some general proposition deduced from the Persistence of Force. And since all phenomena are incidents in the re-distribution of Matter and Motion; and since there are certain general principles, deducible from the Persistence of Force, to which all these re-distributions conform; it seems inferable that ultimately all phenomena, where not classed as consequences of the Persistence of Force, must be classed as consequences of these derivative principles. [499]

144. Of course this development of Science into an organized aggregate of direct and indirect deductions from the Persistence of Force, can be achieved only in the remote future; and indeed cannot be completely achieved even then. Scientific progress is progress in that equilibration of thought and things which we saw is going on, and must continue to go on; but which cannot arrive at perfection in any finite period, because it advances more slowly the further it advances. But though Science can never be entirely reduced to this form; and though only at a far distant time can it be brought nearly to this form; yet much may even now be done in the way of rude approximation. Those who are familiar with the present aspects of Science must recognize in them the broken outlines of a general organization. The possibility of arranging the facts already accumulated, into the order rudely exhibited in the foregoing pages, will itself incline them to the belief that our knowledge may be put into a more connected shape than it at present has. They will see the probability that many now isolated inductions may be reduced to the form of deductions from first principles. They will suspect that inferences drawn from the ultimate laws of force will lead to the investigation and generalization of classes of facts hitherto unexamined. And they will feel not only that a greater degree of certainty must be acquired by Science, as fast as its propositions are directly or indirectly deduced from the highest of all truths; but also that it must so be rendered a more efficient agent of further inquiry.

To bring scientific knowledge to such degree of logical coherence as is at present possible is a task to be achieved only by the combined efforts of many. No one man can possess that encyclopedic informa-

tion required for rightly arranging even the truths already established. But as progress is effected by increments—as all organization,
beginning in faint and blurred outlines, is completed by successive
modifications and additions; advantage may accrue from an [500]
attempt, however rude, to reduce the facts already accumulated—or
rather certain classes of them—to something like co-ordination. Such
must be the plea for the several volumes which are to succeed this.

145. A few closing words must be said, concerning the general
bearings of the doctrines that are now to be further developed. Before
proceeding to interpret the detailed phenomena of Life, and Mind,
and Society, in terms of Matter, Motion, and Force, the reader must
be reminded in what sense the interpretations are to be accepted. In
spite of everything said at the outset, there are probably some who
have gained the impression that those most general truths set forth in
the preceding chapters, together with the truths deducible from
them, claim to be something more than relative truths. And, notwithstanding all evidence to the contrary, there will probably have arisen
in not a few minds, the conviction that the solutions which have been
given, along with those to be derived from them, are essentially materialistic. Let none persist in these misconceptions.

As repeatedly shown in various ways, the deepest truths we can
reach are simply statements of the widest uniformities in our experience of the relations of Matter, Motion, and Force; and Matter,
Motion, and Force are but symbols of the Unknown Reality. That
Power of which the nature remains for ever inconceivable, and to
which no limits in Time or Space can be imagined, works in us certain
effects. These effects have certain likenesses of kind, the most general
of which we class together under the names of Matter, Motion, and
Force; and between these effects there are likenesses of connection,
the most constant of which we class as laws of the highest certainty.
Analysis reduces these several kinds of effect to one kind of effect; and
these several kinds of uniformity to one kind of uniformity. And the
highest achievement of Science is the interpretation of all orders of
phenomena, as differently-conditioned manifestations [501] of this
one kind of effect, under differently-conditioned modes of this one
kind of uniformity. But when Science has done this, it has done
nothing more than systematize our experience; and has in no degree
extended the limits of our experience. We can say no more than
before, whether the uniformities are as absolutely necessary, as they
have become to our thought relatively necessary. The utmost possi-

bility for us, is an interpretation of the process of things as it presents itself to our limited consciousness; but how this process is related to the actual process, we are unable to conceive, much less to know.

Similarly, it must be remembered that while the connection between the phenomenal order and the ontological order is for ever inscrutable, so is the connection between the conditioned forms of being and the unconditioned form of being, for ever inscrutable. The interpretation of all phenomena in terms of Matter, Motion, and Force, is nothing more than the reduction of our complex symbols of thought to the simplest symbols; and when the equation has been brought to its lowest terms the symbols remain symbols still. Hence the reasonings contained in the foregoing pages afford no support to either of the antagonist hypotheses respecting the ultimate nature of things. Their implications are no more materialistic than they are spiritualistic; and no more spiritualistic than they are materialistic. Any argument which is apparently furnished to either hypothesis is neutralized by as good an argument furnished to the other. The Materialist, seeing it to be a necessary deduction from the law of correlation, that what exists in consciousness under the form of feeling, is transformable into an equivalent of mechanical motion, and by consequence into equivalents of all the other forces which matter exhibits; may consider it therefore demonstrated that the phenomena of consciousness are material phenomena. But the Spiritualist, setting out with the same data, may argue with equal cogency that if the forces displayed by matter are cognizable only under the [502] shape of those equivalent amounts of consciousness which they produce, it is to be inferred that these forces, when existing out of consciousness, are of the same intrinsic nature as when existing in consciousness; and that so is justified the spiritualistic conception of the external world, as consisting of something essentially identical with what we call mind. Manifestly, the establishment of correlation between the forces of the outer and the inner worlds may be used to assimilate either to the other; according as we set out with one or other term. But he who rightly interprets the doctrine contained in this work, will see that neither of these terms can be taken as ultimate. He will see that though the relation of subject and object renders necessary to us these antithetical conceptions of Spirit and Matter, the one is no less than the other to be regarded as but a sign of the Unknown Reality which underlies both. [503]

🐝 HERBERT SPENCER

Principles of Biology

Herbert Spencer, *Principles of Biology*, [1864, 1867] New York, D. Appleton & Co., 1871; 2 vols.

GENERAL ASPECTS OF THE EVOLUTION-HYPOTHESIS

LET US PUT OURSELVES for a moment in the position of those who . . . draw inferences respecting the mode of action of that ultimate powei manifested to us through phenomena. We shall find the supposition that each kind of organism was separately designed and put together to be much less consistent with their professed conception of this ultimate power than is the supposition that all kinds of organisms have resulted from one unbroken process. Irregularity of method is a mark of weakness. Uniformity of method is a mark of strength. Continual interposition to alter a pre-arranged set of actions implies defective arrangement in those actions. The maintenance of those actions and the working out by them of the highest results implies completeness of arrangement. If human workmen, whose machines as at first constructed require perpetual adjustment, show their increasing skill by making their machines self-adjusting, then those who figure to themselves the production of the world and its inhabitants by a "Great Artificer" must admit that the achievement of this end by a persistent process, adapted to all contingencies, implies greater skill than its achievement by the process of meeting the contingencies as they severally arise.

So, too, it is with the contrast under its moral aspect. We saw that to the hypothesis of special creations a difficulty is presented by the absence of high forms of life during those immeasurable epochs of the Earth's existence which geology [I, 353] records. But to the hypothesis of evolution, this absence is no such obstacle. Suppose evolution, and this question is necessarily excluded. Suppose special creations, and this question, unavoidably raised, can have no satisfactory answer. Still more marked is this contrast between the two hypotheses, in presence of that vast amount of suffering entailed on all orders of sentient beings, by their imperfect adaptations to their conditions of life; and the further vast amount of suffering entailed on them by enemies and by parasites. We saw that if organisms were severally designed for their respective places in Nature, the inevitable conclusion is that these thousands of kinds of inferior organisms which prey upon superior organisms were intended to inflict all the pain and mortality which results. But the hypothesis of evolution involves us in no such dilemma. Slowly, but surely, evolution brings about an increasing amount of happiness: all evils being but incidental. By its essential nature, the process must everywhere produce greater fitness to the conditions of existence be they what they may. Applying alike to the lowest and the highest forms of organization, there is in all cases a progressive adaptation, and a survival of the most adapted. If, in the uniform working out of the process, there are evolved organisms of low types, which prey on those of higher types, the evils inflicted form but a deduction from the average benefits. The universal and necessary tendency towards supremacy and multiplication of the best, applying to the organic creation as a whole as well as to each species, is ever diminishing the damage done—tends ever to maintain those most superior organisms which, in one way or other, escape the invasions of the inferior, and so tends to produce a type less liable to the invasions of the inferior. Thus the evils accompanying evolution are ever being self-eliminated. Though there may arise the question—Why could they not have been avoided? there does not arise the question—Why were they deliberately [I, 354] inflicted? Whatever may be thought of them, it is clear that they do not imply gratuitous malevolence. [I, 355]

❀ HERBERT SPENCER

The Principles of Sociology

Herbert Spencer, *The Principles of Sociology* [1876–1896], D. Appleton & Co., New York, 1900–1901; 3 vols.

POLITICAL INSTITUTIONS

As CARRIED on throughout the animate world at large, the struggle for existence has been an indispensable means to evolution. Not simply do we see that in the competition among individuals of the same kind survival of the fittest has from the beginning furthered production of a higher type; but we see that to the unceasing warfare between species is mainly due both growth and organization. Without universal conflict there would have been no development of the active powers. The organs of perception and of locomotion have been little by little evolved during the interaction of pursuers and pursued. Improved limbs and senses have furnished better supplies to the viscera, and improved visceral structures have ensured a better supply of aerated blood to the limbs and senses; while a higher nervous system has at each stage been called into play for co-ordinating the actions of these more complex structures. Among predatory animals death by starvation, and among animals preyed upon death by destruction, have carried off the least-favourably modified individuals and varieties. Every advance in strength, speed, agility, or sagacity in creatures of the one class has necessitated a corresponding advance in creatures of the other class; and without never-ending efforts to catch and to escape, with loss of life as the penalty for failure, the progress of neither could have been achieved. [II, 240]

Mark now, however, that while this merciless discipline of nature "red in tooth and claw" has been essential to the progress of sentient life, its persistence through all time with all creatures must not be inferred. The high organization evolved by and for this universal conflict is not necessarily forever employed to like ends. The resulting power and intelligence admit of being far otherwise employed. . . .

[Man's] limbs, teeth, and nails are [by now] but little employed in fight; and his mind is not ordinarily occupied in devising ways of destroying other creatures. . . .

Similarly with social organisms. We must recognize the truth that the struggles for existence between societies have been instrumental to their evolution. Neither the consolidation and re-consolidation of small groups into large ones nor the organization of such compound and doubly compound groups nor the concomitant developments of those aids to a higher life which civilization has brought would have been possible without inter-tribal and inter-national conflicts. Social cooperation is initiated by joint defence, and offence; and from the cooperation thus initiated, all kinds of cooperations have arisen. Inconceivable as have been the horrors caused by this universal antagonism which, beginning with the chronic hostilities of small hordes tens of thousands of years ago, has ended in the occasional vast battles of immense nations, we must nevertheless admit that without it the world would still have been inhabited only by men of feeble types, sheltering in caves and living on wild food. [II, 241]

But now observe that the inter-social struggle for existence which has been indispensable in evolving societies will not necessarily play in the future a part like that which it has played in the past. Recognizing our indebtedness to war for forming great communities and developing their structures, we may yet infer that the acquired powers available for other activities will lose their original activities. While conceding that without these perpetual bloody strifes civilized societies could not have arisen and that an adapted form of human nature, fierce as well as intelligent, was a needful concomitant, we may at the same time hold that such societies having been produced, the brutality of nature . . . which was necessitated by the process, ceasing to be necessary with the cessation of the process, will disappear. While the benefits achieved during the predatory period remain a permanent inheritance, the evils entailed by it will decrease and slowly die out.

Thus, then, contemplating social structures and actions from the evolution point of view, we may preserve that calmness which is needful for scientific interpretation of them without losing our powers of feeling moral reprobation or approbation. [II, 242]

THOMAS H. HUXLEY

Evidence as to Man's Place in Nature

Thomas H. Huxley, *Evidence as to Man's Place in Nature,* New York, D. Appleton & Co., 1863.

[EVERY] LIVING CREATURE commences its existence under a form different from, and simpler than, that which it eventually attains.[74]

The history of the development of any . . . vertebrate animal . . . tells the same story. There is always, to begin with, an egg . . .[75] the yolk of that egg always undergoes . . . *"segmentation"* . . . : the ultimate products of that segmentation constitute the building materials for the body of the young animal. . . . Furthermore, there is a period in which the young of all these animals resemble one another . . . in all essentials of structure, so closely that the differences between them are inconsiderable, while, in their subsequent course they diverge more and more widely from one another. . . .

Thus the study of development affords a clear test of closeness of structural affinity, and one turns with impatience to inquire what results are yielded by the study of the development of Man. Is he something apart? . . . Or does he originate in a similar germ, pass through the same slow and gradually progressive modifications . . . ? The reply . . . has not been doubtful any[80] time these thirty years. Without question, the mode of origin and the early stages of the development of man are identical with those of the animals immediately below him in the scale: without a doubt, in these respects, he is far nearer the Apes than the Apes are to the Dog. . . .[81]

[In] whatever proportion of its limbs the Gorilla differs from Man, the other Apes depart still more widely from the Gorilla. . . .[89]

[For] every constant difference between the Gorilla's skull and the man's, a similar constant difference of the same order . . . may be found between the Gorilla's skull and that of some other ape. So that, for the skull, no less than for the skeleton in general, the proposition holds good, that the differences between Man and the Gorilla are of smaller value than those between the Gorilla and some other Apes. . . .[97]

[Greatly] as the dentition of the highest Ape differs from that of Man, it differs far more widely from that of the lower and lowest Apes. . . . [101]

[People] argue that the vast intellectual chasm between the Apes and Man implies a corresponding structural chasm in the organs of the intellectual functions. . . . [But I shall show] the fallacy of this reasoning. . . . A man born dumb, notwithstanding his great cerebral mass and his inheritance of strong intellectual instincts, would be capable of few higher intellectual manifestations than an Orang or a Chimpanzee, if he were confined to the society of dumb associates. And yet there might not be the slightest discernible difference between his brain and that of a highly intelligent and cultivated person. The dumbness might be the result of a defective structure of the mouth, or of the tongue, or of a mere defective innervation of these parts. . . .

The argument, that because there is an immense difference between a Man's intelligence and an Ape's, therefore there must be an equally immense difference between their brains, appears to me to be about as well based as the reasoning by which one should endeavour to prove that, because there is a "great gulf" between a watch that keeps accurate time and another that will not go at all, there is therefore a great structural hiatus between the two watches. A hair in the balance-wheel . . . , a something so slight that only the practiced eye of the watchmaker can discover it, may be the source of all the difference.

And believing, as I do, with Cuvier, that the possession of articulate speech is the grand distinctive character of man (whether it be absolutely peculiar to him or not), I find it very easy to comprehend, that some equally inconspicuous structural difference may have been the primary cause of the immeasurable and practically infinite divergence of the Human from the Simian Stirps. . . . [122, fn.]

[There] is no existing link between Man and the Gorilla, but do not forget that there is no less sharp line of demarcation, no less complete absence of any transitional form, between the Gorilla and the Orang. . . . The structural differences between Man and the Man-like apes certainly justify our regarding him as constituting a family apart from them; though, inasmuch as he differs less from them than they do from other families of the same order, there can be no justification for placing him in a distinct order. . . .

[Linnaeus is justified in his conclusion] that man is a member of the same order . . . PRIMATES . . . as the Apes. . . . This order is now divisible into seven families. . . .

Perhaps no order of mammals presents us with so extraordinary a series of gradations as this—leading us insensibly from the crown and summit of the animal creation down to creatures, from which there is but a step, as it seems, to the lowest, smallest, and least intelligent of [124] the placental Mammalia. It is as if nature herself had foreseen the arrogance of man, and with Roman severity had provided that his intellect, by its very triumphs, should call into prominence the slaves, admonishing the conqueror that he is but dust. . . . [125]

[The] whole analogy of natural operations furnishes so complete and crushing an argument against the intervention of any but what are termed secondary causes, in the production of all the phenomena of the universe, that, in view of the intimate relations between Man and the rest of the living world, and between the forces exerted by the latter and all other forces, I can see no excuse for doubting that all are co-ordinated terms of Nature's great progression, from the formless to the formed—from the inorganic to the organic—from blind force to conscious intellect and will. [128]

I have endeavoured to show that no absolute structural line of demarcation, wider than that between the animals which immediately succeed us in the scale, can be drawn between the animal world and ourselves. . . . [Even] the highest faculties of feeling and of intellect begin to germinate in lower forms of life. At the same time no one is [129] more strongly convinced than I am of the vastness of the gulf between civilized man and the brutes; or is more certain that whether *from* them or not he is assuredly not *of* them. No one is less disposed to think lightly of the present dignity, or despairingly of the future hopes, of the only consciously intelligent denizen of this world.

We are indeed told . . . that the belief in the unity of origin of man and brutes involves the brutalization and degradation of the former. But is this really so? . . . Is . . . the Poet, or the Philosopher . . . bound to howl and grovel on all fours because . . . he was once an egg, which [130] no ordinary power of discrimination could distinguish from that of a Dog? Or is the philanthropist or the saint to give up his endeavors to lead a noble life, because the simplest study of man's nature reveals, at its foundations, all the selfish passions and fierce appetites of the merest quadruped? . . .

Nay . . ., thoughtful men, once escaped from the blinding influences of traditional prejudice, will find in the lowly stock whence man has sprung, the best evidence of the splendour of his capacities; and will discern in his long progress through the Past, a reasonable ground of faith in his attainment of a nobler Future. [131]

Our reverence for the nobility of manhood will not be lessened by the knowledge that Man is, in substance and in structure, one with the brutes; for, he alone possesses the marvellous endowment of intelligible and rational speech, whereby, in the secular period of his existence, he has slowly accumulated and organized the experience which is almost wholly lost with the cessation of every individual life in other animals; so that now he stands raised upon it as on a mountaintop, far above the level of his humble fellows, and transfigured from his grosser nature by reflecting, here and there, a ray from the infinite source of truth. [132]

❧ THOMAS H. HUXLEY

Science and Christian Tradition

Thomas H. Huxley, *Science and Christian Tradition*, New York, D. Appleton & Co., 1896.

AN EPISCOPAL TRILOGY, 1887

THE BELIEF in the efficacy of prayer depends upon the assumption that there is somebody, somewhere, who is strong enough to deal with the earth and its contents as men deal with the things and events [133] which they are strong enough to modify or control; and who is capable of being moved by appeals such as men make to one another. This belief does not even involve theism; for our earth is an insignificant particle of the solar system, while the solar system is hardly worth speaking of in relation to the All. . . . [134]

[It] is not upon any *a priori* considerations that objections, either to the supposed efficacy of prayer in modifying the course of events, or to the supposed occurrence of miracles, can be scientifically based. The real objection, and, to my mind, the fatal objection, to both these suppositions, is the inadequacy of the evidence to prove any given case of such occurrences which has been adduced. It is a canon of common sense, to say nothing of science, that the more improbable a supposed occurrence, the more cogent ought to be the evidence in its favor. I have looked somewhat carefully into the subject, and I am unable to find in the records of any miraculous event evidence which even approximates to the fulfilment of this requirement. [135]

AGNOSTICISM, 1889

I know of no study which is so unutterably saddening as that of the evolution of humanity, as it is set forth in the annals of history. Out of the darkness of prehistoric ages man emerges with the marks of his lowly origin strong upon him. He is a brute, only more intelligent than the other brutes, a blind prey to impulses, which as often as not lead him to destruction; a victim to endless illusions, which make his mental existence a terror and a burden, and fill his physical life with barren toil and battle. He attains a certain degree of physical comfort, and develops a more or less workable theory of life, in such favorable situations as the plains of Mesopotamia or of Egypt, and then, for thousands and thousands of years, struggles, with varying fortunes, attended by infinite wickedness, bloodshed, and misery, to maintain himself at this point against the greed and the ambition of his fellow-men. He makes a point of killing and otherwise persecuting all those who first try to get him to move on; and [256] when he has moved on a step, foolishly confers post-mortem deification on his victims. He exactly repeats the process with all who want to move a step yet farther. And the best men of the best epochs are simply those who make the fewest blunders and commit the fewest sins. [257]

ॐ HIPPOLYTE A. TAINE

History of English Literature

Hippolyte A. Taine, *History of English Literature* [1865], tr. by H. Van Laun, New York, Holt & Williams, 1871.

INTRODUCTION

IT IS A MISTAKE to study [any single] document as if it were isolated. . . . Behind all, we have neither mythology nor languages, but only men, who arrange words and imagery according to the necessities of their organs and the original bent of their intellects. A dogma is nothing in itself: look at the people who have made it. . . . [2]

[Scholars of the eighteenth century] thought [that] men of every race and century were all but identical . . ., as if they had been turned out of a common mould, and all in conformity to a certain abstract conception which served for the whole human race . . .; they had not seen the infinite diversity and marvellous complexity of souls; they did not know that the moral constitution of a people or an age is as particular and distinct as the physical structure of a family of plants or an order of animals. Nowadays history, like zoology, has found its anatomy; and whatever the branch of history to which you devote yourself—philology, linguistic lore, mythology—it is by these means you must strive to produce new fruit. . . . [5]

[There] is a cause for ambition, for courage, for truth, as there is for digestion, for muscular movement, for animal heat. Vice and virtue are products, like vitriol and sugar; and every complex phenomenon has its springs from other more simple phenomena on which it hangs. Let us then seek the simple phenomena for moral qualities, as we seek them for physical qualities; and let us take the first fact that presents itself: for example, religious music, that of a Protestant Church. There is an inner cause [for] these grave and monotonous melodies . . . : I mean the general idea of the true, external worship which man owes to God. . . . [6] This itself comes from another more general cause, the idea of human conduct in all its comprehensiveness, internal and external. . . . This second idea in its turn depends upon a third still more general, that of moral perfection. . . . That is the master idea, which consists in erecting duty into an absolute king of human life. . . . Here we track the root of man; for to explain this conception it is necessary to consider race itself—that is, the German, the Northman—the structure of his character and intelligence, his general processes of thought and feeling, the sluggishness and cold-ness of sensation which prevent his falling easily and headlong under the sway of pleasure. . . . There the search is at an end; we have ar-rived at a primitive disposition, at a trait proper to all sensations, to all the conceptions of a century or a race, at a particularity inseparable from all the motions of his intellect and his heart. Here lie the grand causes, for they are the universal and permanent causes, present at every moment and in every case, everywhere and always acting, indestructible, and in the end infallibly supreme, since the accidents which thwart them, being limited and partial, end by yielding to the dull and incessant repetition of their force; in such a manner that the general structure of things, and the grand features of events, are their work; and religions, philosophies, poetries, industries, the framework of society and of families, are in fact only the imprints stamped by their zeal.

There is then a system in human sentiments and ideas; and this system has for its motive power certain general traits, certain marks of the intellect and the heart common to men of one race, age, or country. As in mineralogy the crystals, however diverse, spring from certain simply physical forms, so in history, civilizations, however diverse, are [7] derived from certain simple spiritual forms. The one are [sic] explained by a primitive geometrical element, as the others are by a primitive psychological element. . . . [This] kind of ideal picture, geometrical as well as psychological, is hardly complex, and one speedily sees the limits of the outline in which civilizations, like crystals, are constrained to exist. . . . [8]

Three different sources contribute to produce this elementary moral state—the *race*, the *surroundings*, and the *epoch*. What we call the race are the innate and hereditary dispositions which man brings with him to the light, and which, as a rule, are united with the marked differences in the temperament and structure of the body. They vary with various peoples. There is a natural variety of men, as of oxen and horses . . ., some more specially fitted to special works and gifted more richly with particular instincts, as we meet with species of dogs better favoured than others. . . . We have here a distinct force—so distinct that amidst the vast deviations which the other two motive forces produce in him, one can recognize it still. . . . For as soon as an animal begins to exist, it has to reconcile itself with its surroundings; it breathes after a new fashion, renews itself, is differently affected according to the new changes in air, food, temperature. Different climate and situation bring it various needs, and consequently [10] a different course of actions; and this, again, a different set of habits; and still again, a different set of aptitudes and instincts. Man, forced to accommodate himself to circumstances, contracts a temperament and a character corresponding to them; and his character, like his temperament, is so much more stable, as the external impression is made upon him by more numerous repetitions, and is transmitted to his progeny by a more ancient descent. So that at any moment we may consider the character of a people as an abridgment of all its preceding actions and sensations; that is, as a quantity and as a weight, not infinite (as in Spinoza, *Ethics*, Part IV, axiom) since everything in nature is finite, but disproportioned to the rest, and almost impossible to life, since every moment of an almost infinite past has contributed to increase it, and because, in order to raise the scale, one must place in the opposite scale a still greater number of actions and sensations. Such is the first and the richest source of these master-faculties from which historical events take their rise; and one sees at the outset that, if it be powerful, it is because this is no simple spring, but a kind of lake, a deep reservoir wherein other springs have, for a multitude of centuries, discharged their several streams.

Having thus outlined the interior structure of a race, we must consider the surroundings in which it exists. For man is not alone in the world; nature surrounds him, and his fellow-men surround him; accidental and secondary tendencies come to place themselves on his primitive tendencies, and physical or social circumstances disturb or confirm the character committed to their charge. In course of time the climate has had its effect. . . . [We] can assert that the profound differences which are manifest between the German races . . . and the Greek and Latin . . . arise for the most part from the difference between the countries in which they are settled: some in cold moist lands, deep in black marshy forests or on the shores of a wild ocean, caged in by melancholy or violent sensations, prone to drunkenness and gluttony, bent on a fighting, blood-spilling life; others, again, within a lovely landscape, on a bright and laughing sea-coast, enticed to navigation and commerce, exempt from gross cravings of the stomach, inclined from the beginning to social ways, to a settled organization of the state, to feelings and dispositions such as develop the art of oratory, the talent for enjoyment, the inventions of science, letters, arts. Sometimes the state policy has been at work, as in the two Italian civilizations: the first wholly turned to action, conquest, government, legislation, by the original site of its city of refuge, by its border-land emporium, by an armed aristocracy . . . ; the other, shut [11] out from unity and any great political ambition by the stability of its municipal character, the cosmopolitan condition of its pope, and the military intervention of neighbouring nations, directed the whole of its magnificent, harmonious bent towards the worship of pleasure and beauty. Sometimes the social conditions have impressed their mark, as eighteen centuries ago by Christianity, and twenty-five centuries ago by Buddhism, when around the Mediterranean, as in Hindoostan, the extreme results of Aryan conquest and civilization induced an intolerable oppression, the subjugation of the individual, utter despair, a curse upon the world, with the development of metaphysics and myth, so that man in this dungeon of misery, feeling his heart softened, begot the idea of abnegation, charity, tender love, gentleness, humility, brotherly love—there, in a notion of universal nothingness, here under the Fatherhood of God. . . . These are the most efficacious of the visible causes which mould the primitive man: they are to nations what education, career, condition, abode are to individuals; and they seem to comprehend everything, since they comprehend all external powers which shape human matter, and by which the external acts on the internal.

There is yet a third rank of causes. . . . Beside the permanent impulse and the given surroundings, there is the acquired momentum. . . . [12] So it is with a people as with a plant; the same sap, under the same temperature, and in the same soil, produces, at different steps of its progressive development, different formations, buds, flowers . . . in such a manner that the one which follows has always the first for its condition, and grows from its death. . . . The great historical currents are formed after this law—the long dominations of one intellectual pattern, or a master idea, such as . . . the Renaissance. . . . Here as elsewhere we have but a mechanical problem; the total effect is a result, depending entirely on the magnitude and direction of the producing causes. The only difference which separates these moral problems from physical ones is, that the magnitude and direction cannot be valued or computed in the first as in the second. If a need or a faculty is a quantity, capable of degrees, like a pressure or a weight, this quantity is not measurable like the pressure or the weight. We cannot define it in an exact or approximative formula; we cannot have more, or give more, in respect of it, than a literary impression; we are limited to marking and [13] quoting the salient points by which it is manifested, and which indicate approximately . . . the part of the scale which is its position. But though the means of notation are not the same in the moral and physical sciences, yet as in both the matter is the same, equally made up of forces, magnitudes, and directions, we may say that in both the final result is produced after the same method. . . . So much we can say with confidence, that the unknown [literary] creations towards which the current of the centuries conducts us, will be raised up and regulated altogether by the primordial forces; that if these forces could be measured and computed, one might deduce from them as from a formula the specialties of future civilization; and that if . . . we try now to form some idea of our general destiny, it is upon an examination of these forces that we must ground our prophecy. For in enumerating them, we traverse the complete circle of the agencies; and when we have considered race, circumstance, and the acquired momentum, we have exhausted not only the whole of the actual causes, but also the whole of the possible causes of motion. . . . [14]

A civilization forms a body, and its parts are connected with each other like the parts of an organic body. As in an animal, instincts, teeth, limbs, . . . are mutually connected, so that a change in one produces a corresponding change in the rest, and a clever naturalist can by a process of reasoning reconstruct out of a few fragments almost the whole body; even so in a civilization, religion, philosophy, the organization of the family, literature, the arts, make up a system in which every local change induces a general change, so that an experienced historian, studying some particular part of it, sees in advance and half predicts the character of the rest. There is nothing vague in this interdependence. In the living body the regulator is, first, its tendency to manifest a certain primary type; then its necessity for organs whereby to satisfy its wants, and for harmony with itself in order that it may live. In a civilization, the regulator is the presence, in every great human creation, of a productive element, present also in other surrounding creations—to wit, some faculty, aptitude, disposition, effective and discernible, which, being possessed of its proper character, introduces it into all the operations in which it assists, and according to its variations causes all the works in which it cooperates to vary also. [17]

And so . . . every kind of human production— . . . literature, music, the fine arts, philosophy, science, statecraft, industries and the rest . . .—has for its direct cause a moral disposition, or a combination of moral dispositions: the cause given, they appear; the cause withdrawn, they vanish. . . . They are bound up with their causes, as a physical phenomenon with its condition, as the dew with the fall of the variable temperature, as dilatation [sic] with heat. There are such dualities in the moral as in the physical world, as rigorously bound together, and as universally extended in the one as in the other. Whatever develops credulity side by side with poetical thoughts, engenders religion. Thus phenomena have been produced; thus they will be produced. As soon as we know the sufficient and necessary condition of one of these vast occurrences, our understanding grasps the future as well as the past. We can say with confidence in what circumstances it will reappear, foresee without rashness many portions of its future history, and sketch with care some features of its ulterior development. [18]

It was not perceived that [Stendhal alone] explained the most complicated of esoteric mechanisms; that he laid his finger on the mainsprings; that he introduced into the history of the heart scientific processes, the art of notation, decomposition, deduction; that he first marked the fundamental causes of nationality, climate, temperament; in short, that he treated of sentiments as they should be treated—in the manner of the naturalist, namely, and of the natural philosopher, who constructs classifications and weighs forces. [19]

❧ ÉMILE ZOLA

The Experimental Novel

Émile Zola, "The Experimental Novel" [1880] in *The Experimental Novel & Other Essays*, New York, Cassell, 1893.

[THE LATE FRENCH SCIENTIST and author of *Introduction to the Study of Experimental Medicine*] Claude Bernard discusses observation and experiment at great length. There exists . . . a very clear line of demarcation, as follows: "The name of 'observer' is given to him who applies the simple or complex process of investigation in the study of phenomena which he does not vary, and which he gathers, consequently, as nature offers them to him; the name of 'experimentalist' is given to him who employs the simple and complex process of investigation to vary or modify, for an end of some kind, the natural phenomena, and to make them appear under circumstances and conditions in which they are not presented by nature." For instance, astronomy is a science of observation, because you cannot conceive of an astronomer acting upon the stars; while chemistry is an experimental science, as the chemist acts upon nature and modifies it. . . . I repeat [Bernard's] words: [6] ". . . experiment is an observation instigated for the purpose of verification. . . . The observer relates purely and simply the phenomena which he has under his eyes. . . . He should be the photographer of phenomena, his observation should be an exact representation of nature . . . He listens to nature and he writes under its dictation. But once the fact is ascertained and the phenomenon observed, an idea or hypothesis comes into his mind, reason intervenes, and the experimentalist comes forward to interpret the phenomenon. . . ." [7]

Now, to return to the novel, we can easily see that the novelist is equally an observer and an experimentalist. The observer in him gives the facts as he has observed them, suggests the point of departure, displays the solid earth on which his characters are to tread and the phenomena to develop. Then the experimentalist appears and introduces an experiment, . . . sets his characters going in a certain

story so as to show that the succession of facts will be such as the requirement of the determination of the phenomena under examination
call for. . . . I will take as an example the character of the Baron
Hulot in "Cousine Bette," by Balzac. The general fact observed by
Balzac is the ravages that the amorous temperament of a man makes
in his home, in his family, and in society. As soon as he has chosen his
subject, he starts from known facts; then he makes his experiment,
and exposes Hulot to a series of trials, [8] placing him amid certain
surroundings in order to exhibit how the complicated machinery of
his passions works. It is then evident that there is not only observation
there, but that there is also experiment; as Balzac does not remain
satisfied with photographing the facts collected by him, but inter-
feres in a direct way to place his character in certain conditions, and
of these he remains the master. The problem is to know what such a
passion, acting in such a surrounding and under such circumstances,
would produce from the point of view of an individual and of society;
and an experimental novel, 'Cousine Bette,' for example, is simply the
report of the experiment that the novelist conducts before the eyes
of the public. In fact, the whole operation consists in taking facts in
nature, then in studying the mechanism of these facts, acting upon
them, by the modification of circumstances and surroundings, without deviating from the laws of nature. Finally, you possess knowledge
of the man, scientific knowledge of him, in both his individual and
social relations. . . . [9]

A contemptible reproach which they heap upon us naturalistic
writers is the desire to be solely photographers. We have in vain declared that we admit the necessity of an artist's possessing an individual temperament and a personal expression. . . . The idea of
experiment carries with it the idea of modification. We start, indeed,
from the true facts, which are our indestructible basis; but to show
the mechanism of these facts it is necessary for us to produce and
direct the phenomena; this is our share of invention, here is the genius
in the book. . . . [11]

[Bernard] makes doubt the great scientific lever. "The doubter is
the true savant; he doubts only himself and his interpretations; he
believes in science; he even admits in the experimental sciences a cri-
terion or a positive principle, the determinism of phenomena, which
is absolute in living beings as in inanimate bodies." Thus, instead of
confining the novelist within narrow bounds, the experimental

method gives full sway to his intelligence as a thinker, and to his genius as a creator. . . . [12]

[If] the experimental method can be carried from chemistry and physics into physiology and medicine, it can also be carried from physiology into the naturalistic novel.

Cuvier . . . pretended that experiment as applied to inanimate bodies could not be used with living beings. . . . The vitalists even admit a vital force in unceasing battle with the physical and chemical forces neutralizing their action. Claude Bernard, on the contrary, denies all presence of a mysterious force, and affirms that experiment is applicable everywhere. "I propose," he says, "to establish the fact that the science of the phenomena of life can have no other basis than the science of the phenomena of inanimate bodies, and that there are, in this connection, no differences between the principles of biological science and those of physics and chemistry. In fact, the end the experimental method proposes is the same everywhere; it consists in connecting, by experiment, the natural phenomena [14] to their conditions of existence or to their nearest causes. . . . [The vitalists] consider life as a mysterious and supernatural agent, which acts arbitrarily, free from all determinism, and they condemn as materialists all those who endeavor to trace vital phenomena to definite organic and physicochemical conditions. These are false ideas, which it is not easy to root out once they have become [15] domiciled in the mind; only the progress of science can dissipate them." And he lays down this axiom: "With living beings as well as inanimate, the conditions of the existence of each phenomenon are determined in an absolute manner." . . .

Thus you see the progress which science has made. In the last century a more exact application of the experimental method creates physics and chemistry, which then are freed from the irrational and supernatural. Men discover that there are fixed laws, thanks to analysis, and make themselves masters of phenomena. Then . . . living beings, in which the vitalists still admitted a mysterious influence, are in their turn brought under and reduced to the general mechanism of matter. Science proves that the existing conditions of all phenomena are the same in living beings as in inanimate; and from that time on physiology assumes little by little the certainty of chemistry and medicine. But are we going to stop there? Evidently not. When it has been proved that the body of man is a machine, whose machinery can be taken apart and put together again at the will of the experimenter, then we can pass to the passionate and intellectual acts of man. Then we shall enter into the domain which up to the present has belonged to physiology and literature; it will be the decisive conquest by science of the hypotheses of philosophers and writers. We have experimental chemistry and medicine; we shall have an experimental physiology, and later on an experimental novel. It is an inevitable evolution, the goal of which it is easy to see today. [16] All things hang together; it is necessary to start from the determinism of inanimate bodies in order to arrive at the determinism of living beings; and since savants like Claude Bernard demonstrate now that fixed laws govern the human body, we can easily proclaim . . . the hour in which the laws of thought and passion will be formulated in their turn. A like determinism will govern the stones of the roadway and the brain of man. . . . [17]

I consider that the question of heredity has a great influence in the intellectual and passionate manifestations of man. I also attach considerable importance to the suroundings. I ought to touch upon Darwin's theories . . . but I will only say a word on the subject of surroundings. We have just seen the great importance given by Claude Bernard to [19] the study of those inter-organic conditions which must be taken into account if we wish to find the determinism of phenomena in living beings. Well, then! in the study of a family, of a group of living beings, I think that the social condition is of equal importance. Some day the physiologist will explain to us the mechanism of the thoughts and the passions; we shall know how the individual machinery of each man works; how he thinks, how he loves, how he goes from reason to passion and folly; but these phenomena, resulting as they do from the mechanism of the organs, acting under the influence of an interior condition, are not produced in isolation or in the bare void. Man is not alone; he lives in society . . . and consequently, for us novelists, this social condition unceasingly modifies the phenomena. Indeed our great study is just there, in the reciprocal effect of society on the individual and the individual on society. For the physiologist, the exterior and interior conditions are purely chemical and physical, and this aids him in finding the laws which govern them easily. We are not yet able to prove that the social condition is also physical and chemical. It is that certainly, or rather it is the variable product of a group of living beings who themselves are absolutely submissive to the physical and chemical laws which govern alike living beings and inanimate. From this we shall see that we can act upon the social conditions, in acting upon the phenomena of which we have made ourselves master in man. And this is what constitutes the experimental novel: to possess a knowledge of the mechanism of the phenomena inherent in man, to show the machinery of his intellectual and sensory [20] manifestations, under the influences of heredity and environment, such as physiology shall give them to us, and then finally to exhibit man living in social conditions produced by himself, which he modifies daily, and in the heart of which he himself experiences a continual transformation. . . . [21]

[The] dream of the physiologist and the experimental doctor is also that of the novelist, who employs the experimental method in his study of man as a simple individual and as a social animal. Their object is ours; we also desire to master certain phenomena of an intellectual and personal order, to be able to direct them. We are, in a word, experimental moralists, showing by experiment in what way a passion acts in a certain social condition. The day in which we gain control of the mechanism of this passion we can treat it and reduce it, or at least make it as inoffensive as possible. And in this consists the practical utility and high morality of our naturalistic works, which experiment on man, and which dissect piece by piece this human machinery in order to set it going [25] through the influence of the environment. When things have advanced further, when we are in possession of the different laws, it will only be necessary to work upon the individuals and the surroundings if we wish to find the best social condition. In this way we shall construct a practical sociology, and our work will be a help to political and economical sciences. I do not know . . . of a more noble work. . . . To be the master of good and evil, to regulate life, to regulate society, to solve in time all the problems of socialism, above all, to give justice a solid foundation by solving through experiment the questions of criminality—is not this being the most useful and the most moral workers in the human workshop? [26]

Claude Bernard says truly: "The intellectual conquest of man consists in diminishing and driving back indeterminism, and so, gradually, by the aid of the experimental method, gaining ground for determinism." . . . If our work, often cruel, if our terrible pictures needed justification, I should find, indeed, with Claude Bernard this argument conclusive: "You will never reach really fruitful and luminous generalizations on the phenomena of life until you have experimented yourself and stirred up in the hospital, the amphitheatre, and the laboratory the fetid or palpitating sources of life. If it were necessary for me to give a comparison which would explain my sentiments on the science of life, I should say that it is a superb salon, flooded with light, which you can only reach by passing through a long and nauseating kitchen." . . . [27]

They think to crush the naturalistic novelists by treating them as fatalists. How many times have they wished to prove to us that as soon as we did not accept free will, that as soon as man was no more to us than a living machine, acting under the influence of heredity and surroundings, we should fall into gross fatalism, we should debase humanity to the rank of a troop marching under the baton of destiny. It is necessary to define our terms: we are not fatalists, we are determinists, which is not at all the same thing. Claude Bernard explains the two terms very plainly: "We have given the name of determinism to the nearest or determining cause of phenomena. We never act upon the essence of phenomena in nature, but only on their determinism, and by this very fact, that we act upon it, determinism differs from fatalism, upon which we could not act at all. [29] Fatalism assumes that the appearance of any phenomenon is necessary apart from its conditions, while determinism is just the condition essential for the appearance of any phenomenon, and such appearance is never forced. . . ." All we do is to apply this method in our novels, and we are the determinists who experimentally try to determine the condition of the phenomena, without departing in our investigations from the laws of nature. As Claude Bernard very truly says, the moment that we can act, and that we do act, on the determining cause of phenomena—by modifying their surroundings, for example—we cease to be fatalists. [30]

As our power [as novelists] is not the same as that of a savant, as we are experimentalists without being practitioners, we ought to content ourselves with searching out the determinism of social phenomena, and leaving to legislators and to men of affairs the care of controlling sooner or later these phenomena in such a way as to develop the good and reject the bad, from the point of view of their utility to man. . . . Compare with ours the work of the idealistic writers, who rely upon the irrational and the supernatural, and whose every flight upward is followed by a deeper fall into metaphysical chaos. We are the ones who possess strength and morality. . . . [31]

Let it be well understood that I am speaking of the "how" of things and not of the "why." For an experimental savant, the ideal which he is endeavoring to reduce, the indeterminate, is always restricted to the "how." He leaves to philosophers the other ideal, that of the "why," which he despairs of determining. I think that the experimental novelists equally ought not to occupy themselves with this unknown quality, [38] unless they wish to lose themselves in the follies of the poets and the philosophers. It is surely an object large enough to try to know the entire mechanism of nature, without troubling one's self for the time being with the origin of the mechanism. [39]

๕ ARTHUR SCHOPENHAUER

The World as Will and Idea

Arthur Schopenhauer, *The World as Will and Idea* [1818] tr. by R. B. Haldane and J. Kemp, London, Trubner & Co., 1883; 3 vols.

[To] MAN in a state of nature, as to the brutes, [the sexual impulse] is the final end, the highest goal of life. Self-maintenance is his first effort, and as soon as he has made provision for that, he only strives after the propagation of the species: as a merely natural being he can attempt no more. Nature also, the inner being of which is the will to live itself, impels with all her power both man and the brute towards propagation. Then it has attained its end with the individual, and is quite indifferent to its death, for, as the will to live, it cares only for the preservation of the species, the individual is nothing to it. . . . [I, 425]

[The] sexual desire has a very different character from every other; it is not only the strongest, but even specifically of a more powerful kind than any other. . . . For it is the desire which [III, 312] even constitutes the nature of man. In conflict with it no motive is so strong that it would be certain of victory. It is so pre-eminently the chief concern that no other pleasures make up for the deprivation of its satisfaction; and, moreover, for its sake both brute and man undertake every danger and every conflict. . . . [Sex] is really the invisible central point of all action and conduct, and peeps out everywhere in spite of all veils thrown over it. It is the cause of war and the end of peace, the basis of what is serious, and the aim of the jest, the inexhaustible source of wit, the key to all allusions, and the meaning of all . . . stolen glances, the daily meditation of the young, and often also of the old, the hourly thought of the unchaste, and even against their will the constantly recurring imagination of the chaste. . . . [III, 313] [We] see it every moment seat itself, as the true and hereditary lord of the world, out of the fulness of its own strength, upon the ancestral throne, and looking down from thence with scornful glances, laugh at the preparations which have been made to bind it, imprison it, or at least to limit it and wherever it is possible to keep it concealed, or even so to master it that it shall only appear as a subordinate, secondary concern of life. But all this agrees with the fact that the sexual passion is the kernel of the will to live, and consequently the concentration of all desire. . . . Indeed, one may say man is concrete sexual desire . . . and this tendency alone perpetuates and holds together his whole phenomenal existence. The will to live manifests itself indeed primarily as an effort to sustain the individual; yet this is only a step to the effort to sustain the species, and the latter endeavour must be more powerful in proportion as the life of the species surpasses that of the individual in duration, extension, and value. Therefore sexual passion is the most perfect manifestation of the will to live, its most distinctly expressed type; and the origin of the individual in it, and its primacy over all other desires of the natural man, are both in complete agreement with this. . . . [III, 314]

It is a vain and absurd pretence when women assert that they have fallen in love with the mind of a man. . . . Men, on the other hand, are not determined in their instinctive love by the qualities of character of the woman. . . . That a woman of culture and understanding prizes understanding and intellect in a man, that a man from rational reflection should test and have regard to the character of his bride, has nothing to do with the matter with which we are dealing here. Such things lie at the bottom of a rational choice in marriage, but not of the passionate love which is our theme. . . .

[What] is looked to is the rectification of the type of the species, . . . the return to the pure presentation of the type. Here, then, each one loves what he lacks. Starting from the individual constitution, and directed to the individual constitution, the choice which rests

upon [III, 355] such relative considerations is much more definite, decided, and exclusive than that which proceeds merely from the absolute considerations. . . . Accordingly it is not generally precisely
correct and perfect beauties that kindle great passions. For such a
truly passionate inclination to arise something is required which can
only be expressed by a chemical metaphor: two persons must neu-
tralise each other, like acid and alkali, to a neutral salt. The essential
conditions demanded for this are the following. First: all sex is one-
sided. This one-sidedness is more distinctly expressed in one individual than in another; therefore in every individual it can be better sup-
plemented and neutralised by one than by another individual of the
opposite sex, for each one requires a one-sidedness which is the opposite of his own to complete the type of humanity in the new individual
that it to be produced, the constitution of which is always the goal towards which all tends. . . . Accordingly, the neutralisation of two
individualities by each other . . . demands that the definite degree
of *his* manhood shall exactly correspond to the definite degree of *her*
womanhood; so that the one-sidedness of each exactly annuls that of
the other. . . . [III, 356] While . . . the lovers speak pathetically of
the harmony of their souls, the heart of the matter is for the most
part the agreement or suitableness . . . with reference to the being
which is to be produced and its perfection, and which is also clearly
of much more importance than the harmony of their souls, which often, not long after the marriage, resolves itself into a howling dis-
cord. . . . The weaker a man is . . . the more will he seek for strong
women; and the woman on her side will do the same. . . . [III, 357]
Blondes prefer dark persons, or brunettes; but the latter seldom prefer the former. The reason is, that fair hair and blue eyes are in themselves a variation from the type. . . . Therefore in sexual love nature strives to return to dark hair and brown eyes as the primitive
type. . . . Men with excessively slim, long bodies and limbs can
find beauty in a body which is even beyond measure stumpy and
short. The considerations with regard to temperament act in
an [III, 358] analogous manner. Each will prefer the temperament opposed to his own; yet only in proportion as his one is decided. Who-
ever is himself in some respect very perfect does not indeed seek and
love imperfection in this respect, but is yet more easily reconciled
to it than others; because he himself insures the children against
great imperfection of this part. [III, 359]

Part II

INDIVIDUAL AUTHORS

❧ HERMAN MELVILLE

Moby-Dick

Herman Melville, *Moby-Dick: or, The Whale*, New York, Harper & Brothers, 1851.

CHAPTER XLII

The Whiteness of the Whale

WHAT THE WHITE WHALE was to Ahab, has been hinted; what, at times, he was to me, as yet remains unsaid.

Aside from those more obvious considerations touching Moby-Dick, which could not but occasionally awaken in any man's soul some alarm, there was another thought, or rather vague, nameless horror concerning him, which at times by its intensity completely overpowered all the rest; and yet so mystical and well nigh ineffable was it, that I almost despair of putting it in a comprehensible form. It was the whiteness of the whale that above all things appalled me. But how can I hope to explain myself here; and yet, in some dim, random way, explain myself I must, else all these chapters might be naught.

Though in many natural objects, whiteness refiningly enhances beauty, as if imparting some special virtue of its own, as in marbles, japonicas, and pearls; and though various nations have in some way recognised a certain royal pre-eminence in this hue; even the barbaric, grand old kings of Pegu placing the title "Lord of the White Elephants" above all their other magniloquent ascriptions of dominion; and the modern kings of Siam unfurling the same snowy-white quadruped in the royal standard; and the Hanoverian flag bearing the one figure of a snow-white charger; and the great Austrian Empire, Caesarian, heir to overlording Rome, having for the imperial color the same imperial hue; and though this pre-eminence in it applies [207] to the human race itself, giving the white man ideal mastership over every dusky tribe; and though, besides all this, whiteness has been even made significant of gladness, for among the Romans a white stone marked a joyful day; and though in other mortal sympathies and symbolizings, this same hue is made the emblem of many touching, noble things—the innocence of brides, the benignity of age; though among the Red Men of America the giving of the white belt of wampum was the deepest pledge of honor; though in many climes, whiteness typifies the majesty of Justice in the ermine of the Judge, and contributes to the daily state of kings and queens drawn by milk-white steeds; though even in the higher mysteries of the most august religions it has been made the symbol of the divine spotlessness and power; by the Persian fire worshippers, the white forked flame being held the holiest on the altar; and in the Greek mythologies, Great Jove himself being made incarnate in a snow-white bull; and though to the noble Iroquois, the midwinter sacrifice of the sacred White Dog was by far the holiest festival of their theology, that spotless, faithful creature being held the purest envoy they could send to the Great Spirit with the annual tidings of their own fidelity; and though directly from the Latin word for white, all Christian priests derive the name of one part of their sacred vesture, the alb or tunic, worn beneath the cassock; and though among the holy pomps of the Romish faith, white is specially employed in the celebration of the Passion of our Lord; though in the Vision of St. John, white robes are given to the redeemed, and the four-and-twenty elders stand clothed in white before the great white throne, and the Holy One that sitteth there white like wool; yet for all these accumulated associations, with whatever is sweet, and honorable, and sublime, there yet lurks an elusive something in the innermost idea of this hue, which strikes more of panic to the soul than that redness which affrights in blood. [208]

This elusive quality it is, which causes the thought of whiteness, when divorced from more kindly associations, and coupled with any object terrible in itself, to heighten that terror to the furthest bounds. Witness the white bear of the poles, and the white shark of the tropics; what but their smooth, flaky whiteness makes them the transcendent horrors they are? That ghastly whiteness it is which imparts such an abhorrent mildness, even more loathsome than terrific, to the dumb gloating of their aspect. So that not the fierce-fanged tiger in his heraldic coat can so stagger courage as the white-shrouded bear or shark. . . .

Bethink thee of the albatross, whence come those clouds of spiritual wonderment and pale dread, in which that white phantom sails in all imaginations? Not Coleridge first threw that spell; but God's great, unflattering laureate, Nature. . . . [209]

Most famous in our Western annals and Indian traditions is that of the White Steed of the Prairies, a magnificent milk-white charger, large-eyed, small-headed, bluff-chested, and with the dignity of a thousand monarchs in his lofty, overscorning carriage. He was the elected Xerxes of vast herds of wild horses, whose pastures in those days were only fenced by the [210] Rocky Mountains and the Alleghanies. . . . [A]lways to the bravest Indians he was the object of trembling reverence and awe. Nor can it be questioned from what stands on legendary record of this noble horse, that it was his spiritual whiteness chiefly, which so clothed him with divineness; and that this divineness had that in it which, though commanding worship, at the same time enforced a certain nameless terror.

But there are other instances where this whiteness loses all that accessory and strange glory which invests it in the White Steed and Albatross.

What is it that in the Albino man so peculiarly repels and often shocks the eye, as that sometimes he is loathed by his own kith and kin! It is that whiteness which invests him, a thing expressed by the name he bears. The Albino is as well made as other men—has no substantive deformity—and yet this mere aspect of all-pervading whiteness makes him more strangely hideous than the ugliest abortion. Why should this be so? [211]

Nor, in quite other aspects, does Nature in her least palpable but not the less malicious agencies, fail to enlist among her forces this crowning attribute of the terrible. From its snowy aspect, the gauntleted ghost of the Southern Seas has been denominated the White Squall. Nor, in some historic instances, has the art of human malice omitted so potent an auxiliary. How wildly it heightens the effect of that passage in Froissart, when, masked in the snowy symbol of their faction, the desperate White Hoods of Ghent murder their bailiff in the market-place!

Nor, in some things, does the common, hereditary experience of all mankind fail to bear witness to the supernaturalism of this hue. It cannot well be doubted, that the one visible quality in the aspect of the dead which most appals the gazer, is the marble pallor lingering there; as if indeed that pallor were as much like the badge of consternation in the other world, as of mortal trepidation here. And from that pallor of the dead, we borrow the expressive hue of the shroud in which we wrap them. Nor even in our superstitions do we fail to throw the same snowy mantle round our phantoms; all ghosts rising in a milk-white fog—Yea, while these terrors seize us, let us add, that even the king of terrors, when personified by the evangelist, rides on his pallid horse.

Therefore, in his other moods, symbolize whatever grand or gracious thing he will by whiteness, no man can deny that in its profoundest idealized significance it calls up a peculiar apparition to the soul.

But though without dissent this point be fixed, how is mortal man to account for it? . . . [212]

Why to the man of untutored ideality, who happens to be but loosely acquainted with the peculiar character of the day, does the bare mention of Whitsuntide marshal in the fancy such long, dreary, speechless processions of slow-pacing pilgrims, downcast and hooded with new-fallen snow? Or, to the unread, unsophisticated Protestant of the Middle American States, why does the passing mention of a White Friar or a White Nun, evoke such an eyeless statue in the soul?

Or what is there apart from the traditions of dungeoned warriors and kings (which will not wholly account for it) that makes the White Tower of London tell so much more strongly on the imagination of an untravelled American, than those other storied structures, its neighbors—the Byward Tower, or even the Bloody? And those sublimer towers, the White Mountains of New Hampshire, whence, in peculiar moods, comes that gigantic ghostliness over the soul at the bare mention of that name, while the thought of Virginia's Blue Ridge is full of a soft, dewy, distant dreaminess? . . . Or, to choose a wholly unsubstantial instance, purely addressed to the fancy, why, in reading the old fairy tales of Central Europe, does [213] "the tall pale man" of the Hartz forests, whose changeless pallor unrustingly glides through the green of the groves—why is this phantom more terrible than all the whooping imps of the Blocksburg? . . .

I know that, to the common apprehension, this phenomenon of whiteness is not confessed to be the prime agent in exaggerating the terror of objects otherwise terrible; nor to the unimaginative mind is there aught of terror in those appearances whose awfulness to another mind almost solely consists in this one phenomenon, especially when exhibited under any form at all approaching to muteness or universality. What I mean by these two statements may perhaps be respectively elucidated by the following examples.

First: The mariner, when drawing nigh the coasts of foreign lands, if by night he hear the roar of breakers, starts to vigilance, and feels just enough of trepidation to sharpen all his faculties; but under precisely similar circumstances, let him be called from his hammock to view his ship sailing through a midnight sea of milky whiteness —as if from encircling headlands shoals of combed white bears were swimming round him, [214] then he feels a silent, superstitious dread; the shrouded phantom of the whitened waters is horrible to him as a real ghost; in vain the lead assures him he is still off soundings; heart and helm they both go down; he never rests till blue water is under him again. Yet where is the mariner who will tell thee, "Sir, it was not so much the fear of striking hidden rocks, as the fear of that hideous whiteness that so stirred me?"

Second: To the native Indian of Peru, the continual sight of the snow-howdahed Andes conveys naught of dread, except, perhaps in the mere fancying of the eternal frosted desolateness reigning at such vast altitudes, and the natural conceit of what a fearfulness it would be to lose oneself in such inhuman solitudes. Much the same is it with the backwoodsman of the West, who with comparative indifference views an unbounded prairie sheeted with driven snow, no shadow of tree or twig to break the fixed trance of whiteness. Not so the sailor, beholding the scenery of the Antarctic seas; where at times, by some infernal trick of legerdemain in the powers of frost and air, he, shivering and half shipwrecked, instead of rainbows speaking hope and solace to his misery, views what seems a boundless church-yard grinning upon him with its lean ice monuments and splintered crosses.

But thou sayest, methinks this white-lead chapter about whiteness is but a white flag hung out from a craven soul; thou surrenderest to a hypo, Ishmael.

Tell me, why this strong young colt, foaled in some peaceful valley of Vermont, far removed from all beasts of prey—why is it that upon the sunniest day, if you but shake a fresh buffalo robe behind him, so that he cannot even see it, but only smells its wild animal muskiness—why will he start, snort, and with bursting eyes paw the ground in phrensies of affright? There is no remembrance in him of any gorings of wild creatures in his green northern home, so that the strange muskiness he smells cannot recall to him anything associated with the experience [215] of former perils; for what knows he, this New England colt, of the black bisons of distant Oregon? No: but here thou beholdest even in a dumb brute, the instinct of the knowledge of the demonism in the world. Though thousands of miles from Oregon, still when he smells that savage musk, the rending, goring bison herds are as present as to the deserted wild foal of the prairies, which this instant they may be trampling into dust.

Thus, then, the muffled rollings of a milky sea; the bleak rustlings of the festooned frosts of mountains; the desolate shiftings of the windrowed snows of prairies; all these, to Ishmael, are as the shaking of that buffalo robe to the frightened colt!

Though neither knows where lie the nameless things of which the mystic sign gives forth such hints; yet with me, as with the colt, somewhere those things must exist. Though in many of its aspects this visible world seems formed in love, the invisible spheres were formed in fright.

But not yet have we solved the incantation of this whiteness, and learned why it appeals with such power to the soul; and more strange and far more portentous—why, as we have seen, it is at once the most meaning symbol of spiritual things, nay, the very veil of the Christian's Deity; and yet should be as it is, the intensifying agent in things the most appalling to mankind.

Is it that by its indefiniteness it shadows forth the heartless voids and immensities of the universe, and thus stabs us from behind with the thought of annihilation, when beholding the white depths of the milky way? Or is it, that as in essence whiteness is not so much a color as the visible absence of color, and at the same time the concrete of all colors; is it for these reasons that there is such a dumb blankness, full of meaning, in a wide landscape of snows—a colorless, all-color of atheism from which we shrink? And when we consider that other theory of the natural philosophers, that all other earthly hues [216]—every stately or lovely emblazoning—the sweet tinges of sunset skies and woods; yea, and the gilded velvets of butterflies, and the butterfly cheeks of young girls; all these are but subtile deceits, not actually inherent in substances, but only laid on from without; so that all deified Nature absolutely paints like the harlot, whose allurements cover nothing but the charnel-house within; and when we proceed further, and consider that the mystical cosmetic which produces every one of her hues, the great principle of light, for ever remains white or colorless in itself, and if operating without medium upon matter, would touch all objects, even tulips and roses, with its own blank tinge—pondering all this, the palsied universe lies before us a leper; and like wilful travellers in Lapland, who refuse to wear colored and coloring glasses upon their eyes, so the wretched infidel gazes himself blind at the monumental white shroud that wraps all the prospect around him. And of all these things the Albino whale was the symbol. Wonder ye then at the fiery hunt? [217]

✿ HAMLIN GARLAND

Under the Lion's Paw

Hamlin Garland, "Under the Lion's Paw," *Main-Travelled Roads,* Boston, Arena Publishing Co., 1891.*

"Along this main-travelled road trailed an endless line of prairie-schooners, coming into sight at the east, and passing out of sight over the swell to the west. We children used to wonder where they were going and why they went."

IT WAS THE LAST OF AUTUMN and first day of winter coming together. All day long the ploughmen on their prairie farms had moved to and fro in their wide level fields through the falling snow, which melted as it fell, wetting them to the skin—all day, notwithstanding the frequent squalls of snow, the dripping, desolate clouds, and the muck of the furrows, black and tenacious as tar.

Under their dripping harness the horses swung to and fro silently, with that marvellous uncomplaining patience which marks the horse. All day the wild geese, honking wildly, as they sprawled sidewise down the wind, seemed to be fleeing from an enemy behind, and with neck outthrust and wings extended, sailed down the wind, soon lost to sight.

Yet the ploughman behind his plough, though the snow lay on his

* An inexpensive edition of this volume, edited by Thomas A. Bledsoe and following the original text, is published by Rinehart & Co.

ragged great-coat, and the cold clinging mud rose on his heavy boots, fettering [217] him like gyves, whistled in the very beard of the gale. As day passed, the snow, ceasing to melt, lay along the ploughed land, and lodged in the depth of the stubble, till on each slow round the last furrow stood out black and shining as jet between the ploughed land and the gray stubble.

When night began to fall, and the geese, flying low, began to alight invisibly in the near corn-field, Stephen Council was still at work "finishing a land." He rode on his sulky plough when going with the wind, but walked when facing it. Sitting bent and cold but cheery under his slouch hat, he talked encouragingly to his four-in-hand.

"Come round there, boys!—Round agin! We got t' finish this land. Come in there, Dan! *Stiddy*, Kate,—stiddy! None o' y'r tantrums, Kittie. It's purty tuff, but got a be did. *Tchk! tchk!* Step along, Pete! Don't let Kate git y'r single-tree on the wheel. *Once* more!"

They seemed to know what he meant, and that this was the last round, for they worked with greater vigor than before.

"Once more, boys, an' then, sez I, oats an' a nice warm stall, an' sleep f'r all."

By the time the last furrow was turned on the land it was too dark to see the house, and the snow was changing to rain again. The tired and hungry man could see the light from the kitchen shining through the leafless hedge, and lifting a [218] great shout, he yelled, "Sup*per* f'r a half a dozen!"

It was nearly eight o'clock by the time he had finished his chores and started for supper. He was picking his way carefully through the mud, when the tall form of a man loomed up before him with a premonitory cough.

"Waddy ye want?" was the rather startled question of the farmer.

"Well, ye see," began the stranger, in a deprecating tone, "we'd like t' git in f'r the night. We've tried every house f'r the last two miles, but they hadn't any room f'r us. My wife's jest about sick, 'n' the children are cold and hungry——"

"Oh, y' want a stay all night, eh?"

"Yes, sir; it 'ud be a great accom——"

"Waal, I don't make it a practice t' turn anybody way hungry, not on sech nights as this. Drive right in. We ain't got much, but sech as it is——"

But the stranger had disappeared. And soon his steaming, weary team, with drooping heads and swinging single-trees, moved past the well to the block beside the path. Council stood at the side of the "schooner" and helped the children out—two little half-sleeping children—and then a small woman with a babe in her arms.

"There ye go!" he shouted jovially, to the [219] children. "*Now* we're all right! Run right along to the house there, an' tell Mam' Council you wants sumpthin' t' eat. Right this way, Mis'—keep right off t' the right there. I'll go an' git a lantern. Come," he said to the dazed and silent group at his side.

"Mother," he shouted, as he neared the fragrant and warmly lighted kitchen, "here are some wayfarers an' folks who need sumpin' t' eat an' a place t' snooze." He ended by pushing them all in.

Mrs. Council, a large, jolly, rather coarse-looking woman, took the children in her arms. "Come right in, you little rabbits. 'Most asleep, hey? Now here's a drink o' milk f'r each o' ye. I'll have s'm tea in a minute. Take off y'r things and set up t' the fire."

While she set the children to drinking milk, Council got out his lantern and went out to the barn to help the stranger about his team, where his loud, hearty voice could be heard as it came and went between the haymow and the stalls.

The woman came to light as a small, timid, and discouraged-looking woman, but still pretty, in a thin and sorrowful way.

"Land sakes! An' you've travelled all the way from Clear Lake t'-day in this mud! Waal! waal! No wonder you're all tired out. Don't [220] wait f'r the men, Mis'——" She hesitated, waiting for the name.

"Haskins."

"Mis' Haskins, set right up to the table an' take a good swig o' tea whilst I make y' s'm toast. It's green tea, an' it's good. I tell Council as I git older I don't seem to enjoy Young Hyson n'r Gunpowder. I want the reel green tea, jest as it comes off'n the vines. Seems t' have more heart in it, some way. Don't s'pose it has. Council says it's all in m' eye."

Going on in this easy way, she soon had the children filled with bread and milk and the woman thoroughly at home, eating some toast and sweet-melon pickles, and sipping the tea.

"See the little rats!" she laughed at the children. "They're full as they can stick now, and they want to go to bed. Now, don't git up, Mis' Haskins; set right where you are an' let me look after 'em. I know all about young ones, though I'm all alone now. Jane went an' married last fall. But, as I tell Council, it's lucky we keep our health. Set right there, Mis' Haskins; I won't have you stir a finger."

It was an unmeasured pleasure to sit there in the warm, homely kitchen, the jovial chatter of the housewife driving out and holding at bay the growl of the impotent, cheated wind.

The little woman's eyes filled with tears which [221] fell down upon the sleeping baby in her arms. The world was not so desolate and cold and hopeless, after all.

"Now I hope Council won't stop out there and talk politics all night. He's the greatest man to talk politics an' read the *Tribune*. How old is it?"

She broke off and peered down at the face of the babe.

"Two months 'n' five days," said the mother, with a mother's exactness.

"Ye don't say! I want 'o know! The dear little pudzy-wudzy!" she went on, stirring it up in the neighborhood of the ribs with her fat forefinger.

"Pooty tough on 'oo to go gallivant'n' 'cross lots this way——"

"Yes, that's so; a man can't lift a mountain," said Council, entering the door. "Mother, this is Mr. Haskins, from Kansas. He's been eat up 'n' drove out by grasshoppers."

"Glad t' see yeh!—Pa, empty that wash-basin 'n' give him a chance t' wash."

Haskins was a tall man, with a thin, gloomy face. His hair was a reddish brown, like his coat, and seemed equally faded by the wind and sun. And his sallow face, though hard and set, was pathetic somehow. You would have felt [222] that he had suffered much by the line of his mouth showing under his thin, yellow mustache.

"Hain't Ike got home yet, Sairy?"

"Hain't seen 'im."

"W-a-a-l, set right up, Mr. Haskins; wade right into what we've got; 'taint much, but we manage to live on it—she gits fat on it," laughed Council, pointing his thumb at his wife.

After supper, while the women put the children to bed, Haskins and Council talked on, seated near the huge cooking-stove, the steam rising from their wet clothing. In the Western fashion Council told as much of his own life as he drew from his guest. He asked but few questions; but by and by the story of Haskins' struggles and defeat came out. The story was a terrible one, but he told it quietly, seated with his elbows on his knees, gazing most of the time at the hearth.

"I didn't like the looks of the country, anyhow," Haskins said, partly rising and glancing at his wife. "I was ust t' northern Ingyannie, where we have lots o' timber 'n' lots o' rain, 'n' I didn't like the looks o' that dry prairie. What galled me the worst was goin' s' far away acrosst so much fine land layin' all through here vacant."

"And the 'hoppers eat ye four years hand runnin', did they?"

"Eat! They wiped us out. They chawed [223] everything that was green. They jest set around waitin' f'r us to die t' eat us, too. My God! I ust t' dream of 'em sittin' 'round on the bedpost, six feet long, workin' their jaws. They eet the forkhandles. They got worse 'n' worse till they just rolled on one another, piled up like snow in winter. Well, it ain't no use. If I was t' talk all winter I couldn't tell nawthin'. But all the while I couldn't help thinkin' of all that land back here that nobuddy was usin' that I ought 'o had 'stead o' bein' out there in that cussed country."

"Wall, why didn't ye stop an' settle here?" asked Ike, who had come in and was eating his supper.

"Fer the simple reason that you fellers wantid ten 'r fifteen dollars an acre fer the bare land, and I hadn't no money fer that kind o' thing."

"Yes, I do my own work," Mrs. Council was heard to say in the pause which followed. "I'm a gettin' purty heavy t' be on m' laigs all day, but we can't afford t' hire, so I keep rackin' around somehow, like a foundered horse. S' lame—I tell Council he can't tell how lame I am, f'r I'm jest as lame in one laig as t' other." And the good soul laughed at the joke on herself as she took a handful of flour and dusted the biscuit-board to keep the dough from sticking.

"Well, I hain't *never* been very strong," said Mrs. Haskins. "Our folks was Canadians an' [224] small-boned, and then since my last child I hain't got up again fairly. I don't like t' complain. Tim has about all he can bear now—but they was days this week when I jest wanted to lay right down an' die."

"Waal, now, I'll tell ye," said Council, from his side of the stove, silencing everybody with his good-natured roar, "I'd go down and *see* Butler, *anyway*, if I was you. I guess he'd let you have his place purty cheap; the farm's all run down. He's ben anxious t' let t' some-buddy next year. It 'ud be a good chance fer you. Anyhow, you go to bed and sleep like a babe. I've got some ploughing t' do, anyhow, an' we'll see if somethin' can't be done about your case. Ike, you go out an' see if the horses is all right, an' I'll show the folks t' bed."

When the tired husband and wife were lying under the generous quilts of the spare bed, Haskins listened a moment to the wind in the eaves, and then said with a slow and solemn tone:

"There are people in this world who are good enough t' be angels, an' only haff t' die to *be* angels." [225]

II

Jim Butler was one of those men called in the West "land poor." Early in the history of Rock River he had come into the town and started in the grocery business in a small way, occupying a small building in a mean part of the town. At this period of his life he earned all he got, and was up early and late sorting beans, working over butter, and carting his goods to and from the station. But a change came over him at the end of the second year, when he sold a lot of land for four times what he paid for it. From that time forward he believed in land speculation as the surest way of getting rich. Every cent he could save or spare from his trade he put into land at forced sale, or mortgages on land, which were "just as good as wheat," he was accustomed to say.

Farm after farm fell into his hands, until he was recognized as one of the leading landowners of the county. His mortgages were scattered all over Cedar County, and as they slowly but surely fell in he sought usually to retain the former owner as tenant.

He was not ready to foreclose; indeed, he had the name of being one of the "easiest" men in [226] the town. He let the debtor off again and again, extending the time whenever possible.

"I don't want y'r land," he said. "All I'm after is the int'rest on my money—that's all. Now, if y' want 'o stay on the farm, why, I'll give y' a good chance. I can't have the land layin' vacant." And in many cases the owner remained as tenant.

In the meantime he had sold his store; he couldn't spend time in it; he was mainly occupied now with sitting around town on rainy days smoking and "gassin' with the boys," or in riding to and from his farms. In fishing-time he fished a good deal. Doc Grimes, Ben Ashley, and Cal Cheatham were his cronies on these fishing excursions or hunting trips in the time of chickens or partridges. In winter they went to Northern Wisconsin to shoot deer.

In spite of all these signs of easy life Butler persisted in saying he "hadn't enough money to pay taxes on his land," and was careful to convey the impression that he was poor in spite of his twenty farms. At one time he was said to be worth fifty thousand dollars, but land had been a little slow of sale of late, so that he was not worth so much. A fine farm, known as the Higley place, had fallen into his hands in the usual way the previous year, and he had not been able to find a tenant for it. Poor Higley, after working [227] himself nearly to death on it in the attempt to lift the mortgage, had gone off to Dakota, leaving the farm and his curse to Butler.

This was the farm which Council advised Haskins to apply for; and the next day Council hitched up his team and drove down to see Butler.

"You jest let *me* do the talkin'," he said. "We'll find him wearin' out his pants on some salt barrel somew'ers; and if he thought you *wanted* the place he'd sock it to you hot and heavy. You jest keep quiet; I'll fix 'im."

Butler was seated in Ben Ashley's store telling fish yarns when Council sauntered in casually.

"Hello, But; lyin' agin, hey?"

"Hello, Steve! How goes it?"

"Oh, so-so. Too dang much rain these days. I thought it was gon' t' freeze up f'r good last night. Tight squeak if I get m' ploughin' done. How's farmin' with *you* these days?"

"Bad. Ploughin' ain't half done."

"It 'ud be a religious idee f'r you t' go out an' take a hand y'rself."

"I don't haff to," said Butler, with a wink.

"Got anybody on the Higley place?"

"No. Know of anybody?"

"Waal, no; not eggsackly. I've got a relation back t' Michigan who's ben hot an' cold on the [228] idee o' comin' West f'r some time. *Might* come if he could get a good lay-out. What do you talk on the farm?"

"Well, I d' know. I'll rent it on shares or I'll rent it money rent."

"Wall, how much money, say?"

"Well, say ten per cent, on the price—two-fifty."

"Wall, that ain't bad. Wait on 'im till 'e thrashes?"

Haskins listened eagerly to this important question, but Council was coolly eating a dried apple which he had speared out of a barrel with his knife. Butler studied him carefully.

"Well, knocks me out of twenty-five dollars interest."

"My relation'll need all he's got t' git his crops in," said Council, in the same, indifferent way.

"Well, all right; *say* wait," concluded Butler.

"All right; this is the man. Haskins, this is Mr. Butler—no relation to Ben—the hardest-working man in Cedar County."

On the way home Haskins said: "I ain't much better off. I'd like that farm; it's a good farm, but it's all run down, an' so m' I. I could make a good farm of it if I had half a show. But I can't stock it n'r seed it."

"Waal, now don't you worry," roared Council in his ear. "We'll pull y' through somehow till [229] next harvest. He's agreed t' hire it ploughed, an' you can earn a hundred dollars ploughin' an' y' c'n git the seed o' me, an' pay me back when y' can."

Haskins was silent with emotion, but at last he said, "I ain't got nothin' t' live on."

"Now, don't you worry 'bout that. You jest make your headquarters at ol' Steve Council's. Mother'll take a pile o' comfort in havin' y'r wife an' children 'round. Y' see, Jane's married off lately, an' Ike's away a good 'eal, so we'll be darn glad t' have y' stop with us this winter. Nex' spring we'll see if y' can't git a start agin." And he chirruped to the team, which sprang forward with the rumbling, clattering wagon.

"Say, looky here, Council, you can't do this. I never saw——" shouted Haskins in his neighbor's ear.

Council moved about uneasily in his seat and stopped his stammering gratitude by saying: "Hold on, now; don't make such a fuss over a little thing. When I see a man down, an' things all on top of 'm, I jest like t' kick 'em off an' help 'm up. That's the kind of religion I got, an' it's about the *only* kind."

They rode the rest of the way home in silence. And when the red light of the lamp shone out into the darkness of the cold and wintry night, and he thought of this refuge for his children and wife, Haskins could have put his arm around [230] the neck of his burly companion and squeezed him like a lover. But he contented himself with saying, "Steve Council, you'll git y'r pay f'r this some day."

"Don't want any pay. My religion ain't run on such business principles."

The wind was growing colder, and the ground was covered with a white frost, as they turned into the gate of the Council farm, and the children came rushing out, shouting, "Papa's come!" They hardly looked like the same children who sat at the table the night before. Their torpidity, under the influence of sunshine and Mother Council, had given way to a sort of spasmodic cheerfulness, as insects in winter revive when laid on the hearth.

III

Haskins worked like a fiend, and his wife, like the heroic woman that she was, bore also uncomplainingly the most terrible burdens. They rose early and toiled without intermission till the darkness fell on the plain, then tumbled into bed, every bone and muscle aching with fatigue, to rise with the sun next morning to the same round of the same ferocity of labor.

The eldest boy, now nine years old, drove a [231] team all through the spring, ploughing and seeding, milked the cows, and did chores innumerable, in most ways taking the place of a man; an infinitely pathetic but common figure—this boy—on the American farm, where there is no law against child labor. To see him in his coarse clothing, his huge boots, and his ragged cap, as he staggered with a pail of water from the well, or trudged in the cold and cheerless dawn out into the frosty field behind his team, gave the city-bred visitor a sharp pang of sympathetic pain. Yet Haskins loved his boy, and would have saved him from this if he could, but he could not.

By June the first year the result of such Herculean toil began to show on the farm. The yard was cleaned up and sown to grass, the garden ploughed and planted, and the house mended. Council had given them four of his cows.

"Take 'em an' run 'em on shares. I don't want a milk s' many. Ike's away s' much now, Sat'd'ys an' Sund'ys, I can't stand the bother anyhow."

Other men, seeing the confidence of Council in the newcomer, had sold him tools on time; and as he was really an able farmer, he soon had round him many evidences of his care and thrift. At the advice of Council he had taken the farm for three years, with the privilege of re-renting or buying at the end of the term.

"It's a good bargain, an' y' want 'o nail it," [232] said Council. "If you have any kind ov a crop, you c'n pay y'r debts, an' keep seed an' bread."

The new hope which now sprang up in the heart of Haskins and his wife grew almost as a pain by the time the wide field of wheat began to wave and rustle and swirl in the winds of July. Day after day he would snatch a few moments after supper to go and look at it.

"Have ye seen the wheat t'-day, Nettie?" he asked one night as he rose from supper.

"No, Tim, I ain't had time."

"Well, take time now. Le's go look at it."

She threw an old hat on her head—Tommy's hat—and looking almost pretty in her thin, sad way, went out with her husband to the hedge.

"Ain't it grand, Nettie? Just look at it."

It was grand. Level, russet here and there, heavy-headed, wide as a lake, and full of multitudinous whispers and gleams of wealth, it stretched away before the gazers like the fabled field of the cloth of gold.

"Oh, I think—I *hope* we'll have a good crop, Tim; and oh, how good the people have been to us!"

"Yes; I don't know where we'd be t'-day if it hadn't ben f'r Council and his wife."

"They're the best people in the world," said the little woman, with a great sob of gratitude.

"We'll be in the field on Monday, sure," said [233] Haskins, gripping the rail of fences as if already at the work of the harvest.

The harvest came, bounteous, glorious, but the winds came and blew it into tangles, and the rain matted it here and there close to the ground, increasing the work of gathering it threefold.

Oh, how they toiled in those glorious days! Clothing dripping with sweat, arms aching, filled with briers, fingers raw and bleeding, backs broken with the weight of heavy bundles, Haskins and his man toiled on. Tommy drove the harvester, while his father and a hired man bound on the machine. In this way they cut ten acres every day, and almost every night after supper, when the hand went to bed, Haskins returned to the field shocking the bound grain in the light of the moon. Many a night he worked till his anxious wife came out at ten o'clock to call him in to rest and lunch.

At the same time she cooked for the men, took care of the children, washed and ironed, milked the cows at night, made the butter, and sometimes fed the horses and watered them while her husband kept at the shocking. No slave in the Roman galleys could have toiled so frightfully and lived, for this man thought himself a free man, and that he was working for his wife and babes.

When he sank into his bed with a deep groan [234] of relief, too tired to change his grimy, dripping clothing, he felt that he was getting nearer and nearer to a home of his own, and pushing the wolf of want a little farther from his door.

There is no despair so deep as the despair of a homeless man or woman. To roam the roads of the country or the streets of the city, to feel there is no rood of ground on which the feet can rest, to halt weary and hungry outside lighted windows and hear laughter and song within—these are the hungers and rebellions that drive men to crime and women to shame.

It was the memory of this homelessness, and the fear of its coming again, that spurred Timothy Haskins and Nettie, his wife, to such ferocious labor during that first year.

IV

"'M, yes; 'm, yes; first-rate," said Butler, as his eye took in the neat garden, the pig-pen, and the well-filled barnyard. "You're gitt'n quite a stock around yeh. Done well, eh?"

Haskins was showing Butler around the place. He had not seen it for a year, having spent the year in Washington and Boston with Ashley, his brother-in-law, who had been elected to Congress.

"Yes, I've laid out a good deal of money durin' [235] the last three years. I've paid out three hundred dollars f'r fencin'."

"Um—h'm! I see, I see," said Butler, while Haskins went on.

"The kitchen there cost two hundred; the barn ain't cost much in money, but I've put a lot o' time on it. I've dug a new well, and I——"

"Yes, yes, I see. You've done well. Stock worth a thousand dollars," said Butler, picking his teeth with a straw.

"About that," said Haskins, modestly. "We begin to feel's if we was gitt'n' a home f'r ourselves; but we've worked hard. I tell ye we begin to feel it, Mr. Butler, and we're goin' t' begin to ease up purty soon. We've been kind of plannin' a trip back t' *her* folks after the fall ploughin's done."

"*Eggs*-actly!" said Butler, who was evidently thinking of something else. "I suppose you've kine o' kalklated on stayin' here three years more?"

"Well, yes. Fact is, I think I c'n buy the farm this fall, if you'll give me a reasonable show."

"Um—m! What do you call a reasonable show?"

"Waal; say a quarter down and three years' time."

Butler looked at the huge stacks of wheat which filled the yard,

over which the chickens were fluttering [236] and crawling, catching
grasshoppers, and out of which the crickets were singing innumer-
ably. He smiled in a peculiar way as he said, "Oh, I won't be hard on
yer. But what did you expect to pay f'r the place?"

"Why, about what you offered it for before, two thousand five
hundred, or *possibly* three thousand dollars," he added quickly, as
he saw the owner shake his head.

"This farm is worth five thousand and five hundred dollars," said
Butler, in a careless and decided voice.

"*What!*" almost shrieked the astounded Haskins. "What's that? Five
thousand? Why, that's double what you offered it for three years
ago."

"Of course, and it's worth it. It was all run down then; now it's in
good shape. You've laid out fifteen hundred dollars in improvements,
according to your own story."

"But *you* had nothin' t' do about that. It's my work an' my money."

"You bet it was; but it's my land."

"But what's to pay me for all my——"

"Ain't you had the use of 'em?" replied Butler, smiling calmly into
his face.

Haskins was like a man struck on the head with a sandbag; he
couldn't think; he stammered as he tried to say: "But—I never'd git
the use— You'd rob me! More'n that: you [237] agreed—you promised
that I could buy or rent at the end of three years at——"

"That's all right. But I didn't say I'd let you carry off the improvements, nor that I'd go on renting the farm at two-fifty. The land is
doubled in value, it don't matter how; it don't enter into the question;
an' now you can pay me five hundred dollars a year rent, or take it
on your own terms at fifty-five hundred, or—git out."

He was turning away when Haskins, the sweat pouring from his
face, fronted him, saying again:

"But *you've* done nothing to make it so. You hain't added a cent.
I put it all there myself, expectin' to buy. I worked an' sweat to improve it. I was workin' for myself an' babes——"

"Well, why didn't you buy when I offered to sell? What y' kickin'
about?"

"I'm kickin' about payin' you twice f'r my own things,—my own
fences, my own kitchen, my own garden."

Butler laughed. "You're too green t' eat, young feller. *Your* improvements! The law will sing another tune."

"But I trusted your word."

"Never trust anybody, my friend. Besides, I didn't promise not to do this thing. Why, man, don't look at me like that. Don't take me for a thief. It's the law. The reg'lar thing. Everybody does it."

"I don't care if they do. It's stealin' jest the [238] same. You take three thousand dollars of my money. The work o' my hands and my wife's." He broke down at this point. He was not a strong man mentally. He could face hardship, ceaseless toil, but he could not face the cold and sneering face of Butler.

"But I don't take it," said Butler, coolly. "All you've got to do is to go on jest as you've been a-doin', or give me a thousand dollars down, and a mortgage at ten per cent on the rest."

Haskins sat down blindly on a bundle of oats near by, and with staring eyes and drooping head went over the situation. He was under the lion's paw. He felt a horrible numbness in his heart and limbs. He was hid in a mist, and there was no path out.

Butler walked about, looking at the huge stacks of grain, and pulling now and again a few handfuls out, shelling the heads in his hands and blowing the chaff away. He hummed a little tune as he did so. He had an accommodating air of waiting.

Haskins was in the midst of the terrible toil of the last year. He was walking again in the rain and the mud behind his plough; he felt the dust and dirt of the threshing. The ferocious husking-time, with its cutting wind and biting, clinging snows, lay hard upon him. Then he thought of his wife, how she had cheerfully cooked and baked, without holiday and without rest. [239]

"Well, what do you think of it?" inquired the cool, mocking, insinuating voice of Butler.

"I think you're a thief and a liar!" shouted Haskins, leaping up. "A black-hearted houn'!" Butler's smile maddened him; with a sudden leap he caught a fork in his hands, and whirled it in the air. "You'll never rob another man, damn ye!" he grated through his teeth, a look of pitiless ferocity in his accusing eyes.

Butler shrank and quivered, expecting the blow; stood, held hypnotized by the eyes of the man he had a moment before despised—a man transformed into an avenging demon. But in the deadly hush between the lift of the weapon and its fall there came a gush of faint, childish laughter and then across the range of his vision, far away and dim, he saw the sun-bright head of his baby girl, as, with the pretty, tottering run of a two-year-old, she moved across the grass of the dooryard. His hands relaxed; the fork fell to the ground; his head lowered.

"Make out y'r deed an' morgige, an' git off'n my land, an' don't ye never cross my line agin; if y' do, I'll kill ye."

Butler backed away from the man in wild haste, and climbing into his buggy with trembling limbs, drove off down the road, leaving Haskins seated dumbly on the sunny pile of sheaves, his head sunk into his hands. [240]

❧ STEPHEN CRANE

Maggie: A Girl of the Streets

Stephen Crane, *Maggie: A Girl of the Streets* [1893], New York, D. Appleton & Co., 1896.

THE JOHNSON FAMILY

CHAPTER III

[*The Parents*]

THE OLD WOMAN was a gnarled and leathery personage who could don at will an expression of great virtue. She possessed a small music-box capable of one tune, and a collection of "God bless yeh's" pitched in assorted keys of fervency. Each day she took a position upon the stones of Fifth Avenue, [19] where she crooked her legs under her and crouched, immovable and hideous, like an idol. She received daily a small sum in pennies. It was contributed, for the most part, by persons who did not make their homes in that vicinity.

Once, when a lady had dropped her purse on the sidewalk, the gnarled woman had grabbed it and smuggled it with great dexterity beneath her cloak. When she was arrested she had cursed the lady into a partial swoon, and with her aged limbs, twisted from rheumatism, had kicked the breath out of a huge policeman whose conduct upon that occasion she referred to when she said, "The police, damn 'em!"

"Eh, Jimmie, it's a shame," she said. "Go, now, like a dear, an' buy me a can, an' if yer mudder raises 'ell all night yehs can sleep here."

Jimmie took a tendered tin pail and seven pennies and departed. He passed into the side door of a saloon and went to the bar. [20] Straining up on his toes he raised the pail and pennies as high as his arms would let him. He saw two hands thrust down to take them. Directly the same hands let down the filled pail, and he left.

In front of the gruesome doorway he met a lurching figure. It was his father, swaying about on uncertain legs.

"Give me deh can. See?" said the man.

"Ah, come off! I got dis can fer dat ol' woman, an' it'd be dirt teh swipe it. See?" said Jimmie.

The father wrenched the pail from the urchin. He grasped it in both hands and lifted it to his mouth. He glued his lips to the under edge and tilted his head. His throat swelled until it seemed to grow near his chin. There was a tremendous gulping movement and the beer was gone.

The man caught his breath and laughed. He hit his son on the head with the empty pail. As it rolled clanging into the street, [21] Jimmie began to scream, and kicked repeatedly at his father's shins.

"Look at deh dirt what yeh done me," he yelled. "Deh ol' woman'll be trowin fits."

He retreated to the middle of the street, but the old man did not pursue. He staggered toward the door.

"I'll paste yeh when I ketch yeh!" he shouted, and disappeared.

During the evening he had been standing against a bar drinking whiskies, and declaring to all comers confidentially: "My home reg'lar livin' hell! Why do I come an' drin' whisk' here thish way? 'Cause home reg'lar livin' hell!"

Jimmie waited a long time in the street and then crept warily up through the building. He passed with great caution the door of the gnarled woman, and finally stopped outside his home and listened.

He could hear his mother moving heavily about among the furniture of the room. She was chanting in a mournful voice, occasionally [22] interjecting bursts of volcanic wrath at the father, who, Jimmie judged, had sunk down on the floor or in a corner.

"Why deh blazes don' cher try teh keep Jim from fightin'? I'll break yer jaw!" she suddenly bellowed.

The man mumbled with drunken indifference. "Ah, w'at's bitin' yeh? W'a's odds? Wha' makes kick?"

"Because he tears 'is clothes, yeh fool!" cried the woman in supreme wrath.

The husband seemed to become aroused. "Go chase yerself!" he thundered fiercely in reply. There was a crash against the door, and something broke into clattering fragments. Jimmie partially suppressed a yell and darted down the stairway. Below he paused and listened. He heard howls and curses, groans and shrieks—a confused chorus as if a battle were raging. With it all there was the crash of splintering furniture. The eyes of the urchin glared in his fear that one of them would discover him. [23]

Curious faces appeared in doorways, and whispered comments passed to and fro. "Ol' Johnson's playin' horse agin."

Jimmie stood until the noises ceased and the other inhabitants of the tenement had all yawned and shut their doors. Then he crawled upstairs with the caution of an invader of a panther's den. Sounds of labored breathing came through the broken doorpanels. He pushed the door open and entered, quaking.

A glow from the fire threw red hues over the bare floor, the cracked and soiled plastering, and the overturned and broken furniture. In the middle of the floor lay his mother asleep. In one corner of the room his father's limp body hung across the seat of a chair.

The urchin stole forward. He began to shiver in dread of awakening his parents. His mother's great chest was heaving painfully. Jimmie paused and looked down at [24] her. Her face was inflamed and swollen from drinking. Her yellow brows shaded eyelids that had grown blue. Her tangled hair tossed in waves over her forehead. Her mouth was set in the same lines of vindictive hatred that it had, perhaps, borne during the fight. Her bare red arms were thrown out above her head in an attitude of exhaustion, something, mayhap, like that of a sated villain.

The urchin bent over his mother. He was fearful lest she should open her eyes, and the dread within him was so strong that he could not forbear to stare, but hung as if fascinated over the woman's grim face.

Suddenly her eyes opened. The urchin found himself looking straight into an expression which, it would seem, had the power to change his blood to salt. He howled piercingly and fell backward.

The woman floundered for a moment, tossed her arms about her head as if in combat, and again began to snore. [25]

Jimmie crawled back into the shadows and waited. A noise in the next room had followed his cry at the discovery that his mother was awake. He grovelled in the gloom, his eyes riveted upon the intervening door.

He heard it creak, and then the sound of a small voice came to him. "Jimmie! Jimmie! Are yehs dere?" it whispered. The urchin started. The thin white face of his sister looked at him from the doorway of the other room. She crept to him across the floor.

The father had not moved, but lay in the same death-like sleep. The mother writhed in an uneasy slumber, her chest wheezing as if she were in the agonies of strangulation. Out at the window a florid moon was peering over dark roofs, and in the distance the waters of a river glimmered pallidly.

The small frame of the ragged girl was quivering. Her features were haggard from weeping, and her eyes gleamed with fear. [26] She grasped the urchin's arm in her little trembling hands and they huddled in a corner. The eyes of both were drawn, by some force, to stare at the woman's face, for they thought she need only to awake and all the fiends would come from below.

They crouched until the ghost mists of dawn appeared at the window, drawing close to the panes, and looking in at the prostrate, heaving body of the mother. [27]

CHAPTER IV

[The Son]

The babe, Tommie, died. He went away in an insignificant coffin, his small waxen hand clutching a flower that the girl, Maggie had stolen from an Italian.

She and Jimmie lived.

The inexperienced fibers of the boy's eyes were hardened at an early age. He became a young man of leather. He lived some red years without laboring. During that time his sneer became chronic. He studied human nature in the gutter, and found it no worse than he thought he had reason to believe it. He never conceived a respect for the world, because he had begun with no idols that it had smashed.

He clad his soul in armor by means of happening hilariously in at
a mission church [28] where a man composed his sermons of "you's."
Once a philosopher asked this man why he did not say "we" instead
of "you." The man replied, "What?"

While they got warm at the stove he told his hearers just where he
calculated they stood with the Lord. Many of the sinners were impatient over the pictured depths of their degradation. They were
waiting for soup-tickets.

A reader of the words of wind demons might have been able to
see the portions of a dialogue pass to and fro between the exhorter
and his hearers.

"You are damned," said the preacher. And the reader of sounds
might have seen the reply go forth from the ragged people: "Where's
our soup?"

Jimmie and a companion sat in a rear seat and commented upon
the things that didn't concern them, with all the freedom of English
tourists. When they grew thirsty and went out, their minds confused
the speaker with Christ. [29]

Momentarily, Jimmie was sullen with thoughts of a hopeless alti-
tude where grew fruit. His companion said that if he should ever go to
heaven he would ask for a million dollars and a bottle of beer.

Jimmie's occupation for a long time was to stand at street corners
and watch the world go by, dreaming blood-red dreams at the passing
of pretty women. He menaced mankind at the intersections of streets.

At the corners he was in life and of life. The world was going on
and he was there to perceive it.

He maintained a belligerent attitude toward all well-dressed men.
To him fine raiment was allied to weakness, and all good coats
covered faint hearts. He and his orders were kings, to a certain extent, over the men of untarnished clothes, because these latter
dreaded, perhaps, to be either killed or laughed at.

Above all things he despised obvious Christians and ciphers with
the chrysanthemums [30] of aristocracy in their buttonholes. He considered himself above both of these classes. He was afraid of nothing.

When he had a dollar in his pocket his satisfaction with existence
was the greatest thing in the world. So, eventually, he felt obliged to
work. His father died, and his mother's years were divided up into
periods of thirty days.

He became a truck driver. There was given to him the charge of a
painstaking pair of horses and a large rattling truck. He invaded the

turmoil and tumble of the downtown streets, and learned to breathe maledictory defiance at the police, who occasionally used to climb up, drag him from his perch, and punch him.

In the lower part of the city he daily involved himself in hideous tangles. If he and his team chanced to be in the rear he preserved a demeanor of serenity, crossing his legs and bursting forth into yells when foot passengers took dangerous dives beneath the [31] noses of his champing horses. He smoked his pipe calmly, for he knew that his pay was marching on.

If his charge was in the front, and if it became the key-truck of chaos, he entered terrifically into the quarrel that was raging to and fro among the drivers on their high seats, and sometimes roared oaths and violently got himself arrested.

After a time his sneer grew so that it turned its glare upon all things. He became so sharp that he believed in nothing. To him the police were always actuated by malignant impulses, and the rest of the world was composed, for the most part, of despicable creatures who were all trying to take advantage of him, and with whom, in defence, he was obliged to quarrel on all possible occasions. He himself occupied a down-trodden position, which had a private but distinct element of grandeur in its isolation.

The greatest cases of aggravated idiocy were, to his mind, rampant upon the front [32] platforms of all street-cars. At first his tongue strove with these beings, but he eventually became superior. In him grew a majestic contempt for those strings of street-cars that followed him like intent bugs.

He fell into the habit, when starting on a long journey, of fixing his eye on a high and distant object, commanding his horses to start, and then going into a trance of oblivion. Multitudes of drivers might howl in his rear, and passengers might load him with opprobrium, but he would not awaken until some blue policeman turned red and began frenziedly to seize bridles and beat the soft noses of the responsible horses.

When he paused to contemplate the attitude of the police toward himself and his fellows, he believed that they were the only men in the city who had no rights. When driving about, he felt that he was held liable by the police for anything that might occur in the streets, and that he was the common [33] prey of all energetic officials. In revenge, he resolved never to move out of the way of anything, until formidable circumstances or a much larger man than himself forced him to it.

Foot passengers were mere pestering flies with an insane disregard for their legs and his convenience. He could not comprehend their desire to cross the streets. Their madness smote him with eternal amazement. He was continually storming at them from his throne. He sat aloft and denounced their frantic leaps, plunges, dives, and straddles.

When they would thrust at, or parry, the noses of his champing horses, making them swing their heads and move their feet, and thus disturbing a stolid, dreamy repose, he swore at the men as fools, for he himself could perceive that Providence had caused it to be clearly written that he and his team had the inalienable right to stand in the proper path of the sun-chariot and, if they [34] so minded, to obstruct its mission or take a wheel off.

And if the god driver had had a desire to step down, put up his flame-colored fists, and manfully dispute the right of way, he would have probably been immediately opposed by a scowling mortal with two sets of hard knuckles.

It is possible, perhaps, that this young man would have derided, in an axle-wide alley, the approach of a flying ferryboat. Yet he achieved a respect for a fire-engine. As one charged toward his truck, he would drive fearfully upon a sidewalk, threatening untold people with annihilation. When an engine struck a mass of blocked trucks, splitting it into fragments as a blow annihilates a cake of ice, Jimmie's team could usually be observed high and safe, with whole wheels, on the sidewalk. The fearful coming of the engine could break up the most intricate muddle of heavy vehicles at which the police had been storming for half an hour. [35]

A fire-engine was enshrined in his heart as an appalling thing that he loved with a distant, dog-like devotion. It had been known to overturn a street-car. Those leaping horses, striking sparks from the cobbles in their forward lunge, were creatures to be ineffably admired. The clang of the going pierced his breast like a noise of remembered war.

When Jimmie was a little boy he began to be arrested. Before he reached a great age, he had a fair record.

He developed too great a tendency to climb down from his truck and fight with other drivers. He had been in quite a number of miscellaneous fights, and in some general barroom rows that had become known to the police. Once he had been arrested for assaulting a Chinaman. Two women in different parts of the city, and entirely unknown to each other, caused him considerable annoyance by breaking forth, simultaneously, at fateful intervals, into wailings [36] about marriage and support and infants.

Nevertheless, he had, on a certain star-lit evening, said wonderingly and quite reverently, "Deh moon looks like hell, don't it?" [37]

CHAPTER V

[The Daughter]

The girl, Maggie, blossomed in a mud-puddle. She grew to be a most rare and wonderful production of a tenement district, a pretty girl.

None of the dirt of Rum Alley seemed to be in her veins. The philosophers, upstairs, downstairs, and on the same floor, puzzled over it.

When a child, playing and fighting with gamins in the street, dirt disgusted her. Attired in tatters and grime, she went unseen.

There came a time, however, when the young men of the vicinity said, "Dat Johnson goil is a putty good looker." About this period her brother remarked to her: "Mag, I'll tell yeh dis! See? Yeh've eeder got t'go on d'toif er go t' work!" Whereupon [38] she went to work, having the feminine aversion to the alternative.

By a chance, she got a position in an establishment where they made collars and cuffs. She received a stool and a machine in a room where sat twenty girls of various shades of yellow discontent. She perched on the stool and treadled at her machine all day, turning out collars with a name which might have been noted for its irrelevancy to anything connected with collars. At night she returned home to her mother.

Jimmie grew large enough to take the vague position of head of the family. As incumbent of that office, he stumbled upstairs late at night, as his father had done before him. He reeled about the room, swearing at his relations, or went to sleep on the floor.

The mother had gradually risen to such a degree of fame that she could bandy words with her acquaintances among the police justices. Court officials called her by her first name. When she appeared they pursued a [39] course which had been theirs for months. They in-

evitably grinned, and cried out, "Hello, Mary, you here again?" Her
grey head wagged in many courts. She always besieged the bench
with voluble excuses, explanations, apologies, and prayers. Her flam-
ing face and rolling eyes were a familiar sight on the island. She
measured time by means of sprees, and was swollen and dishevelled.

One day the young man Pete, who as a lad had smitten the Devil's
Row urchin in the back of the head and put to flight the antagonists
of his friend Jimmie, strutted upon the scene. He met Jimmie one day
on the street, promised to take him to a boxing match in Williamsburg,
and called for him in the evening.

Maggie observed Pete.

He sat on a table in the Johnson home, and dangled his checked
legs with an enticing nonchalance. His hair was curled down over his
forehead in an oiled bang. His pugged [40] nose seemed to revolt from
contact with a bristling moustache of short, wire-like hairs. His blue
double-breasted coat, edged with black braid, was buttoned close to a
red puff tie, and his patent leather shoes looked like weapons.

His mannerisms stamped him as a man who had a correct sense of
his personal superiority. There were valor and contempt for circumstances in the glance of his eye. He waved his hands like a man of the
world who dismisses religion and philosophy, and says "Rats!" He had
certainly seen everything, and with each curl of his lip he declared
that it amounted to nothing. Maggie thought he must be a very "ele-
gant" bartender.

He was telling tales to Jimmie.

Maggie watched him furtively, with half-closed eyes lit with a
vague interest.

"Hully gee! Dey makes me tired," he said. "Mos' e'ry day some
farmer comes in an' tries t' run d' shop. See? But d' gits t'rowed right
out. I jolt dem right out in [41] d' street before dey knows where dey
is. See?"

"Sure," said Jimmie.

"Dere was a mug come in d' place d' odder day wid an idear he
was goin' t' own d' place. Hully gee! he was goin' t' own d' place. I see
he had a still on, an' I didn' wanna give 'im no stuff, so I says, 'Git
outa here an' don' make no trouble,' I says like dat. See? 'Git outa here
an' don' make no trouble'; like dat. 'Git outa here,' I says. See?"

Jimmie nodded understandingly. Over his features played an eager
desire to state the amount of his valor in a similar crisis, but the nar-
rator proceeded.

"Well, deh blokie he says: 'T' blazes wid it! I ain' lookin' for no scrap,' he says—see?—'but,' he says, 'I'm 'spectable cit'zen an' I wanna drink, an' quick, too.' See? 'Aw, go ahn!' I says, like dat. 'Aw, go ahn,' I says. See? 'Don' make no trouble,' I says, like dat. 'Don' make no trouble.' See? [42] Den d' mug, he squared off an' said he was fine as silk wid his dukes—see?—an' he wan'ed a drink—quick. Dat's what he said. See?"

"Sure," repeated Jimmie.

Pete continued. "Say, I jes' jumped d' bar, an' d' way I plunked dat blokie was outa sight. See? Dat's right! In d' jaw! See? Hully gee! he t'rowed a spittoon t'rough d' front windee. Say, I taut I'd drop dead. But d' boss, he comes in after, an' he says: 'Pete, yehs done jes' right! Yeh've gotta keep order, an' it's all right.' See? 'It's all right,' he says. Dat's what he said."

The two held a technical discussion.

"Dat bloke was a dandy," said Pete, in conclusion, "but he hadn' oughta made no trouble. Dat's what I says t' dem: 'Don' come in here an' make no trouble,' I says, like dat. 'Don' make no trouble.' See?"

As Jimmie and his friend exchanged tales descriptive of their prowess, Maggie leaned back in the shadow. Her eyes dwelt wonderingly and rather wistfully upon Pete's face. [43] The broken furniture, grimy walls, and general disorder and dirt of her home of a sudden appeared before her and began to take a potential aspect. Pete's aristocratic person looked as if it might soil. She looked keenly at him, occasionally wondering if he was feeling contempt. But Pete seemed to be enveloped in reminiscence.

"Hully gee!" said he, "dose mugs can't phase me. Dey knows I kin wipe up d' street wid any tree of dem."

When he said, "Ah, what d' hell!" his voice was burdened with disdain for the inevitable and contempt for anything that fate might compel him to endure.

Maggie perceived that here was the ideal man. Her dim thoughts were often searching for far-away lands where the little hills sing together in the morning. Under the trees of her dream-gardens there had always walked a lover. [44]

❧ STEPHEN CRANE

The Open Boat

Stephen Crane, "The Open Boat," *Scribner's Magazine*, XXI
(June, 1897).

*A Tale Intended to be after the Fact. Being the Experience of Four
Men from the Sunk Steamer* COMMODORE.

NONE OF THEM KNEW the color of the sky. Their eyes glanced level,
and were fastened upon the waves that swept toward them. These
waves were of the hue of slate, save for the tops, which were of foam-
ing white, and all of the men knew the colors of the sea. The horizon
narrowed and widened, and dipped and rose, and at all times its edge
was jagged with waves that seemed thrust up in points like rocks.

Many a man ought to have a bathtub larger than the boat which
here rode upon the sea. These waves were most wrongfully and bar-
barously abrupt and tall, and each froth-top was a problem in small-
boat navigation.

The cook squatted in the bottom and looked with both eyes at the
six inches of gunwale which separated him from the ocean. His sleeves
were rolled over his fat forearms, and the two flaps of his unbuttoned
vest dangled as he bent to bail out the boat. Often he said, "Gawd!
that was a narrow clip." As he remarked it he invariably gazed east-
ward over the broken sea.

The oiler, steering with one of the two oars in the boat, sometimes
raised himself suddenly to keep clear of water that swirled in over the
stern. It was a thin little oar and it seemed often ready to snap.

The correspondent, pulling at the other oar, watched the waves and
wondered why he was there.

The injured captain, lying in the bow, was at this time buried in that
profound dejection and indifference which comes, temporarily at
least, to even the bravest and most enduring when, willy nilly, the
firm fails, the army loses, the ship goes down. The mind of the master
of a vessel is rooted deep in the timbers of her, though he command

for a day or a decade; and this captain had on him the stern impression of a scene in the grays of dawn of seven turned faces, and later a stump of a top-mast with a white ball on it, that slashed to and fro at the waves, went low and lower, and down. Thereafter there was something strange in his voice. Although steady, it was deep with mourning, and of a quality beyond oration or tears.

"Keep 'er a little more south, Billie," said he.

" 'A little more south,' sir," said the oiler in the stern.

A seat in this boat was not unlike a seat upon a bucking broncho, and, by the same token, a broncho is not much smaller. The craft pranced and reared, and plunged like an animal. As each wave came, and she rose for it, she seemed like a horse making at a fence outrageously high. The manner of her scramble over these walls of water is a mystic thing, and, moreover, at the top of them were ordinarily these problems in white water, the foam racing down from the summit of each wave, requiring a new leap, and a leap from the air. Then, after scornfully bumping a crest, she would slide, and race, and splash down a long incline, and arrive bobbing and nodding in front of the next menace.

A singular disadvantage of the sea lies in the fact that after successfully surmounting one wave you discover that there is another behind it just as important and just as nervously anxious to do something effective in the way of swamping boats. In a ten-foot dinghy one can get an idea of the resources of the sea in the line of waves that is not probable to the average experience, which is never at sea in a dinghy. As each slaty wall of water approached, it shut all else from the view of the men in the boat, and it was not difficult to imagine that this particular wave [728] was the final outburst of the ocean, the last effort of the grim water. There was a terrible grace in the move of the waves, and they came in silence, save for the snarling of the crests.

In the wan light the faces of the men must have been gray. Their eyes must have glinted in strange ways as they gazed steadily astern. Viewed from a balcony, the whole thing would doubtlessly have been weirdly picturesque. But the men in the boat had no time to see it, and if they had had leisure, there were other things to occupy their minds. The sun swung steadily up the sky, and they knew it was broad day because the color of the sea changed from slate to emerald-green, streaked with amber lights, and the foam was like tumbling snow. The process of the breaking day was unknown to them. They were

aware only of this effect upon the color of the waves that rolled
toward them.

In disjointed sentences the cook and the correspondent argued as
to the difference between a life-saving station and a house of refuge.
The cook had said: "There's a house of refuge just north of the Mosquito Inlet Light, and as soon as they see us they'll come off in their
boat and pick us up."

"As soon as who see us?" said the correspondent.

"The crew," said the cook.

"Houses of refuge don't have crews," said the correspondent. "As I
understand them, they are only places where clothes and grub are
stored for the benefit of shipwrecked people. They don't carry crews."

"Oh, yes, they do," said the cook.

"No, they don't," said the correspondent.

"Well, we're not there yet, anyhow," said the oiler, in the stern.

"Well," said the cook, "perhaps it's not a house of refuge that I'm
thinking of as being near Mosquito Inlet Light. Perhaps it's a life-
saving station."

"We're not there yet," said the oiler in the stern.

II

As the boat bounced from the top of each wave the wind tore
through the hair of the hatless men, and as the craft plopped her stern
down again the spray slashed past them. The crest of each of these
waves was a hill, from the top of which the men surveyed, for a moment, a broad tumultuous expanse, shining and wind-riven. It was
probably splendid, it was probably glorious, this play of the free sea,
wild with lights of emerald and white and amber.

"Bully good thing it's an on-shore wind," said the cook. "If not,
where would we be? Wouldn't have a show."

"That's right," said the correspondent.

The busy oiler nodded his assent.

Then the captain, in the bow, chuckled in a way that expressed
humor, contempt, tragedy, all in one. "Do you think we've got much
of a show now, boys?" said he.

Whereupon the three were silent, save for a trifle of hemming and
hawing. To express any particular optimism at this time they felt to
be childish and stupid, but they all doubtless possessed this sense of
the situation in their minds. A young man thinks doggedly at such

times. On the other hand, the ethics of their condition was decidedly against any open suggestion of hopelessness. So they were silent.

"Oh, well," said the captain, soothing his children, "we'll get ashore all right."

But there was that in his tone which made them think; so the oiler quoth, "Yes! if this wind holds."

The cook was bailing. "Yes! if we don't catch hell in the surf."

Canton-flannel gulls flew near and far. Sometimes they sat down on the sea, near patches of brown seaweed that rolled over the waves with a movement like carpets on a line in a gale. The birds sat comfortably in groups, and they were envied by some in the dinghy, for the wrath of the sea was no more to them than it was to a covey of prairie chickens a thousand miles inland. Often they came very close and stared at the men with black bead-like eyes. At these times they were uncanny and sinister in their unblinking scrutiny, and the men hooted angrily at them, telling them to be gone. One came, and evidently decided to alight on the top of the captain's head. The bird flew parallel to the boat and did not circle, but made short sidelong jumps in the air in chicken fashion. His black eyes were wistfully [729] fixed upon the captain's head. "Ugly brute," said the oiler to the bird. "You look as if you were made with a jackknife." The cook and the correspondent swore darkly at the creature. The captain naturally wished to knock it away with the end of the heavy painter, but he did not dare do it, because anything resembling an emphatic gesture would have capsized this freighted boat; and so, with his open hand, the captain gently and carefully waved the gull away. After it had been discouraged from the pursuit the captain breathed easier on account of his hair, and others breathed easier because the bird struck their minds at this time as being somehow gruesome and ominous.

In the meantime the oiler and the correspondent rowed; and also they rowed. They sat together in the same seat, and each rowed an oar. Then the oiler took both oars; then the correspondent took both oars, then the oiler; then the correspondent. They rowed and they rowed. The very ticklish part of the business was when the time came for the reclining one in the stern to take his turn at the oars. By the very last star of truth, it is easier to steal eggs from under a hen than it was to change seats in the dinghy. First the man in the stern slid his hand along the thwart and moved with care, as if he were of Sèvres. Then the man in the rowing-seat slid his hand along the other thwart. It was all done with the most extraordinary care. As the two sidled past each other, the whole party kept watchful eyes on the coming wave, and the captain cried: "Look out, now! Steady, there!"

The brown mats of seaweed that appeared from time to time were like islands, bits of earth. They were travelling, apparently, neither one way nor the other. They were, to all intents, stationary. They informed the men in the boat that it was making progress slowly toward the land.

The captain, rearing cautiously in the bow after the dinghy soared on a great swell, said that he had seen the lighthouse at Mosquito Inlet. Presently the cook remarked that he had seen it. The correspondent was at the oars then, and for some reason he too wished to look at the lighthouse; but his back was toward the far shore, and the waves were important, and for some time he could not seize an opportunity to turn his head. But at last there came a wave more gentle than the others, and when at the crest of it he swiftly scoured the western horizon.

"See it?" said the captain.

"No," said the correspondent, slowly; "I didn't see anything."

"Look again," said the captain. He pointed. "It's exactly in that direction."

At the top of another wave the correspondent did as he was bid, and this time his eyes chanced on a small, still thing on the edge of the swaying horizon. It was precisely like the point of a pin. It took an anxious eye to find a lighthouse so tiny.

"Think we'll make it, Captain?"

"If this wind holds and the boat don't swamp, we can't do much else," said the captain.

The little boat, lifted by each towering sea and splashed viciously by the crests, made progress that in the absence of seaweed was not apparent to those in her. She seemed just a wee thing wallowing, miraculously top up, at the mercy of five oceans. Occasionally a great spread of water, like white flames, swarmed into her.

"Bail her, cook," said the captain, serenely.

"All right, Captain," said the cheerful cook.

III

It would be difficult to describe the subtle brotherhood of men that was here established on the seas. No one said that it was so. No one mentioned it. But it dwelt in the boat, and each man felt it warm him.

They were a captain, an oiler, a cook, and a correspondent, and they were friends—friends in a more curiously iron-bound degree than may be common. The hurt captain, lying against the water-jar in the bow, spoke always in a low voice and calmly; but he could never command a more ready and swiftly obedient crew than the motley three of the dinghy. It was more than a mere recognition of what was best for the common safety. There was surely in it a quality that was personal and heart-felt. And after this devotion to the commander of the boat, there was this comradeship, that the correspondent, for instance, who had been taught to be cynical of men, knew even at the time was the best [730] experience of his life. But no one said that it was so. No one mentioned it.

"I wish we had a sail," remarked the captain. "We might try my overcoat on the end of an oar, and give you two boys a chance to rest." So the cook and the correspondent held the mast and spread wide the overcoat; the oiler steered; and the little boat made good way with her new rig. Sometimes the oiler had to scull sharply to keep a sea from breaking into the boat, but otherwise sailing was a success.

Meanwhile the lighthouse had been growing slowly larger. It had now almost assumed color, and appeared like a little gray shadow on the sky. The man at the oars could not be prevented from turning his head rather often to try for a glimpse of this little gray shadow.

At last, from the top of each wave, the men in the tossing boat could see land. Even as the lighthouse was an upright shadow on the sky, this land seemed but a long black shadow on the sea. It certainly was thinner than paper. "We must be about opposite New Smyrna," said the cook, who had coasted this shore often in schooners. "Captain, by the way, I believe they abandoned that life-saving station there about a year ago."

"Did they?" said the captain.

The wind slowly died away. The cook and the correspondent were not now obliged to slave in order to hold high the oar. But the waves continued their old impetuous swooping at the dinghy, and the little craft, no longer under way, struggled woundily over them. The oiler or the correspondent took the oars again.

Shipwrecks are *apropos* of nothing. If men could only train for them and have them occur when the men had reached pink condition, there would be less drowning at sea. Of the four in the dinghy none had slept any time worth mentioning for two days and two nights previous to embarking in the dinghy, and in the excitement of clambering about the deck of a foundering ship they had also forgotten to eat heartily.

For these reasons, and for others, neither the oiler nor the correspondent was fond of rowing at this time. The correspondent wondered ingenuously how in the name of all that was sane could there be people who thought it amusing to row a boat. It was not an amusement; it was a diabolical punishment, and even a genius of mental aberrations could never conclude that it was anything but a horror to the muscles and a crime against the back. He mentioned to the boat in general how the amusement of rowing struck him, and the weary-faced oiler smiled in full sympathy. Previously to the foundering, by the way, the oiler had worked a double watch in the engine-room of the ship.

"Take her easy now, boys," said the captain. "Don't spend yourselves. If we have to run a surf you'll need all your strength, because we'll sure have to swim for it. Take your time."

Slowly the land arose from the sea. From a black line it became a line of black and a line of white—trees and sand. Finally the captain said that he could make out a house on the shore. "That's the house of refuge, sure," said the cook. "They'll see us before long, and come out after us."

The distant lighthouse reared high. "The keeper ought to be able to make us out now, if he's looking through a glass," said the captain. "He'll notify the life-saving people."

"None of those other boats could have got ashore to give word of the wreck," said the oiler, in a low voice, "else the life-boat would be out hunting us."

Slowly and beautifully the land loomed out of the sea. The wind came again. It had veered from the northeast to the southeast. Finally a new sound struck the ears of the men in the boat. It was the low thunder of the surf on the shore. "We'll never be able to make the lighthouse now," said the captain. "Swing her head a little more north, Billie."

" 'A little more north,' sir," said the oiler.

Whereupon the little boat turned her nose once more down the wind, and all but the oarsman watched the shore grow. Under the influence of this expansion doubt and direful apprehension was [sic] leaving the minds of the men. The management of the boat was still most absorbing, but it could not prevent a quiet cheerfulness. In an hour, perhaps, they would be ashore.

Their backbones had become thoroughly [731] used to balancing in the boat, and they now rode this wild colt of a dinghy like circus men. The correspondent thought that he had been drenched to the skin, but happening to feel in the top pocket of his coat, he found therein eight cigars. Four of them were soaked with sea-water; four were perfectly scatheless. After a search, somebody produced three dry matches; and thereupon the four waifs rode in their little boat and, with an assurance of an impending rescue shining in their eyes, puffed at the big cigars, and judged well and ill of all men. Everybody took a drink of water.

IV

"Cook," remarked the captain, "there don't seem to be any signs of life about your house of refuge."

"No," replied the cook. "Funny they don't see us!"

A broad stretch of lowly coast lay before the eyes of the men. It was of low dunes topped with dark vegetation. The roar of the surf was plain, and sometimes they could see the white lip of a wave as it spun up the beach. A tiny house was blocked out black upon the sky. Southward, the slim lighthouse lifted its little gray length.

Tide, wind, and waves were swinging the dinghy northward. "Funny they don't see us," said the men.

The surf's roar was here dulled, but its tone was nevertheless thunderous and mighty. As the boat swam over the great rollers the men sat listening to this roar. "We'll swamp sure," said everybody.

It is fair to say here that there was not a life-saving station within twenty miles in either direction; but the men did not know this fact, and in consequence they made dark and opprobrious remarks concerning the eyesight of the nation's life-savers. Four scowling men sat in the dinghy and surpassed records in the invention of epithets.

"Funny they don't see us."

The light-heartedness of a former time had completely faded. To their sharpened minds it was easy to conjure pictures of all kinds of incompetency and blindness and, indeed, cowardice. There was the shore of the populous land, and it was bitter and bitter to them that from it came no sign.

"Well," said the captain, ultimately, "I suppose we'll have to make a try for ourselves. If we stay out here too long, we'll none of us have strength left to swim after the boat swamps."

And so the oiler, who was at the oars, turned the boat straight for the shore. There was a sudden tightening of muscles. There was some thinking.

"If we don't all get ashore," said the captain—"if we don't all get ashore, I suppose you fellows know where to send news of my finish?"

They then briefly exchanged some addresses and admonitions. As for the reflections of the men, there was a great deal of rage in them. Perchance they might be formulated thus: "If I am going to be drowned—if I am going to be drowned—if I am going to be drowned, why, in the name of the seven mad gods who rule the sea, was I allowed to come thus far and contemplate sand and trees? Was I brought here merely to have my nose dragged away as I was about to nibble the sacred cheese of life? It is preposterous. If this old ninny-woman, Fate, cannot do better than this, she should be deprived of the management of men's fortunes. She is an old hen who knows not her intention. If she has decided to drown me, why did she not do it in the beginning and save me all this trouble? The whole affair is absurd. . . . But no; she cannot mean to drown me. She dare not drown me. She cannot drown me. Not after all this work." Afterward the man might have had an impulse to shake his fist at the clouds. "Just drown me, now, and then hear what I call you!"

The billows that came at this time were more formidable. They seemed always just about to break and roll over the little boat in a turmoil of foam. There was a preparatory and long growl in the speech of them. No mind unused to the sea would have concluded that the dinghy could ascend these sheer heights in time. The shore was still afar. The oiler was a wily surfman. "Boys," he said swiftly, "she won't live three minutes more, and we're too far out to swim. Shall I take her to sea again, Captain?"

"Yes; go ahead!" said the captain.

This oiler, by a series of quick miracles and fast and steady oarsmanship, turned [732] the boat in the middle of the surf and took her safely to sea again.

There was a considerable silence as the boat bumped over the furrowed sea to deeper water. Then somebody in gloom spoke: "Well, anyhow, they must have seen us from the shore by now."

The gulls went in slanting flight up the wind toward the gray, desolate east. A squall, marked by dingy clouds and clouds brick-red, like smoke from a burning building, appeared from the southeast.

"What do you think of those life-saving people? Ain't they peaches?"

"Funny they haven't seen us."

"Maybe they think we're out here for sport! Maybe they think we're fishin'. Maybe they think we're damned fools."

It was a long afternoon. A changed tide tried to force them southward, but wind and wave said northward. Far ahead, where coastline, sea, and sky formed their mighty angle, there were little dots which seemed to indicate a city on the shore.

"St. Augustine?"

The captain shook his head. "Too near Mosquito Inlet."

And the oiler rowed, and then the correspondent rowed; then the oiler rowed. It was a weary business. The human back can become the seat of more aches and pains than are registered in books for the composite anatomy of a regiment. It is a limited area, but it can become the theater of innumerable muscular conflicts, tangles, wrenches, knots, and other comforts.

"Did you ever like to row, Billie?" asked the correspondent.

"No," said the oiler; "hang it!"

When one exchanged the rowing-seat for a place in the bottom of the boat, he suffered a bodily depression that caused him to be careless of everything save an obligation to wiggle one finger. There was cold sea-water swashing to and fro in the boat, and he lay in it. His head, pillowed on a thwart, was within an inch of the swirl of a wavecrest, and sometimes a particularly obstreperous sea came inboard and drenched him once more. But these matters did not annoy him. It is almost certain that if the boat had capsized he would have tumbled comfortably out upon the ocean as if he felt sure that it was a great soft mattress.

"Look! There's a man on the shore!"

"Where?"

"There! See 'im? See 'im?"

"Yes, sure! He's walking along."

"Now he's stopped. Look! He's facing us!"

"He's waving at us!"

"So he is! By thunder!"

"Ah, now we're all right! Now we're all right! There'll be a boat out here for us in half an hour."

"He's going on. He's running. He's going up to that house there."

The remote beach seemed lower than the sea, and it required a searching glance to discern the little black figure. The captain saw a floating stick, and they rowed to it. A bath towel was by some weird chance in the boat, and, tying this on the stick, the captain waved it. The oarsman did not dare turn his head, so he was obliged to ask questions.

"What's he doing now?"

"He's standing still again. He's looking, I think. . . . There he goes again—toward the house. . . . Now he's stopped again."

"Is he waving at us?"

"No, not now; he was, though."

"Look! There comes another man!"

"He's running."

"Look at him go, would you!"

"Why, he's on a bicycle. Now he's met the other man. They're both waving at us. Look!"

"There comes something up the beach."

"What the devil is that thing?"

"Why, it looks like a boat."

"Why, certainly, it's a boat."

"No; it's on wheels."

"Yes, so it is. Well, that must be the life-boat. They drag them along shore on a wagon."

"That's the life-boat, sure."

"No, by —d, it's—it's an omnibus."

"I tell you it's a life-boat."

"It is not! It's an omnibus. I can see it plain. See? One of those big hotel omnibuses."

"By thunder, you're right. It's an omnibus, sure as fate. What do you suppose they are doing with an omnibus? Maybe they are going around collecting the life-crew, hey?"

"That's it, likely. Look! There's a fellow waving a little black flag. He's standing on the steps of the omnibus. [733] There come those other two fellows. Now they're all talking together. Look at the fellow with the flag. Maybe he ain't waving it!"

"That ain't a flag, is it? That's his coat. Why, certainly, that's his coat."

"So it is; it's his coat. He's taken it off and is waving it around his head. But would you look at him swing it!"

"Oh, say, there isn't any life-saving station there. That's just a winter-resort hotel omnibus that has brought over some of the boarders to see us drown."

"What's that idiot with the coat mean? What's he signalling, any-how?"

"It looks as if he were trying to tell us to go north. There must be a life-saving station up there."

"No; he thinks we're fishing. Just giving us a merry hand. See? Ah, there, Willie!"

"Well, I wish I could make something out of those signals. What do you suppose he means?"

"He don't mean anything; he's just playing."

"Well, if he'd just signal us to try the surf again, or to go to sea and wait, or go north, or go south, or go to hell, there would be some reason in it. But look at him! He just stands there and keeps his coat revolving like a wheel. The ass!"

"There come more people."

"Now there's quite a mob. Look! Isn't that a boat?"

"Where? Oh, I see where you mean. No, that's no boat."

"That fellow is still waving his coat."

"He must think we like to see him do that. Why don't he quit it? It don't mean anything."

"I don't know. I think he is trying to make us go north. It must be that there's a life-saving station there somewhere."

"Say, he ain't tired yet. Look at 'im wave!"

"Wonder how long he can keep that up. He's been revolving his coat ever since he caught sight of us. He's an idiot. Why aren't they getting men to bring a boat out? A fishing-boat—one of those big yawls—could come out here all right. Why don't he do something?"

"Oh, it's all right now."

"They'll have a boat out here for us in less than no time, now that they've seen us."

A faint yellow tone came into the sky over the low land. The shadows on the sea slowly deepened. The wind bore coldness with it, and the men began to shiver.

"Holy smoke!" said one, allowing his voice to express his impious mood, "if we keep on monkeying out here! If we've got to flounder out here all night!"

"Oh, we'll never have to stay here all night! Don't you worry. They've seen us now, and it won't be long before they'll come chasing out after us."

The shore grew dusky. The man waving a coat blended gradually into this gloom, and it swallowed in the same manner the omnibus and the group of people. The spray, when it dashed uproariously over the side, made the voyagers shrink and swear like men who were being branded.

"I'd like to catch the chump who waved the coat. I feel like soaking him one, just for luck."

"Why? What did he do?"

"Oh, nothing, but then he seemed so damned cheerful."

In the meantime the oiler rowed, and then the correspondent rowed, and then the oiler rowed. Gray-faced and bowed forward, they mechanically, turn by turn, plied the leaden oars. The form of the lighthouse had vanished from the southern horizon, but finally a pale star appeared, just lifting from the sea. The streaked saffron in the west passed before the all-merging darkness, and the sea to the east was black. The land had vanished, and was expressed only by the low and drear thunder of the surf.

"If I am going to be drowned—if I am going to be drowned—if I am going to be drowned, why, in the name of the seven mad gods who rule the sea, was I allowed to come thus far and contemplate sand and trees? Was I brought here merely to have my nose dragged away as I was about to nibble the sacred cheese of life?"

The patient captain, drooped over the water-jar, was sometimes obliged to speak to the oarsman.

"Keep her head up! Keep her head up!"

" 'Keep her head up,' sir." The voices were weary and low.

This was surely a quiet evening. All save the oarsman lay heavily and listlessly in the boat's bottom. As for him, his eyes [734] were just capable of noting the tall black waves that swept forward in a most sinister silence, save for an occasional subdued growl of a crest.

The cook's head was on a thwart, and he looked without interest at the water under his nose. He was deep in other scenes. Finally he spoke. "Billie," he murmured, dreamfully, "what kind of pie do you like best?"

V

"Pie!" said the oiler and the correspondent, agitatedly. "Don't talk about those things, blast you!"

"Well," said the cook, "I was just thinking about ham sandwiches, and—"

A night on the sea in an open boat is a long night. As darkness settled finally, the shine of the light, lifting from the sea in the south, changed to full gold. On the northern horizon a new light appeared, a small bluish gleam on the edge of the waters. These two lights were the furniture of the world. Otherwise there was nothing but waves.

Two men huddled in the stern, and distances were so magnificent in the dinghy that the rower was enabled to keep his feet partly warm by thrusting them under his companions. Their legs indeed extended far under the rowing-seat until they touched the feet of the captain forward. Sometimes, despite the efforts of the tired oarsman, a wave came piling into the boat, an icy wave of the night, and the chilling water soaked them anew. They would twist their bodies for a moment and groan, and sleep the dead sleep once more, while the water in the boat gurgled about them as the craft rocked.

The plan of the oiler and the correspondent was for one to row until he lost the ability, and then arouse the other from his sea-water couch in the bottom of the boat.

The oiler plied the oars until his head drooped forward and the overpowering sleep blinded him; and he rowed yet afterward. Then he touched a man in the bottom of the boat, and called his name. "Will you spell me for a little while?" he said meekly.

"Sure, Billie," said the correspondent, awaking and dragging himself to a sitting position. They exchanged places carefully, and the oiler, cuddling down in the sea-water at the cook's side, seemed to go to sleep instantly.

The particular violence of the sea had ceased. The waves came without snarling. The obligation of the man at the oars was to keep the boat headed so that the tilt of the rollers would not capsize her, and to preserve her from filling when the crests rushed past. The black waves were silent and hard to be seen in the darkness. Often one was almost upon the boat before the oarsman was aware.

In a low voice the correspondent addressed the captain. He was not sure that the captain was awake, although this iron man seemed to be always awake. "Captain, shall I keep her making for that light north, sir?"

The same steady voice answered him. "Yes. Keep it about two points off the port bow."

The cook had tied a life-belt around himself in order to get even the warmth which this clumsy cork contrivance could donate, and he seemed almost stove-like when a rower, whose teeth invariably chattered wildly as soon as he ceased his labor, dropped down to sleep.

The correspondent, as he rowed, looked down at the two men sleeping underfoot. The cook's arm was around the oiler's shoulders, and, with their fragmentary clothing and haggard faces, they were the babes of the sea—a grotesque rendering of the old babes in the wood.

Later he must have grown stupid at his work, for suddenly there was a growling of water, and a crest came with a roar and a swash into the boat, and it was a wonder that it did not set the cook afloat in his life-belt. The cook continued to sleep, but the oiler sat up, blinking his eyes and shaking with the new cold.

"Oh, I'm awful sorry, Billie," said the correspondent, contritely.

"That's all right, old boy," said the oiler, and lay down again and was asleep.

Presently it seemed that even the captain dozed, and the correspondent thought that he was the one man afloat on all the oceans. The wind had a voice as it came over the waves, and it was sadder than the end.

There was a long, loud swishing astern of the boat, and a gleaming trail of phosphorescence, like blue flame, was furrowed [735] on the black waters. It might have been made by a monstrous knife.

Then there came a stillness, while the correspondent breathed with the [sic] open mouth and looked at the sea.

Suddenly there was another swish and another long flash of bluish light, and this time it was alongside the boat, and might almost have been reached with an oar. The correspondent saw an enormous fin speed like a shadow through the water, hurling the crystalline spray and leaving the long glowing trail.

The correspondent looked over his shoulder at the captain. His face was hidden, and he seemed to be asleep. He looked at the babes of the sea. They certainly were asleep. So, being bereft of sympathy, he leaned a little way to one side and swore softly into the sea.

But the thing did not then leave the vicinity of the boat. Ahead or astern, on one side or the other, at intervals long or short, fled the long sparkling streak, and there was to be heard the *whirroo* of the dark fin. The speed and power of the thing was greatly to be admired. It cut the water like a gigantic and keen projectile.

The presence of this biding thing did not affect the man with the same horror that it would if he had been a picnicker. He simply looked at the sea dully and swore in an undertone.

Nevertheless, it is true that he did not wish to be alone with the thing. He wished one of his companions to awake by chance and keep him company with it. But the captain hung motionless over the water-jar, and the oiler and the cook in the bottom of the boat were plunged in slumber.

VI

"If I am going to be drowned—if I am going to be drowned—if I am going to be drowned, why, in the name of the seven mad gods of the sea, was I allowed to come thus far and contemplate sand and trees?"

During this dismal night, it may be remarked that a man would conclude that it was really the intention of the seven mad gods to drown him, despite the abominable injustice of it. For it was certainly an abominable injustice to drown a man who had worked so hard, so hard. The man felt it would be a crime most unnatural. Other people had drowned at sea since galleys swarmed with painted sails, but still—

When it occurs to a man that nature does not regard him as important, and that she feels she would not maim the universe by disposing of him, he at first wishes to throw bricks at the temple, and he hates deeply the fact that there are no bricks and no temples. Any visible expression of nature would surely be pelleted with his jeers.

Then, if there be no tangible thing to hoot, he feels, perhaps, the desire to confront a personification and indulge in pleas, bowed to one knee, and with hands supplicant, saying, "Yes, but I love myself."

A high cold star on a winter's night is the word he feels that she says to him. Thereafter he knows the pathos of his situation.

The men in the dinghy had not discussed these matters, but each had, no doubt, reflected upon them in silence and according to his mind. There was seldom any expression upon their faces save the general one of complete weariness. Speech was devoted to the business of the boat.

To chime the notes of his emotion, a verse mysteriously entered the correspondent's head. He had even forgotten that he had forgotten this verse, but it suddenly was in his mind.

A soldier of the Legion lay dying in Algiers;
There was lack of woman's nursing, there was dearth of woman's
    tears;
But a comrade stood beside him, and he took that comrade's hand,
And he said, "I shall never see my own, my native land."

In his childhood the correspondent had been made acquainted with
the fact that a soldier of the Legion lay dying in Algiers, but he had
never regarded the fact as important. Myriads of his school-fellows
had informed him of the soldier's plight, but the dinning had naturally
ended by making him perfectly indifferent. He had never considered
it his affair that a soldier of the Legion lay dying in Algiers, nor had it
appeared to him as a matter for sorrow. It was less to him than breaking of a pencil's point. [736]

Now, however, it quaintly came to him as a human, living thing. It
was no longer merely a picture of a few throes in the breast of a poet,
meanwhile drinking tea and warming his feet at the grate; it was an
actuality—stern, mournful, and fine.

The correspondent plainly saw the soldier. He lay on the sand with
his feet out straight and still. While his pale left hand was upon his
chest in an attempt to thwart the going of his life, the blood came between his fingers. In the far Algerian distance, a city of low square
forms was set against a sky that was faint with the last sunset hues.
The correspondent, plying the oars and dreaming of the slow and
slower movements of the lips of the soldier, was moved by a profound
and perfectly impersonal comprehension. He was sorry for the soldier
of the Legion who lay dying in Algiers.

The thing which had followed the boat and waited had evidently
grown bored at the delay. There was no longer to be heard the slash
of the cutwater, and there was no longer the flame of the long trail.
The light in the north still glimmered, but it was apparently no nearer
to the boat. Sometimes the boom of the surf rang in the correspondent's ears, and he turned the craft seaward then and rowed harder.
Southward, some one had evidently built a watch-fire on the beach. It
was too low and too far to be seen, but it made a shimmering, roseate
reflection upon the bluff in back of it, and this could be discerned
from the boat. The wind came stronger, and sometimes a wave suddenly raged out like a mountain-cat, and there was to be seen the
sheen and sparkle of a broken crest.

The captain, in the bow, moved on his water-jar and sat erect.
"Pretty long night," he observed to the correspondent. He looked at
the shore. "Those life-saving people take their time."

"Did you see that shark playing around?"

"Yes, I saw him. He was a big fellow, all right."

"Wish I had known you were awake."

Later the correspondent spoke into the bottom of the boat. "Billie!"

There was a slow and gradual disentanglement. "Billie, will you spell me?"

"Sure," said the oiler.

As soon as the correspondent touched the cold, comfortable sea-water in the bottom of the boat and had huddled close to the cook's life-belt he was deep in sleep, despite the fact that his teeth played all the popular airs. This sleep was so good to him that it was but a moment before he heard a voice call his name in a tone that demonstrated the last stages of exhaustion. "Will you spell me?"

"Sure, Billie."

The light in the north had mysteriously vanished, but the correspondent took his course from the wide-awake captain.

Later in the night they took the boat farther out to sea, and the captain directed the cook to take one oar at the stern and keep the boat facing the seas. He was to call out if he should hear the thunder of the surf. This plan enabled the oiler and the correspondent to get respite together. "We'll give those boys a chance to get into shape again," said the captain. They curled down and, after a few preliminary chatterings and trembles, slept once more the dead sleep. Neither knew they had bequeathed to the cook the company of another shark, or perhaps the same shark.

As the boat caroused on the waves, spray occasionally bumped over the side and gave them a fresh soaking, but this had no power to break their repose. The ominous slash of the wind and the water affected them as it would have affected mummies.

"Boys," said the cook, with the notes of every reluctance in his voice, "she's drifted in pretty close. I guess one of you had better take her to sea again." The correspondent, aroused, heard the crash of the toppled crests.

As he was rowing, the captain gave him some whiskey-and-water, and this steadied the chills out of him. "If I ever get ashore and anybody shows me even a photograph of an oar—"

At last there was a short conversation.

"Billie! . . . Billie, will you spell me?"

"Sure," said the oiler.

VII

When the correspondent again opened his eyes, the sea and the sky were each of the gray hue of the dawning. Later, carmine [737] and gold was painted upon the waters. The morning appeared finally, in its splendor, with a sky of pure blue, and the sunlight flamed on the tips of the waves.

On the distant dunes were set many little black cottages, and a tall white windmill reared above them. No man, nor dog, nor bicycle appeared on the beach. The cottages might have formed a deserted village.

The voyagers scanned the shore. A conference was held in the boat. "Well," said the captain, "if no help is coming, we might better try a run through the surf right away. If we stay out here much longer we will be too weak to do anything for ourselves at all." The others silently acquiesced in this reasoning. The boat was headed for the beach. The correspondent wondered if none ever ascended the tall wind-tower, and if then they never looked seaward. This tower was a giant, standing with its back to the plight of the ants. It represented in a degree, to the correspondent, the serenity of nature amid the struggles of the individual—nature in the wind, and nature in the vision of men. She did not seem cruel to him then, nor beneficent, nor treacherous, nor wise. But she was indifferent, flatly indifferent. It is, perhaps, plausible that a man in this situation, impressed with the unconcern of the universe, should see the innumerable flaws of his life, and have them taste wickedly in his mind, and wish for another chance. A distinction between right and wrong seems absurdly clear to him, then, in this new ignorance of the grave-edge, and he understands that if he were given another opportunity he would mend his conduct and his words, and be better and brighter during an introduction or at a tea.

"Now, boys," said the captain, "she is going to swamp sure. All we can do is to work her in as far as possible, and then when she swamps, pile out and scramble for the beach. Keep cool now, and don't jump until she swamps sure."

The oiler took the oars. Over his shoulders he scanned the surf. "Captain," he said, "I think I'd better bring her about and keep her head-on to the seas and back her in."

"All right, Billie," said the captain. "Back her in." The oiler swung the boat then, and seated in the stern, the cook and the correspondent were obliged to look over their shoulders to contemplate the lonely and indifferent shore.

The monstrous inshore rollers heaved the boat high until the men were again enabled to see the white sheets of water scudding up the slanted beach. "We won't get in very close," said the captain. Each time a man could wrest his attention from the rollers, he turned his glance toward the shore, and in the expression of the eyes during this contemplation there was a singular quality. The correspondent, observing the others, knew that they were not afraid, but the full meaning of their glances was shrouded.

As for himself, he was too tired to grapple fundamentally with the fact. He tried to coerce his mind into thinking of it, but the mind was dominated at this time by the muscles, and the muscles said they did not care. It merely occurred to him that if he should drown it would be a shame.

There were no hurried words, no pallor, no plain agitation. The men simply looked at the shore. "Now, remember to get well clear of the boat when you jump," said the captain.

Seaward the crest of a roller suddenly fell with a thunderous crash, and the long white comber came roaring down upon the boat.

"Steady now," said the captain. The men were silent. They turned their eyes from the shore to the comber and waited. The boat slid up the incline, leaped at the furious top, bounced over it, and swung down the long back of the wave. Some water had been shipped, and the cook bailed it out.

But the next crest crashed also. The tumbling, boiling flood of white water caught the boat and whirled it almost perpendicular. Water swarmed in from all sides. The correspondent had his hands on the gunwale at this time, and when the water entered at that place he swiftly withdrew his fingers, as if he objected to wetting them.

The little boat, drunken with this weight of water, reeled and snuggled deeper into the sea.

"Bail her out, cook! Bail her out!" said the captain.

"All right, Captain," said the cook.

"Now, boys, the next one will do for [738] us sure," said the oiler. "Mind to jump clear of the boat."

The third wave moved forward, huge, furious, implacable. It fairly swallowed the dinghy, and almost simultaneously the men tumbled into the sea. A piece of life-belt had lain in the bottom of the boat, and as the correspondent went overboard he held this to his chest with his left hand.

The January water was icy, and he reflected immediately that it was colder than he had expected to find it off the coast of Florida. This appeared to his dazed mind as a fact important enough to be noted at the time. The coldness of the water was sad; it was tragic. This fact was somehow mixed and confused with his opinion of his situation, so that it seemed almost a proper reason for tears. The water was cold.

When he came to the surface he was conscious of little but the noisy water. Afterward he saw his companions in the sea. The oiler was ahead in the race. He was swimming strongly and rapidly. Off to the correspondent's left, the cook's great white and corked back bulged out of the water; and in the rear the captain was hanging with his one good hand to the keel of the overturned dinghy.

There is a certain immovable quality to a shore, and the correspondent wondered at it amid the confusion of the sea.

It seemed also very attractive; but the correspondent knew that it was a long journey, and he paddled leisurely. The piece of life-preserver lay under him, and sometimes he whirled down the incline of a wave as if he were on a hand-sled.

But finally he arrived at a place in the sea where travel was beset with difficulty. He did not pause swimming to inquire what manner of current had caught him, but there his progress ceased. The shore was set before him like a bit of scenery on a stage, and he looked at it and understood with his eyes each detail of it.

As the cook passed, much farther to the left, the captain was calling to him, "Turn over on your back, cook! Turn over on your back and use the oar."

"All right, sir." The cook turned on his back, and, paddling with an oar, went ahead as if he were a canoe.

Presently the boat also passed to the left of the correspondent, with the captain clinging with one hand to the keel. He would have appeared like a man raising himself to look over a board fence if it were not for the extraordinary gymnastics of the boat. The correspondent marvelled that the captain could still hold to it.

They passed on nearer to shore—the oiler, the cook, the captain —and following them went the water-jar, bouncing gaily over the seas.

The correspondent remained in the grip of this strange new enemy, a current. The shore, with its white slope of sand and its green bluff topped with little silent cottages, was spread like a picture before him. It was very near to him then, but he was impressed as one who, in a gallery, looks at a scene from Brittany or Algiers.

He thought: "I am going to drown? Can it be possible? Can it be possible? Can it be possible?" Perhaps an individual must consider his own death to be the final phenomenon of nature.

But later a wave perhaps whirled him out of this small deadly current, for he found suddenly that he could again make progress toward the shore. Later still he was aware that the captain, clinging with one hand to the keel of the dinghy, had his face turned away from the shore and toward him, and was calling his name. "Come to the boat! Come to the boat!"

In his struggle to reach the captain and the boat, he reflected that when one gets properly wearied drowning must really be a comfortable arrangement—a cessation of hostilities accompanied by a large degree of relief; and he was glad of it, for the main thing in his mind for some moments had been horror of the temporary agony; he did not wish to be hurt.

Presently he saw a man running along the shore. He was undressing with most remarkable speed. Coat, trousers, shirt, everything flew magically off him.

"Come to the boat!" called the captain.

"All right, Captain." As the correspondent paddled, he saw the captain let himself down to bottom and leave the boat. Then the correspondent performed his one little marvel of the voyage. A large wave caught him and flung him with ease and supreme speed completely over the boat and far beyond it. It struck him even then as an event in gymnastics and a true miracle of the sea. An overturned boat in the surf is not a plaything to a swimming man. [739]

The correspondent arrived in water that reached only to his waist, but his condition did not enable him to stand for more than a moment. Each wave knocked him into a heap, and the undertow pulled at him.

Then he saw the man who had been running and undressing, and undressing and running, come bounding into the water. He dragged ashore the cook, and then waded toward the captain; but the captain waved him away and sent him to the correspondent. He was naked —naked as a tree in winter; but a halo was about his head, and he shone like a saint. He gave a strong pull, and a long drag, and a bully heave at the correspondent's hand. The correspondent, schooled in the minor formulae, said, "Thanks, old man." But suddenly the man cried, "What's that?" He pointed a swift finger. The correspondent said, "Go."

In the shallows, face downward, lay the oiler. His forehead touched
sand that was periodically, between each wave, clear of the sea.

The correspondent did not know all that transpired afterward.
When he achieved safe ground he fell, striking the sand with each
particular part of his body. It was as if he had dropped from a roof,
but the thud was grateful to him.

It seems that instantly the beach was populated with men with
blankets, clothes, and flasks, and women with coffee-pots and all the
remedies sacred to their minds. The welcome of the land to the men
from the sea was warm and generous; but a still and dripping shape
was carried slowly up the beach, and the land's welcome for it could
only be the different and sinister hospitality of the grave.

When it came night, the white waves paced to and fro in the moon-
light, and the wind brought the sound of the great sea's voice to the
men on the shore, and they felt that they could then be interpret-
ers. [740]

✥ STEPHEN CRANE

Black Riders and Other Lines

Stephen Crane, *Black Riders and Other Lines,* Boston, Cope-
land and Day, 1895.

[GOD FASHIONED THE SHIP OF THE WORLD]

God fashioned the ship of the world carefully.
With the infinite skill of an All-Master
Made He the hull and the sails,
Held He the rudder
Ready for adjustment.
Erect stood He, scanning His work proudly.
Then—at fateful time—a wrong called,
And God turned, heeding.
Lo, the ship, at this opportunity, slipped slyly.

Making cunning noiseless travel down the ways.
So that, for ever rudderless, it went upon the seas.
Going ridiculous voyages,
Making quaint progress,
Turning as with serious purpose
Before stupid winds.
And there were many in the sky
Who laughed at this thing. [6-7]

❧ STEPHEN CRANE

War Is Kind

Stephen Crane, *War Is Kind*, New York, Frederick A. Stokes, 1899.

[TO THE MAIDEN]

To the maiden
The sea was blue meadow
Alive with little froth-people
Singing.

To the sailor, wrecked,
The sea was dead gray walls
Superlative in vacancy,
Upon which nevertheless at fateful time
Was written
The grim hatred of nature. [19-20]

[A NEWSPAPER IS A COLLECTION]

A newspaper is a collection of half-injustices
Which, bawled by boys from mile to mile,
Spreads its curious opinion

To a million merciful and sneering men,
While families cuddle the joys of the fireside
When spurred by tale of dire lone agony.
A newspaper is a court
Where everyone is kindly and unfairly tried
By a squalor of honest men.
A newspaper is a market
Where wisdom sells its freedom
And melons are crowned by the crowd.
A newspaper is a game
Where his error scores the player victory
While another's skill wins death.
A newspaper is a symbol;
It is feckless life's chronicle,
A collection of loud tales
Concentrating eternal stupidities,
That in remote ages lived unhaltered,
Roaming through a fenceless world. [40]

[A MAN SAID TO THE UNIVERSE]

A man said to the universe:
"Sir, I exist!"
"However," replied the universe,
"The fact has not created in me
A sense of obligation." [56]

[THE TREES IN THE GARDEN]

The trees in the garden rained flowers.
Children ran there joyously.
They gathered the flowers
Each to himself.
Now there were some
Who gathered great heaps—
Having opportunity and skill—
Until, behold, only chance blossoms
Remained for the feeble.
Then a little spindling tutor

Ran importantly to the father, crying:
"Pray, come hither!
See this unjust thing in your garden!"
But when the father had surveyed,
He admonished the tutor:
"Not so, small sage!
This thing is just.
For, look you,
Are not they who possess the flowers
Stronger, bolder, shrewder
Than they who have none?
Why should the strong—
The beautiful strong—
Why should they not have the flowers?"
Upon reflection, the tutor bowed to the ground,
"My lord," he said,
"The stars are displaced
By this towering wisdom." [65-66]

[GOD IS COLD]* [189?]

A man adrift on a slim spar
A horizon smaller than the rim of a bottle
Tented waves rearing lashy dark points
The near whine of froth in circles.
                   God is cold.

The incessant raise and swing of the sea
And growl after growl of crest
The sinkings, green, seething, endless
The upheaval half-completed.
                   God is cold.

The seas are in the hollow of Thy Hand;
Oceans may be turned to a spray
Raining down through the stars

* The poem above was posthumously printed in *The Bookman*, April, 1929. It is reprinted from *The Collected Poems of Stephen Crane*, edited by Wilson Follett, by permission of Alfred A. Knopf, Inc., Copyright © 1930, by Alfred A. Knopf, Inc.

Because of a gesture of pity toward a babe.
Oceans may become grey ashes,
Die with a long moan and a roar
Amid the tumult of the fishes
And the cries of the ships,
Because The Hand beckons the mice.
A horizon smaller than a doomed assassin's cap,
Inky, surging tumults
A reeling, drunken sky and no sky
A pale hand sliding from a polished spar.
God is cold.

The puff of a coat imprisoning air:
A face kissing the water-death
A weary slow sway of a lost hand
And the sea, the moving sea, the sea.
God is cold. [129-130]

✿ JACK LONDON

The White Silence

Jack London, "The White Silence: Another Story of Malemute Kid," *Overland Monthly*, XXXIII (February, 1899).

"CARMEN WON'T LAST more than a couple of days." Mason spat out a chunk of ice and surveyed the poor animal ruefully, then put her foot in his mouth and proceeded to bite out the ice which clustered cruelly between the toes.

"I never saw a dog with a highfalutin name that ever was worth a rap," he said, as he concluded his task and shoved her aside. "They just fade away and die under the responsibility. Did ye ever see one go wrong with a sensible name like Cassiar, Siwash, or Husky? No, sir! Take a look at Shookum here, he's——"

Snap! The lean brute flashed up, the white teeth just missing Mason's throat.

"Ye will, will ye?" A shrewd clout behind the ear with the butt of the dog-whip stretched the animal in the snow, quivering softly, a yellow slaver dripping from its fangs.

"As I was saying, just look at Shookum, here—he's got the spirit. Bet ye he eats Carmen before the week's out."

"I'll bank another proposition against that," replied Malemute Kid, reversing the frozen bread placed before the fire to thaw. "We'll eat Shookum before the trip is over. What d' ye say, Ruth?"

The Indian woman settled the coffee with a piece of ice, glanced from Malemute Kid to her husband, then at the dogs, but vouchsafed no reply. It was such a palpable truism that none was necessary. Two hundred miles of unbroken trail in prospect, with a scant six days' grub for themselves and none for the dogs, could admit no other alternative. The two men and the woman grouped about the fire and began their meager meal. The dogs lay in their harnesses, for it was a mid-day halt, and watched each mouthful enviously.

"No more lunches after to-day," said Malemute Kid. "And we've got to keep a close eye on the dogs,—they're getting vicious. They'd just as soon pull a fellow down as not, if they get a chance."

"And I was president of an Epworth once, and taught in the Sunday-school." Having irrelevantly delivered himself of this, Mason fell into a dreamy contemplation of his steaming moccasins, but was aroused by Ruth filling his cup. "Thank God, we've got slathers of tea! I've seen it growing, down in Tennessee. What wouldn't I give for a hot corn pone just now! Never mind, Ruth; you won't starve much longer, nor wear moccasins either."

The woman threw off her gloom at this, and in her eyes welled up a great love for her white lord,—the first white man she had ever seen,—the first man whom she had known to treat a woman as something better than a mere animal or beast of burden.

"Yes, Ruth," continued her husband, having recourse to the macaronic jargon in which it was alone possible for them to understand each other, and which it is impossible to reproduce; "wait till we clean up and pull for the Outside. We'll take the White Man's canoe and go to the Salt Water. Yes, bad water, rough water,—great mountains dance up and down all the time. And so big, so far, so far away, —you travel ten sleep, twenty sleep, forty sleep," (he graphically enumerated the days on his fingers,) "all the time water, bad water

Then you come to great village, plenty people, just the same mosquitoes next summer. Wigwams oh, so high,—ten, twenty pines. Hi-yu skookum!"

He paused impotently, cast an appealing glance at Malemute Kid, then laboriously placed the twenty pines, end on end, by sign language. Malemute Kid smiled with cheery cynicism; but Ruth's eyes were wide with wonder, and with pleasure; for she half believed he was joking, and such condescensions pleased her poor woman's heart.

"And then you step into a—a box, and pouf! up you go." He tossed his empty cup in the air by way of illustration, and as he deftly caught it, cried: "And biff! down you come. Oh, great medicine-men! You go Fort Yukon, I go Arctic City,—twenty-five sleep,—big string, all the time.—I catch him string,—I say, 'Hello Ruth! How are ye?'—and you say, 'Is that my good husband?'—and I say 'Yes,'—and you say, 'No can bake good bread, no more soda,'—then I say, 'Look in cache, under flour; good-by.' You look and catch plenty soda. All the time you Fort Yukon, me Arctic City. Hi-yi medicine-man!"

Ruth smiled so ingenuously at the fairy story, that both men burst into laughter. A row among the dogs cut short the wonders of the Outside, and by the time the snarling combatants were separated, she had lashed the sleds and all was ready for the trail.

"Mush! Baldy! Hi! Mush on!" Mason worked his whip smartly, and as the dogs whined low in the traces, broke out the sled with the gee-pole. Ruth followed with the second team, leaving Malemute Kid, who had helped her start, to bring up the rear. Strong man, noble brute that he was, capable of felling an ox at a blow, he could not bear to beat the poor animals, but humored them as a dog-driver rarely does,—nay, almost wept with them in their misery.

"Come, mush on there, you poor sore-footed brutes," he murmured, after several ineffectual attempts to start the load. But his patience was at last rewarded, and though whimpering with pain, they hastened to join their fellows.

No more conversation; the toil of the trail will not permit such extravagance. And of all deadening labors, that of the Northland trail is the worst. Happy is the man who can weather a day's travel at the price of silence, and that on a beaten track.

And of all heart-breaking labors, that of breaking trail is the worst. At every step the great webbed shoe sinks till the snow is level with the knee. Then up, straight up, the deviation of a fraction of an inch being a certain precursor of disaster, the snow-shoe must be lifted till the surface is cleared; then forward, down, and the other foot is raised perpendicularly for the matter of half a yard. He who tries this for the first time, if haply he avoids bringing his shoes in danger-ous propinquity and measures not his length on the treacherous foot-ing, will give up exhausted at the end of a hundred yards; he who can keep out of the way of the dogs for a whole day may well crawl into his sleeping-bag with a clear conscience, and a pride which passeth all understanding; and he who travels twenty sleeps on the Long Trail is a man whom the gods may envy.

The afternoon wore on, and with the awe, born of the White Si-lence, the voiceless travelers bent to their work. Nature has many tricks wherewith she convinces man of his finity,—the ceaseless flow of the tides, the fury of the storm, the shock of the earthquake, the long role of heaven's artillery,—but the most tremendous, the most stupefying of all, is the passive phase of the White Silence. All move-ment ceases, the sky clears, the heavens are as brass; the slightest whisper seems sacrilege, and man becomes timid, affrighted at the sound of his own voice. Sole speck of life journeying across the ghostly wastes of a dead world, he trembles at his audacity, realizes that his is a maggot's life, nothing more. Strange thoughts arise unsummoned, and the mystery of all things strives for utterance. And the fear of death, of God, of the universe, comes over him,—the hope of the Resurrection and the Life, the yearning for immortality, the vain striving of the imprisoned essence, it is then, if ever, man walks alone with God.

So wore the day away. The river took a great bend, and Mason headed his team for the cut-off across the narrow neck of land. But the dogs balked at the high bank. Again and again, though Ruth and Malemute Kid were shoving on the sled, they slipped back. Then came the concerted effort. The miserable creatures, weak from hunger, exerted their last strength. Up—up—the sled poised on the top of the bank; but the leader swung the string of dogs behind him to the right, fouling Mason's snow-shoes. The result was grievous. Mason was whipped off his feet; one of the dogs fell in the traces; and the sled toppled back, dragging everything to the bottom again.

Slash! the whip fell among the dogs cruelly, especially upon the one which had fallen.

"Don't, Mason," entreated Malemute Kid; "the poor devil's on its last legs. Wait and we'll put my team on."

Mason deliberately withheld the whip till the last word had fallen, then out flashed the long lash, completely curling about the offending creature's body. Carmen,—for it was Carmen,—cowered in the snow, cried piteously, then rolled over on her side.

It was a tragic moment, a pitiful incident of the trail,—a dying dog, two comrades in anger. Ruth glanced solicitously from man to man. But Malemute Kid restrained himself, though there was a world of reproach in his eyes, and bending over the dog, cut the traces. No word was spoken. The teams were double-spanned and the difficulty overcome; the sleds were under way again, the dying dog dragging herself along in the rear. As long as an animal can travel, it is not shot, and this last chance is accorded it,—the crawling into camp, if it can, in the hope of a moose being killed.

Already penitent for his angry action, but too stubborn to make amends, Mason toiled on at the head of the cavalcade, little dreaming that danger hovered in the air. The timber clustered thick in the sheltered bottom, and through this they threaded their way. Fifty feet or more from the trail towered a lofty pine. For generations it had stood there, and for generations destiny had had this one end in view,—perhaps the same had been decreed of Mason.

He stooped to fasten the loosened thong of his moccasin. The sleds came to a halt and the dogs lay down in the snow without a whimper. The stillness was weird; not a breath rustled the frost-encrusted forest; the cold and silence of outer space had chilled the heart and smote the trembling lips of nature. A sigh pulsed through the air,— they did not seem to actually hear it, but rather felt it, like the premonition of movement in a motionless void. Then the great tree, burdened with its weight of years and snow, played its last part in the tragedy of life. He heard the warning crash and attempted to spring up, but almost erect, caught the blow squarely on the shoulder.

The sudden danger; the quick death,—how often had Malemute Kid faced it! The pine needles were still quivering as he gave his commands and sprang into action. Nor did the Indian girl faint or raise her voice in idle wailing, as would many of her white sisters. At his order, she threw her weight on the end of a quickly extemporized handspike, easing the pressure and listening to her husband's groans, while Malemute Kid attacked the tree with his ax. The steel rang merrily as it bit into the frozen trunk, each stroke being accompanied by a forced, audible respiration, the "Huh!" "Huh!" of the woodsman.

At last the Kid laid the pitiable thing that was once a man in the snow. But worse than his comrade's pain, was the dumb anguish in the woman's face, the blended look of hopeful, hopeless query. Little was said; those of the Northland are early taught the futility of words and the inestimable value of deeds. With the temperature at sixty-five below zero, a man cannot lie many minutes in the snow and live. So the sled-lashings were cut, and the sufferer, rolled in furs, laid on a couch of boughs. Before him roared a fire, built of the very wood which wrought the mishap. Behind and partially over him was stretched the primitive fly,—a piece of canvas, which caught the radiating heat and threw it back and down upon him,—a trick which men may know who study physics at the fount.

And men who have shared their bed with death know when the call is sounded. Mason was terribly crushed. The most cursory examination revealed it. His right arm, leg, and back, were broken; his limbs were paralyzed from the hips; and the likelihood of internal injuries was large. An occasional moan was his only sign of life.

No hope; nothing to be done. The pitiless night crept slowly by,— Ruth's portion, the despairing stoicism of her race, and Malemute Kid adding new lines to his face of bronze. In fact, Mason suffered least of all, for he spent his time in Eastern Tennessee, in the Great Smoky Mountains, living over the scenes of his childhood. And most pathetic was the melody of his long-forgotten Southern vernacular, as he raved of swimming-holes and coon-hunts and watermelon raids. It was as Greek to Ruth, but the Kid understood and felt,—felt as only one can feel who has been shut out for years from all that civilization means.

Morning brought consciousness to the stricken man, and Malemute Kid bent closer to catch his whispers.

"You remember when we foregathered on the Tanana, four years come next ice-run? I didn't care so much for her then. It was more like she was pretty, and there was a smack of excitement about it, I think. But d' ye know, I've come to think a heap of her. She's been a good wife to me, always at my shoulder in the pinch. And when it comes to trading, you know there isn't her equal. D' ye recollect the time she shot the Moosehorn Rapids to pull you and me off that rock, the bullets whipping the water like hailstones?—and the time of the famine at Nuklukyeto?—or when she raced the ice-run to bring the news? Yes, she's been a good wife to me, better 'n that other one. Didn't know I'd been there? Never told you, eh? Well, I tried it once, down in the States. That's why I'm here. Been raised together, too. I came away to give her a chance for divorce. She got it.

"But that's got nothing to do with Ruth. I had thought of cleaning up and pulling for the Outside next year,—her and I,—but it's too late. Don't send her back to her people, Kid. It's beastly hard for a woman to go back. Think of it!—nearly four years on our bacon and beans and flour and dried fruit, and then to go back to her fish and cariboo. It's not good for her to have tried our ways, to come to know they're better'n her people's, and then return to them. Take care of her, Kid,—why don't you,—but no, you always fought shy of them, —and you never told me why you came to this country. Be kind to her, and send her back to the States as soon as you can. But fix it so as she can come back,—liable to get homesick, you know.

"And the youngster—it's drawn us closer, Kid. I only hope it is a boy. Think of it!—flesh of my flesh, Kid. He mustn't stop in this country. And if it's a girl, why she can't. Sell my furs; they'll fetch at least five thousand, and I've got as much more with the company. And handle my interests with yours. I think that bench claim will show up. See that he gets a good schooling; and Kid, above all, don't let him come back. This country was not made for white men.

"I'm a gone man, Kid. Three or four sleeps at the best. You've got to go on. You must go on! Remember, it's my wife, it's my boy,—O God! I hope it's a boy! You can't stay by me,—and I charge you, a dying man, that you pull on."

"Give me three days," pleaded Malemute Kid. "You may change for the better; something may turn up."

"No."

"Just three days."

"You must pull on."

"Two days."

"It's my wife and my boy, Kid. You would not ask it."

"One day."

"No, no! I charge—"

"Only one day. We can shave it through on the grub, and I might knock over a moose."

"No,—all right; one day, but not a minute more. And Kid, don't— don't leave me to face it alone. Do as you would ask of me. Just a shot, one pull on the trigger. You understand. Think of it! Think of it! Flesh of my flesh, and I'll never live to see him!

"Send Ruth here. I want to say good-by and tell her that she must think of the boy and not wait till I'm dead. She might refuse to go with you if I didn't. Good-by, old man; good-by.

"Kid! I say—a—sink a hole above pup, next to the slide. I panned out forty cents on my shovel there.

"And Kid," he stooped lower to catch the last faint words, the dying man's surrender of his pride. "I'm sorry—for—you know—Carmen."

Leaving the girl crying softly over her man, Malemute Kid slipped into his parka and snow-shoes, tucked his rifle under his arm, and crept away into the forest. He was no tyro in the stern sorrows of the Northland, but never had he faced so stiff a problem as this. In the abstract, it was a plain, mathematical proposition,—three possible lives as against one doomed one. But now he hesitated. For five years, shoulder to shoulder, on the rivers and trails, in the camps and mines, facing death by field and flood and famine, had they knitted the bonds of their comradeship. So close was the tie, that he had often been conscious of a vague jealousy of Ruth, from the first time she had come between. And now the severance must be hastened by his own hand.

Though he prayed for a moose, just one moose, all game seemed to have deserted the land, and nightfall found the exhausted man crawling into camp, light-handed, heavy-hearted. An uproar from the dogs and shrill cries from Ruth hastened him.

Bursting into the camp, he saw the girl in the midst of the snarling pack, laying about her with an ax. The dogs had broken the iron rule of their masters and were rushing the grub. He joined the issue with his rifle reversed, and the hoary game of natural selection was played with all the ruthlessness of its primeval environment. Rifle and ax went up and down, hit or missed with monotonous regularity; lithe bodies flashed, with wild eyes and dripping fangs; and man and beast fought for supremacy to the bitterest conclusion. Then the beaten brutes crept to the edge of the firelight, licking their wounds, voicing their misery to the stars.

The whole stock of dried salmon had been devoured, and perhaps five pounds of flour remained to tide them over two hundred miles of wilderness. Ruth returned to her husband, while Malemute Kid cut up the warm body of one of the dogs, the skull of which had been crushed by the ax. Every portion was carefully put away, save the hide and offal, cast to his fellows of the moment before.

Morning brought fresh trouble. The animals were turning on each other. Carmen, who still clung to her slender thread of life, was downed by the pack. The lash fell among them unheeded. They cringed and cried under the blows, but refused to scatter till the last wretched bit had disappeared,—bones, hide, hair, everything.

Malemute Kid went about his work, listening to Mason, who was back in Tennessee, delivering tangled discourses and wild exhortations to his brethren of other days.

Taking advantage of neighboring pines, he worked rapidly, and Ruth watched him make a cache similar to those sometimes used by hunters to preserve their meat from the wolverines and dogs. One after the other, he bent the tops of two small pines toward each other and nearly to the ground, making them fast with thongs of moose-hide. Then he beat the dogs into submission and harnessed them to two of the sleds, loading the same with everything but the furs which enveloped Mason. These he wrapped and lashed tightly about him, fastening either end of the robes to the bent pines. A single stroke of his hunting-knife would release them and send the body high in the air.

Ruth had received her husband's last wishes and made no struggle. Poor girl, she had learned the lesson of obedience well. From a child, she had bowed and seen all women bow to the lords of creation, and it did not seem in the nature of things for woman to resist. The Kid permitted her one outburst of grief, as she kissed her husband,—her own people had no such custom,—then led her to the foremost sled and helped her into her snowshoes. Blindly, instinctively, she took the gee-pole and whip, and "mushed" the dogs out on the trail. Then he returned to Mason, who had fallen into a coma, and long after she was out of sight, he crouched by the fire, waiting, hoping, praying for his comrade to die.

It is not pleasant to be alone with painful thoughts in the White Silence. The silence of gloom is merciful, shrouding one as with protection and breathing a thousand intangible sympathies; but the bright White Silence, clear and cold, under steely skies, is pitiless.

An hour passed,—two hours,—but the man would not die. At high noon, the sun, without raising its rim above the southern horizon, threw a suggestion of fire athwart the heavens, then quickly drew it back. Malemute Kid roused and dragged himself to his comrade's side. He cast one glance about him. The White Silence seemed to sneer, and a great fear came upon him. There was a sharp report; Mason swung into his aerial sepulcher; and Malemute Kid, sole speck of life, lashed the dogs into a wild gallop as he fled across the snow.

✪ FRANK NORRIS

McTeague

Frank Norris, *McTeague: A Story of San Francisco,* New York, Doubleday & McClure Co., 1899.*

[A PORTRAIT OF McTEAGUE]

FOR THIRTEEN DAYS of each fortnight his father was a steady, hardworking shift-boss of the mine. Every other Sunday he became an irresponsible animal, a beast, a brute, crazy with alcohol. . . . [2]

McTeague was a young giant, carrying his huge shock of blond hair six feet three inches from the ground; moving his immense limbs, heavy with ropes of muscle, slowly, ponderously. His hands were enormous, red, and covered with a fell of stiff yellow hair; they were hard as wooden mallets, strong as vises, the hands of the old-time car-boy [in the mines]. . . . His head was square-cut, angular; the jaw salient, like that of the carnivora.

McTeague's mind was as his body, heavy, slow to act, sluggish. Yet there was nothing vicious about the man. Altogether he suggested the draught horse immensely strong, stupid, docile, obedient. . . . [3]

[An early dental patient named] Trina was McTeague's first experience. With her the feminine element suddenly entered his little world. It was not only her that he saw and felt, it was the woman, the whole sex, an entire new humanity, strange and alluring, that he seemed to have discovered. How had he ignored it so long? . . . His whole rude idea of life had to be changed. The male virile desire in him tardily awakened, aroused itself, strong and brutal. It was

* A reliable, inexpensive re-issue of this book, edited by Carvel Collins, is published by Rinehart & Co.

resistless, untrained, a thing not to be held in leash an instant. . . . [27]
While at his work McTeague was every minute obliged to bend
closely over her; his hands touched her face . . . her lips pressed
against his fingers. She breathed warmly on his forehead and on his
eyelids, while the odor of her hair, a charming feminine perfume,
sweet, heavy, enervating, came to his nostrils, so penetrating, so delicious, that his flesh pricked and tingled with it; a veritable sensation
of faintness passed over this huge, callous fellow. . . . He drew a
short breath through his nose; his jaws suddenly gripped together
vise-like. . . . [28] For some time he stood watching her as she lay
there [anaesthetized], unconscious and helpless, and very pretty. . . .
Suddenly the animal in the man stirred and woke; the evil instincts
that in him were so close to the surface leaped to life, shouting and
clamoring. . . . [29] Blindly, and without knowing why, McTeague
fought against it, moved by an unreasoned instinct of resistance.
Within him, a certain second self, another better McTeague rose with
the brute; both were strong, with the huge crude strength of the man
himself. The two were at grapples. . . . It was the old battle, old as
the world, wide as the world—the sudden panther leap of the animal,
lips drawn, fangs aflash, hideous, monstrous, not to be resisted, and
the simultaneous arousing of the other man, the better self. . . . [30]
The struggle was bitter; his teeth ground themselves together with a
little rasping sound; the blood sang in his ears; his face flushed scarlet;
his hands twisted themselves together like the knotting of cables. The
fury in him was as the fury of a young bull in the heat of high summer. . . . [31] Below the fine fabric of all that was good in him ran
the foul stream of hereditary evil, like a sewer. The vices and sins
of his father and of his father's father, to the third and fourth and five
hundredth generation, tainted him. The evil of an entire race flowed
in his veins. Why should it be? He did not desire it. Was he to blame?

[McTeague, an overnight guest in Trina's home, ventures into her
clothes closet.] He went farther into the closet, touching the clothes
gingerly, stroking them softly with his huge leathern palms. As he
stirred them a delicate perfume disengaged itself from the folds. Ah,
that exquisite odor! It was not only her hair now, it was Trina herself
—her mouth, her hands, her neck; the indescribably sweet, fleshly
aroma that was a part of her, pure and clean, and redolent of youth
and freshness. All at once, seized with an unreasoned impulse, Mc-
Teague opened his huge arms and gathered the little garments close

to him, plunging his face deep amongst them, savoring their delicious odor with long breaths of luxury and supreme content.

[A PORTRAIT OF TRINA]

[She recalls that first meeting with McTeague] . . . this blond giant had appeared, this huge, stolid fellow, with his immense, crude strength. She had not loved him at first. . . . But he had only to take her in his arms, to crush down [87] her struggle with his enormous strength, to subdue her, conquer her by sheer brute force, and she gave up in an instant. But why—why . . .? Why did she feel the desire, the necessity of being conquered . . .? Why did it please her? Why had it suddenly thrilled her from head to foot with a quick, terrifying gust of passion, the like of which she had never known? . . . When McTeague had all at once caught her in his huge arms, something had leaped to life in her—something that had hitherto lain dormant, something strong and overpowering. It frightened her now as she thought of it, this second self that had wakened within her. . . . Was it something to be ashamed of? Was it not, after all, natural, clean, spontaneous? . . . She was frank, straightforward, a healthy, natural human being, without sex as yet. She was almost like a boy. At once there had been a mysterious disturbance. The woman within her suddenly awoke. . . . [88] McTeague had awakened the Woman, and, whether she would or no, she was his now irrevocably; struggle against it as she would, she belonged to him. . . . She had not sought it, she had not desired it. The spell was laid upon her. Was it a blessing? Was it a curse? . . . [89]

[THE TWO LOVERS]

The very act of submission that bound the woman to him forever had made her seem less desirable in his eyes. Their undoing had already begun. Yet neither of them was to blame. From the first they had not sought each other. Chance had brought them face to face, and mysterious instincts as ungovernable as the winds of heaven were at work knitting their lives together. Neither of them had asked that this thing should be—that their destinies, their very souls, should be the sport of chance. If they could have known, they would have shunned the fearful risk. But they were allowed no voice in the matter. Why should it all be? [89]

❧ FRANK NORRIS

The Octopus

Frank Norris, *The Octopus: A Story of California,* New York, Doubleday, Page & Co., 1901.*

ALL THAT DIVISION of the great ranch was thick with . . . wonderful wheat. Never had Los Muertos [Magnus Derrick's ranch] been more generous, never a season more successful. S. Behrman ["agent" of the railroad—the "octopus"] drew a long breath of satisfaction. He knew just how great was his share in the lands which had just been absorbed by the corporation he served, just how many thousands of bushels of this marvellous crop were his property. Through all these years of confusion, bickerings, open hostility and, at last, actual warfare he had waited, nursing his patience, calm with the firm assurance of ultimate success. The end, at length, had come; he had entered into his reward and saw himself at last installed in the place he had so long, so silently coveted; saw himself chief of a principality, the Master of the Wheat. . . . [615]

[Behrman has gone to Port Costa to watch the wheat loaded on board the ship that is to take it to India, where there is famine.]

Directly in front of where he sat on the platform was the chute from the cleaner, and from this into the mouth of a half-full sack spouted an unending gush of grain, winnowed, cleaned, threshed, ready for the mill.

The pour from the chute of the cleaner had for S. Behrman an immense satisfaction. Without an instant's pause, a thick rivulet of wheat rolled and dashed tumultuous into the sack. In half a minute— sometimes in twenty seconds—the sack was full, was passed over to the second sewer, the mouth reeved up, and the sack dumped out upon the ground, to be picked up by the wagons and hauled to the railroad.

S. Behrman, hypnotized, sat watching that river of grain. All that

* Available in the Riverside Edition (Houghton Mifflin Company), edited by Kenneth S. Lynn.

shrieking, bellowing machinery, all that gigantic organism, all the months of labour, the ploughing, the planting, the prayers for rain, the years of preparation, the heartaches, the anxiety, the foresight, all the whole business of the ranch, the work of horses, of steam, of men and boys, looked to this spot—the grain chute from the harvester into the sacks. Its volume was the index of failure or success, of riches or poverty. And at this point, the labour of the rancher ended. Here, at the lip of the chute, he parted company with his grain, and from here the wheat streamed forth to feed the world. The yawning mouths of the sacks might well stand for the unnumbered mouth of the People, all agape for food; and here, into these sacks, at first so lean, so flaccid, attenuated like starved stomachs, rushed the living stream [617] of food, insistent, interminable, filling the empty, fattening the shrivelled, making it sleek and heavy and solid. . . . [618]

S. Behrman went forward to the hatch that opened down into the vast hold of the ship. A great iron chute connected this hatch with the elevator, and through it was rushing a veritable cataract of wheat.

It came from some gigantic bin within the elevator itself, rushing down the confines of the chute to plunge into the roomy, gloomy interior of the hold with an incessant, metallic roar, persistent, steady, inevitable. No men were in sight. The place was deserted. No human agency seemed to be back of the movement of the wheat. Rather, the grain seemed impelled with a force of its own, a resistless, huge force, eager, vivid, impatient for the sea.

S. Behrman stood watching, his ears deafened with the roar of the hard grains against the metallic lining of the chute. He put his hand once into the rushing tide, and the contact rasped the flesh of his fingers and like an undertow drew his hand after it in its impetuous dash.

Cautiously he peered down into the hold. A musty odour rose to his nostrils, the vigorous, pungent aroma [641] of the raw cereal. It was dark. He could see nothing; but all about and over the opening of the hatch the air was full of a fine, impalpable dust that blinded the eyes and choked the throat and nostrils.

As his eyes became used to the shadows of the cavern below him, he began to distinguish the grey mass of the wheat, a great expanse, almost liquid in its texture, which, as the cataract from above plunged into it, moved and shifted in long, slow eddies. As he stood there, this cataract on a sudden increased in volume. He turned about, casting his eyes upward toward the elevator to discover the cause.

His foot caught in a coil of rope, and he fell headforemost into the hold.

The fall was a long one and he struck the surface of the wheat with the sodden impact of a bundle of damp clothes. For the moment he was stunned. All the breath was driven from his body. He could neither move nor cry out. But, by degrees, his wits steadied themselves and his breath returned to him. He looked about and above him. The daylight in the hold was dimmed and clouded by the thick chaff-dust thrown off by the pour of grain, and even this dimness dwindled to twilight at a short distance from the opening of the hatch, while the remotest quarters were lost in impenetrable blackness. He got upon his feet only to find that he sank ankle deep in the loose-packed mass underfoot.

"Hell," he muttered, "here's a fix."

Directly underneath the chute, the wheat, as it poured in, raised itself in a conical mound, but from the sides of this mound it shunted away incessantly in thick layers, flowing in all directions with the nimbleness of water. Even as S. Behrman spoke, a wave of grain poured around his legs and rose rapidly to the level of his knees. He stepped quickly back. To stay near the chute would soon bury him to the waist. [642]

No doubt, there was some other exit from the hold, some companion ladder that led up to the deck. He scuffled and waded across the wheat, groping in the dark with outstretched hands. With every inhalation he choked, filling his mouth and nostrils more with dust than with air. At times he could not breathe at all, but gagged and gasped, his lips distended. But search as he would, he could find no outlet to the hold, no stairway, no companion ladder. Again and again, staggering along in the black darkness, he bruised his knuckles and forehead against the iron sides of the ship. He gave up the attempt to find any interior means of escape and returned laboriously to the space under the open hatchway. Already he could see that the level of the wheat was raised.

"God," he said, "this isn't going to do at all." He uttered a great shout. "Hello, on deck there, somebody! For God's sake."

The steady, metallic roar of the pouring wheat drowned out his voice. He could scarcely hear it himself above the rush of the cataract. Besides this, he found it impossible to stay under the hatch. The flying grains of wheat, spattering as they fell, stung his face like wind-driven particles of ice. It was a veritable torture; his hands smarted with it. Once he was all but blinded. Furthermore, the succeeding waves of wheat, rolling from the mound under the chute, beat him back, swirling and dashing against his legs and knees, mounting swiftly higher, carrying him off his feet.

Once more he retreated, drawing back from beneath the hatch. He stood still for a moment and shouted again. It was in vain. His voice returned upon him, unable to penetrate the thunder of the chute, and horrified, he discovered that so soon as he stood motionless upon the wheat, he sank into it. Before he knew it, he [643] was knee-deep again, and a long swirl of grain sweeping outward from the ever-breaking, ever-reforming pyramid below the chute, poured around his thighs, immobilizing him.

A frenzy of terror suddenly leaped to life within him. The horror of death, the Fear of The Trap, shook him like a dry reed. Shouting, he tore himself free of the wheat and once more scrambled and struggled toward the hatchway. He stumbled as he reached it and fell directly beneath the pour. Like a storm of small shot, mercilessly, pitilessly, the unnumbered multitude of hurtling grains flagellated and beat and tore his flesh. Blood streamed from his forehead and, thickening with the powder-like chaff-dust, blinded his eyes. He struggled to his feet once more. An avalanche from the cone of wheat buried him to his thighs. He was forced back and back and back, beating the air, falling, rising, howling for aid. He could no longer see; his eyes, crammed with dust, smarted as if transfixed with needles whenever he opened them. His mouth was full of the dust, his lips were dry with it; thirst tortured him, while his outcries choked and gagged in his rasped throat.

And all the while without stop, incessantly, inexorably, the wheat, as if moving with a force all its own, shot downward in a prolonged roar, persistent, steady, inevitable.

He retreated to a far corner of the hold and sat down with his back against the iron hull of the ship and tried to collect his thoughts, to calm himself. Surely there must be some way of escape; surely he was not to die like this, die in this dreadful substance that was neither solid nor fluid. What was he to do? How make himself heard?

But even as he thought about this, the cone under the chute broke again and sent a great layer of grain rippling [644] and tumbling toward him. It reached him where he sat and buried his hand and one foot.

He sprang up trembling and made for another corner.

"By God," he cried, "by God, I must think of something pretty quick!"

Once more the level of the wheat rose and the grains began piling deeper about him. Once more he retreated. Once more he crawled staggering to the foot of the cataract, screaming till his ears sang and his eyeballs strained in their sockets, and once more the relentless tide drove him back.

Then began that terrible dance of death; the man dodging, doubling, squirming, hunted from one corner to another, the wheat slowly, inexorably flowing, rising, spreading to every angle, to every nook and cranny. It reached his middle. Furious and with bleeding hands and broken nails, he dug his way out to fall backward, all but exhausted, gasping for breath in the dust-thickened air. Roused again by the slow advance of the tide, he leaped up and stumbled away, blinded with the agony in his eyes, only to crash against the metal hull of the vessel. He turned about, the blood streaming from his face, and paused to collect his senses, and with a rush, another wave swirled about his ankles and knees. Exhaustion grew upon him. To stand still meant to sink; to lie or sit meant to be buried the quicker; and all this in the dark, all this in an air that could scarcely be breathed, all this while he fought an enemy that could not be gripped, toiling in a sea that could not be stayed.

Guided by the sound of the falling wheat, S. Behrman crawled on hands and knees toward the hatchway. Once more he raised his voice in a shout for help. His bleeding throat and raw, parched lips refused to utter but a wheezing moan. Once more he tried to look toward the one patch of faint light above him. His eyelids, clogged with [645] chaff, could no longer open. The Wheat poured about his waist as he raised himself upon his knees.

Reason fled. Deafened with the roar of the grain, blinded and made dumb with its chaff, he threw himself forward with clutching fingers, rolling upon his back, and lay there, moving feebly, the head rolling from side to side. The Wheat, leaping continuously from the chute, poured around him. It filled the pockets of the coat, it crept up the sleeves and trouser legs, it covered the great, protuberant stomach, it ran at last in rivulets into the distended, gasping mouth. It covered the face.

Upon the surface of the Wheat, under the chute, nothing moved but the Wheat itself. There was no sign of life. Then, for an instant, the surface stirred. A hand, fat, with short fingers and swollen veins, reached up, clutching, then fell limp and prone. In another instant it was covered. In the hold of the Swanhilda there was no movement but the widening ripples that spread flowing from the ever-breaking, ever-reforming cone; no sound, but the rushing of the Wheat that continued to plunge incessantly from the iron chute in a prolonged roar, persistent, steady, inevitable. . . . [646]

The drama was over. The fight of Ranch and Railroad had been wrought out to its dreadful close. It was true, as Shelgrim had said, that forces rather than men had locked horns in that struggle, but for all that the men of the Ranch and not the men of the Railroad had suffered. Into the prosperous valley, into the quiet community of farmers, that galloping monster, that terror of steel and steam had burst, shooting athwart the horizons, flinging the echo of its thunder over all the ranches of the valley, leaving blood and destruction in its path.

Yes, the Railroad had prevailed. The ranches had been seized in the tentacles of the octopus; the iniquitous burden of extortionate freight rates had been imposed like a yoke of iron. The monster had killed Harran, had killed Osterman, had killed Broderson, had killed Hooven. It had beggared Magnus and had driven him to a state of semi-insanity after he had wrecked his honour in the vain attempt to do evil, that good might come. It had enticed Lyman into its toils to pluck from him his manhood and his honesty, corrupting him and poisoning him beyond redemption; it had hounded Dyke from his legitimate employment and had made of him a highwayman and criminal. It had cast forth Mrs. Hooven to starve to death upon the city streets. It had driven Minna to prostitution. It had slain Annixter at the very moment when painfully and manfully he had at last achieved his own salvation and stood forth resolved to do right, to act unselfishly and to live for others. It had widowed Hilma in the very dawn of her happiness. It had killed the very [650] babe within the mother's womb, strangling life ere yet it had been born, stamping out the spark ordained by God to burn through all eternity.

What, then, was left? Was there no hope, no outlook for the future, no rift in the black curtain, no glimmer through the night? Was good to be thus overthrown? Was evil thus to be strong and to prevail? Was nothing left? . . .

Men—motes in the sunshine—perished, were shot down in the very noon of life, hearts were broken, little children started in life lamentably handicapped; young girls were brought to a life of shame;

old women died in the heart of life for lack of food. In that little, isolated group of human insects, misery, death, and anguish spun like a wheel of fire.

But the Wheat remained. Untouched, unassailable, undefiled, that mighty world-force, that nourisher of nations, wrapped in Nirvanic calm, indifferent to the human swarm, gigantic, resistless, moved onward in its appointed grooves. Through the welter of blood at the irrigating ditch, through the sham charity and shallow philanthropy of famine-relief committees, the great harvest of Los Muertos rolled like a flood from the Sierras to the Himalayas to feed thousands of starving scarecrows on the barren plains of India.

Falseness dies; injustice and oppression in the end of everything fade and vanish away. Greed, cruelty, selfishness, and inhumanity are short-lived; the individual [651] suffers, but the race goes on. Annixter dies, but in a far-distant corner of the world a thousand lives are saved. The larger view always and through all shams, all wickedness, discovers the Truth that will in the end prevail, and all things, surely, inevitably, resistlessly work together for good. [652]

❧ FRANK NORRIS

A Deal in Wheat

Frank Norris, "A Deal in Wheat," in *A Deal in Wheat and Other Stories of the New and Old West*, New York, Doubleday, Page and Co., 1903.*

I

The Bear—Wheat at Sixty-two

As SAM LEWISTON backed the horse into the shafts of his buckboard and began hitching the tugs to the whiffletree, his wife came out from the kitchen door of the house and drew near, and stood for some time

* Copyright © 1903, 1931, by Doubleday & Co., Inc. Reprinted by permission. of the publisher.

at the horse's head, her arms folded and her apron rolled around them. For a long moment neither spoke. They had talked over the situation so long and so comprehensively the night before that there seemed to be nothing more to say.

The time was late in the summer, the place a ranch in southwestern Kansas, and Lewiston and his wife were two of a vast population of farmers, wheat growers, who at that moment were passing through a crisis—a crisis that at any moment might culminate in tragedy. Wheat was down to sixty-six.

At length Emma Lewiston spoke.

"Well," she hazarded, looking vaguely out [3] across the ranch toward the horizon, leagues distant; "well, Sam, there's always that offer of brother Joe's. We can quit—and go to Chicago—if the worst comes."

"And give up!" exclaimed Lewiston, running the lines through the torets. "Leave the ranch! Give up! After all these years!"

His wife made no reply for the moment. Lewiston climbed into the buckboard and gathered up the lines. "Well, here goes for the last try, Emmie," he said. "Good-bye, girl. Maybe things will look better in town to-day."

"Maybe," she said gravely. She kissed her husband good-by and stood for some time looking after the buckboard traveling toward the town in a moving pillar of dust.

"I don't know," she murmured at length; "I don't know just how we're going to make out."

When he reached town, Lewiston tied the horse to the iron railing in front of the Odd Fellows' Hall, the ground floor of which was occupied by the post-office, and went across the street and up the stairway of a building of brick and granite—quite the most pretentious structure of the town—and knocked at a door upon the first landing. The door was furnished with a pane of frosted glass, on which, in gold [4] letters, was inscribed "Bridges & Co., Grain Dealers."

Bridges himself, a middle-aged man who wore a velvet skullcap and who was smoking a Pittsburg stogie, met the farmer at the counter and the two exchanged perfunctory greetings.

"Well," said Lewiston, tentatively, after a while.

"Well, Lewiston," said the other, "I can't take that wheat of yours at any better than sixty-two."

"Sixty-*two*."

"It's the Chicago price that does it, Lewiston. Truslow is bearing the stuff for all he's worth. It's Truslow and the bear clique that stick the knife into us. The price broke again this morning. We've just got a wire."

"Good heavens," murmured Lewiston, looking vaguely from side to side. "That—that ruins me. I *can't* carry my grain any longer— what with storage charges and—and—Bridges, I don't see just how I'm going to make out. Sixty-two cents a bushel! Why, man, what with this and with that it's cost me nearly a dollar a bushel to raise that wheat, and now Truslow—"

He turned away abruptly with a quick gesture of infinite discouragement.

He went down the stairs, and making his [5] way to where his buckboard was hitched, got in, and, with eyes vacant, the reins slipping and sliding in his limp, half-open hands, drove slowly back to the ranch. His wife had seen him coming, and met him as he drew up before the barn.

"Well?" she demanded.

"Emmie," he said as he got out of the buckboard, laying his arm across her shoulder, "Emmie, I guess we'll take up with Joe's offer. We'll go to Chicago. We're cleaned out!" [6]

II

The Bull—Wheat at a Dollar-ten

. . . —and said Party of the Second Part further covenants and agrees to merchandise such wheat in foreign ports, it being understood and agreed between the Party of the First Part and the Party of the Second Part that the wheat hereinbefore mentioned is released and sold to the Party of the Second Part for export purposes only, and not for consumption or distribution within the boundaries of the United States of America or of Canada.

"Now, Mr. Gates, if you will sign for Mr. Truslow, I guess that'll be all," remarked Hornung when he had finished reading.

Hornung affixed his signature to the two documents and passed them over to Gates, who signed for his principal client, Truslow—or, as he had been called ever since he had gone into the fight against Hornung's corner—the Great Bear. Hornung's secretary was called

in and witnessed the signatures, and Gates thrust the contract into his
Gladstone bag and stood up, smoothing his hat. [7]

"You will deliver the warehouse receipts for the grain," began
Gates.

"I'll send a messenger to Truslow's office before noon," interrupted
Hornung. "You can pay by certified check through the Illinois Trust
people."

When the other had taken himself off, Hornung sat for some
moments gazing abstractedly toward his office windows, thinking
over the whole matter. He had just agreed to release to Truslow, at
the rate of one dollar and ten cents per bushel, one hundred thousand
out of the two million and odd bushels of wheat that he, Hornung,
controlled, or actually owned. And for the moment he was wondering,
if, after all, he had done wisely in not goring the Great Bear to actual
financial death. He had made him pay one hundred thousand dollars.
Truslow was good for this amount. Would it not have been better
to have put a prohibitive figure on the grain and forced the Bear into
bankruptcy? True, Hornung would then be without his enemy's
money, but Truslow would have been eliminated from the situation,
and that—so Hornung told himself—was always a consummation
most devoutly, strenuously and diligently to be striven for. Truslow
once dead was dead, but the Bear was never more dangerous than
when desperate. [8]

"But so long as he can't get *wheat*," muttered Hornung at the end
of his reflections, "he can't hurt me. And he can't get it. That I *know*."

For Hornung controlled the situation. So far back as the February
of that year an "unknown bull" had been making his presence felt on
the floor of the Board of Trade. By the middle of March the commercial reports of the daily press had begun to speak of "the powerful
bull clique"; a few weeks later that legendary condition of affairs
implied and epitomized in the magic words "Dollar Wheat" had been
attained, and by the first of April, when the price had been boosted
to one dollar and ten cents a bushel. Hornung had disclosed his
hand, and in place of mere rumors, the definite and authoritative
news that May wheat had been cornered in the Chicago Pit went
flashing around the world from Liverpool to Odessa and from Duluth
to Buenos Ayres.

It was—as the veteran operators were persuaded—Truslow himself who had made Hornung's corner possible. The Great Bear had

for once overreached himself, and, believing himself all-powerful, had hammered the price just the fatal fraction too far down. Wheat had gone to sixty-two—for the time, and under the circumstances, an abnormal price. [9] When the reaction came it was tremendous. Hornung saw his chance, seized it, and in a few months had turned the tables, had cornered the product, and virtually driven the bear clique out of the pit.

On the same day that the delivery of the hundred thousand bushels was made to Truslow, Hornung met his broker at his lunch club.

"Well," said the latter, "I see you let go that line of stuff to Truslow."

Hornung nodded; but the broker added:

"Remember, I was against it from the very beginning. I know we've cleared up over a hundred thou'. I would have fifty times preferred to have lost twice that and *smashed Truslow dead*. Bet you what you like he makes us pay for it somehow."

"Huh!" grunted his principal. "How about insurance and warehouse charges, and carrying expenses on that lot? Guess we'd have had to pay those, too, if we'd held on."

But the other put up his chin, unwilling to be persuaded. "I won't sleep easy," he declared, "till Truslow is busted." [10]

III

The Pit

Just as Going mounted the steps on the edge of the pit the great gong struck, a roar of a hundred voices developed with the swiftness of successive explosions, the rush of a hundred men surging downward to the centre of the pit filled the air with the stamp and grind of feet, a hundred hands in eager strenuous gestures tossed upward from out of the brown of the crowd, the official reporter in his cage on the margin of the pit leaned far forward with straining ear to catch the opening bid, and another day of battle was begun.

Since the sale of the hundred thousand bushels of wheat to Truslow the "Hornung crowd" had steadily shouldered the price higher until on this particular morning it stood at one dollar and a half. That was Hornung's price. No one else had any grain to sell.

But not ten minutes after the opening Going was surprised out of all countenance to hear shouted from the other side of the pit these words: [11]

"Sell May at one-fifty."

Going was for the moment touching elbows with Kimbark on one side and with Merriam on the other, all three belonging to the "Hornung crowd." Their answering challenge of "*Sold*" was as the voice of one man. They did not pause to reflect upon the strangeness of the circumstance. (That was for afterward.) Their response to the offer was as unconscious as reflex action and almost as rapid, and before the pit was well aware of what had happened the transaction of one thousand bushels was down upon Going's trading-card and fifteen hundred dollars had changed hands. But here was a marvel— the whole available supply of wheat cornered, Hornung master of the situation, invincible, unassailable; yet behold a man willing to sell, a Bear bold enough to raise his head.

"That was Kennedy, wasn't it, who made that offer?" asked Kimbark, as Going noted down the trade—"Kennedy, that new man?"

"Yes; who do you suppose he's selling for; who's willing to go short at this stage of the game?"

"Maybe he ain't short."

"Short! Great heavens, man; wher'd he get the stuff?"

"Blamed if I know. We can account for [12] every handful of May. Steady! Oh, there he goes again."

"Sell a thousand May at one-fifty," vociferated the bear-broker, throwing out his hand, one finger raised to indicate the number of "contracts" offered. This time it was evident that he was attacking the Hornung crowd deliberately, for, ignoring the jam of traders that swept toward him, he looked across the pit to where Going and Kimbark were shouting "*Sold! Sold!*" and nodded his head.

A second time Going made memoranda of the trade, and either the Hornung holdings were increased by two thousand bushels of May wheat or the Hornung bank account swelled by at least three thousand dollars of some unknown short's money.

Of late—so sure was the bull crowd of its position—no one even thought of glancing at the inspection sheet on the bulletin board. But now one of Going's messengers hurried up to him with the announcement that this sheet showed receipts at Chicago for that morning of twenty-five thousand bushels, and not credited to Hornung. Some one had got hold of a line of wheat overlooked by the "clique" and was dumping it upon them.

"Wire the chief," said Going over his shoulder to Merriam. This one struggled out [13] of the crowd, and on a telegraph blank scribbled:

"Strong bear movement—New Man—Kennedy—Selling in lots of five contracts—Chicago receipts twenty-five thousand."

The message was despatched, and in a few moments the answer came back, laconic, of military terseness.

"Support the market."

And Going obeyed, Merriam and Kimbark following, the new broker fairly throwing the wheat at them in thousand-bushel lots.

"Sell May at 'fifty; sell May; sell May." A moment's indecision, an instant's hesitation, the first faint suggestion of weakness, and the market would have broken under them. But for the better part of four hours they stood their ground, taking all that was offered, in constant communication with the Chief, and from time to time stimulated and steadied by his brief unvarying command:

"Support the market."

At the close of the session they had bought in the twenty-five thousand bushels of May. Hornung's position was as stable as a rock, and the price closed even with the opening figure—one dollar and a half.

But the morning's work was the talk of all La Salle Street. Who was back of that raid? What was the meaning of this unexpected selling? For weeks the Pit trading had been merely nominal. Truslow, the Great Bear, from whom the most serious attack might have been expected, had gone to his country seat at Geneva Lake, in Wisconsin, declaring himself to be out of the market entirely. He went bass fishing every day. [15]

IV

The Belt Line

On a certain day toward the middle of the month, at a time when the mysterious Bear had unloaded some eighty thousand bushels upon Hornung, a conference was held in the library of Hornung's home. His broker attended it, and also a clean-faced, bright-eyed individual whose name of Cyrus Ryder might have been found upon the payroll of a rather well-known detective agency. For upward of half an hour after the conference began the detective spoke, the other two listening attentively, gravely.

"Then, last of all," concluded Ryder, "I made out I was a hobo, and began stealing rides on the Belt Line Railroad. Know the road? It just circles Chicago. Truslow owns it. Yes? Well, then I began to catch on. I noticed that cars of certain numbers—thirty-one naught thirty-four, thirty-two one ninety—well, the numbers don't matter, but anyhow, these cars were always switched on to the sidings by Mr. Truslow's main elevator D soon [16, 17] as they came in. The wheat was shunted in, and they were pulled out again. Well, I spotted one car and stole a ride on her. Say, look here, *that car went right around the city on the Belt, and came back to D again, and the same wheat in her all the time.* The grain was reinspected—it was raw, I tell you—and the warehouse receipts made out just as though the stuff had come in from Kansas or Iowa."

"The same wheat all the time!" interrupted Hornung.

"The same wheat—your wheat, that you sold to Truslow."

"Great snakes!" ejaculated Hornung's broker. "Truslow never took it abroad at all."

"Took it abroad! Say, he's been running it around Chicago, like the supers in 'Shenandoah,' round an' round so you'd think it was a new lot, an' selling it back to you again."

"No wonder we couldn't account for so much wheat."

"Bought it from us at one-ten, and made us buy it back—our own wheat—at one-fifty."

Hornung and his broker looked at each other in silence for a moment. Then all at once Hornung struck the arm of his chair with his fist and exploded in a roar of laughter. The [18] broker stared for one bewildered moment, then followed his example.

"Sold! Sold!" shouted Hornung almost gleefully. "Upon my soul it's as good as a Gilbert and Sullivan show. And we—Oh, Lord! Billy, shake on it, and hats off to my distinguished friend, Truslow. He'll be President some day. Hey! What? Prosecute him? Not I."

"He's done us out of a neat hatful of dollars for all that," observed the broker, suddenly grave.

"Billy, it's worth the price."

"We've got to make it up somehow."

"Well, tell you what. We were going to boost the price to one seventy-five next week, and make that our settlement figure."

"Can't do it now. Can't afford it."

"No. Here; we'll let out a big link; we'll put wheat at two dollars, and let it go at that."

"Two it is, then," said the broker. [19]

V

The Bread Line

The street was very dark and absolutely deserted. It was a district on the "South Side," not far from the Chicago River, given up largely to wholesale stores, and after nightfall was empty of all life. The echoes slept but lightly hereabouts, and the slightest footfall, the faintest noise, woke them upon the instant and sent them clamoring up and down the length of the pavement between the iron-shuttered fronts. The only light visible came from the side door of a certain "Vienna" bakery, where at one o'clock in the morning loaves of bread were given away to any who should ask. Every evening about nine o'clock the outcasts began to gather about the side door. The stragglers came in rapidly, and the line—the "bread line," as it was called —began to form. By midnight it was usually some hundred yards in length, stretching almost the entire length of the block.

Toward ten in the evening, his coat collar turned up against the fine drizzle that pervaded [20, 21] the air, his hands in his pockets, his elbows gripping his sides, Sam Lewiston came up and silently took his place at the end of the line.

Unable to conduct his farm upon a paying basis at the time when Truslow, the "Great Bear," had sent the price of grain down to sixty-two cents a bushel, Lewiston had turned over his entire property to his creditors, and, leaving Kansas for good, had abandoned farming, and had left his wife at her sister's boarding-house in Topeka with the understanding that she was to join him in Chicago so soon as he found a steady job. Then he had come to Chicago and had turned workman. His brother Joe conducted a small hat factory on Archer Avenue, and for a time he found there a meagre employment. But difficulties had occurred, times were bad, the hat factory was involved in debts, the repealing of a certain import duty on manufactured felt overcrowded the home market with cheap Belgian and French products, and in the end his brother had resigned and gone to Milwaukee.

Thrown out of work, Lewiston drifted aimlessly about Chicago, from pillar to post, working a little, earning here a dollar, there a dime, but always sinking, sinking, till at last the ooze of the lowest bottom dragged at his feet and the rush of the great ebb went over him and [22] engulfed him and shut him from the light, and a park bench became his home and the "bread line" his chief makeshift of subsistence.

He stood now in the infolding drizzle, sodden, stupefied with fatigue. Before and behind stretched the line. There was no talking. There was no sound. The street was empty. It was so still that the passing of a cable-car in the adjoining thoroughfare grated like prolonged rolling explosions, beginning and ending at immeasurable distances. The drizzle descended incessantly. After a long time midnight struck.

There was something ominous and gravely impressive in this interminable line of dark figures, close-pressed, soundless; a crowd, yet absolutely still; a close-packed, silent file, waiting, waiting in the vast deserted night-ridden street; waiting without a word, without a movement, there under the night and under the slow-moving mists of rain.

Few in the crowd were professional beggars. Most of them were workmen, long since out of work, forced into idleness by long-continued "hard times," by ill luck, by sickness. To them the "bread line" was a godsend. At least they could not starve. Between jobs here in the end was something to hold them up—a small platform, as it were, above the sweep [23] of black water, where for a moment they might pause and take breath before the plunge.

The period of waiting on this night of rain seemed endless to those silent, hungry men; but at length there was a stir. The line moved. The side door opened. Ah, at last! They were going to hand out the bread.

But instead of the usual white-aproned under-cook with his crowded hampers there now appeared in the doorway a new man— a young fellow who looked like a bookkeeper's assistant. He bore in his hand a placard, which he tacked to the outside of the door. Then he disappeared within the bakery, locking the door after him.

A shudder of poignant despair, an unformed, inarticulate sense of calamity, seemed to run from end to end of the line. What had happened? Those in the rear, unable to read the placard, surged forward, a sense of bitter disappointment clutching at their hearts.

The line broke up, disintegrated into a shapeless throng—a throng that crowded forward and collected in front of the shut door whereon the placard was affixed. Lewiston, with the others, pushed forward. On the placard he read these words:

"Owing to the fact that the price of grain has been increased to two dollars a bushel, there will be no [24] distribution of bread from this bakery until further notice."

Lewiston turned away, dumb, bewildered. Till morning he walked the streets, going on without purpose, without direction. But now at last his luck had turned. Overnight the wheel of his fortunes had creaked and swung upon its axis, and before noon he had found a job in the street-cleaning brigade. In the course of time he rose to be first shift-boss, then deputy inspector, then inspector, promoted to the dignity of driving a red wagon with rubber tires and drawing a salary instead of mere wages. The wife was sent for and a new start made.

But Lewiston never forgot. Dimly he began to see the significance of things. Caught once in the cogs and wheels of a great and terrible engine, he had seen—none better—its workings. Of all the men who had vainly stood in the "breadline" on that rainy night in early summer, he, perhaps, had been the only one who had struggled up to the surface again. How many others had gone down in the great ebb? Grim question; he dared not think how many.

He had seen the two ends of a great wheat operation—a battle between Bear and Bull. The stories (subsequently published in the [25] city's press) of Truslow's counter move in selling Hornung his own wheat, supplied the unseen section. The farmer—he who raised the wheat—was ruined upon one hand; the working-man— he who consumed it—was ruined upon the other. But between the two, the great operators, who never saw the wheat they traded in, bought and sold the world's food, gambled in the nourishment of entire nations, practiced their tricks, their chicanery and oblique shifty "deals," were reconciled in their differences, and went on through their appointed way, jovial, contented, enthroned, and unassailable. [26]

𝕮 THEODORE DREISER

Sister Carrie

Theodore Dreiser, *Sister Carrie*, New York, Doubleday, Page & Co., 1900.*

[CAROLINE MEEBER has left her home in Wisconsin to seek her fortune in Chicago.] Caroline, or Sister Carrie, as she had been half affectionately termed by the family, was possessed of a mind rudimentary in its power of observation and analysis. Self-interest with her was high, but not strong. It was, nevertheless, her guiding characteristic. Warm with the fancies of youth, pretty with the insipid prettiness of the formative period, possessed of a figure promising eventual shapeliness and an eye alight with certain native intelligence, she was a fair example of the middle American class— two generations removed from the emigrant. Books were beyond her interest—knowledge a sealed book. In the intuitive graces she was still crude. She [2] could scarcely toss her head gracefully. Her hands were almost ineffectual. The feet, though small, were set flatly. And yet she was interested in her charms, quick to understand the keener pleasures of life, ambitious to gain in material things. A half-equipped little knight she was, venturing to reconnoitre the mysterious city and dreaming wild dreams. . . . [3]

[Carrie inspects a department store, "The Fair."] Carrie passed along the busy aisles, much affected by the remarkable displays of trinkets, dress goods, stationery, and jewelry. Each separate counter was a show place of dazzling interest and attraction. She could not help feeling the claim of each trinket and valuable upon her personally. . . . There was nothing there . . . which she did not long to own. The dainty slippers and stockings, the delicately frilled skirts and petticoats, the laces, ribbons, hair-combs, purses, all touched her with individual desire. . . . [24]

[Almost penniless, with winter near, Carrie accepts money for warm clothing from Charles Drouet, a chance acquaintance.] To her,

* Available in a new (Rinehart) edition, edited by Kenneth S. Lynn.

and indeed to all the world, he was a nice, good-hearted man. There was nothing evil in the fellow. He gave her the money out of a good heart. . . . Femininity affected his feelings. He was the creature of an inborn desire. . . . He had no mental process in him worthy the dignity of [the terms "speculation" or "philosophising"]. In his good clothes and fine health, he was a merry, unthinking moth of the lamp. Deprived of his position, and struck by a few of the involved and baffling forces which sometimes play upon man, he would have been as helpless as Carrie . . . , as pitiable. . . .

Now, in regard to his pursuit of women, he meant them no harm, because he did not conceive of the relation which he hoped to hold with them as being harmful. He loved to make advances to women, to have them succumb to his charms, not because he was a cold-blooded, dark, scheming villain, but because his inborn desire urged him to that as a chief delight. He was vain, he was boastful, he was as deluded by fine clothes as any silly-headed girl. [71] A truly deep-dyed villain could have hornswaggled him as readily as he could have flattered a pretty shop-girl. His fine success as a salesman lay in his geniality and the thoroughly reputable standing of his house. He bobbed about among men, a veritable bundle of enthusiasm—no power worthy the name of intellect, no thoughts worthy the adjective noble, no feelings long continued in one strain. . . .

The best proof that there was something open and commendable about the man was the fact that Carrie took the money. No deep, sinister soul with ulterior motives could have given her fifteen cents under the guise of friendship. The unintellectual are not so helpless. Nature has taught the beasts of the field to fly when some unheralded danger threatens. She has put into the small, unwise head of the chipmunk the untutored fear of poisons. "He keepeth His creatures whole," was not written of beasts alone. Carrie was unwise, and, therefore, like the sheep in its unwisdom, strong in feeling. The instinct of self-protection, strong in all such natures, was roused but feebly, if at all, by the overtures of Drouet. . . . [72]

[With regard to Carrie's decision to live with Drouet] Among the forces which sweep and play throughout the universe, untutored man is but a wisp in the wind. Our civilisation is still in a middle stage, scarcely beast, in that it is no longer wholly guided by instinct; scarcely human, in that it is not yet wholly guided by reason. On the tiger no responsibility rests. We see him aligned by nature with the forces of life—he is born into their keeping and without thought he is protected. We see man far removed from the lairs of the jungles, his innate instinct dulled by too near an approach to free-will, his free-will not sufficiently developed to replace his instincts and afford him perfect guidance. He is becoming too wise to hearken always to instincts and desires; he is still too weak to always pre-vail against them. As a beast, the forces of life aligned him with them; as a man, he has not yet wholly learned to align himself with the forces. In this intermediate stage he wavers—neither drawn in harmony with nature by his instincts nor yet wisely putting himself into harmony by his own free will. He is even as a wisp in the wind, moved by every breath of passion, acting now by his will and now by his instincts, erring with one, only to retrieve by the other, falling by one, only to rise by the other—a creature of incal-culable variability. We have the consolation of knowing that evolu-tion is ever in action, that the ideal is a light that cannot fail. He will not forever balance thus between good and evil. When [83] this jan-gle of free-will and instinct shall have been adjusted, when perfect understanding has given the former power to replace the latter en-tirely, man will no longer vary. The needle of understanding will yet point steadfast and unwavering to the distinct pole of truth. . . . [84]

[Carrie has become Drouet's mistress. It is winter in Chicago.] In the light of the world's attitude toward woman and her duties, the nature of Carrie's mental state deserves consideration. Actions such as hers are measured by an arbitrary scale. Society possesses a con-ventional standard whereby it judges all things. All men should be good, all women virtuous. Wherefore, villain, hast thou failed?

For all the liberal analysis of Spencer and our modern naturalistic philosophers, we have but an infantile perception of morals. There is more in the subject than mere conformity to a law of evolution. It is yet deeper than conformity to things of earth alone. . . . Answer, first, why the heart thrills; explain wherefore some plaintive note goes wandering about the world, undying; make clear the rose's subtle al-chemy evolving its ruddy lamp in light and rain. In the essence of these facts lie the first principles of morals. . . .

In the view of a certain stratum of society, Carrie was [101] com-fortably established—in the eyes of the starveling, beaten by every wind and gusty sheet of rain, she was safe in a halcyon harbour. . . . The rooms were comfortably enough furnished. . . . The whole place was cosey. . . . By her industry and natural love of order, which now developed, the place maintained an air pleasing in the extreme. . . . [102]

She looked into her glass and saw a prettier Carrie than she had seen before; she looked into her mind . . . and saw a worse. Between these two images she wavered, hesitating which to believe.

"My, but you're a little beauty," Drouet was wont to exclaim to her. . . . Her conscience, however, was not a Drouet, interested to praise. There she heard a different voice, with which she argued, pleaded, excused. It was no just and sapient counsellor, in its last analysis. It was only an average little conscience, a thing which represented the world, her past environment, habit, convention, in a confused way. With it, the voice of the people was truly the voice of God.

"Oh, thou failure!" said the voice. . . . "You had not tried before you failed."

It was when Carrie was alone, looking out across the park, that she would be listening to this. . . . [103] It was somewhat clear in utterance at first, but never wholly convincing. There was always an answer, always the December days threatened. . . . There seems to be something in the chill breezes which scurry through the long, narrow thoroughfares productive of rueful thoughts. Not poets alone . . . feel this, but dogs and all men. . . . The sparrow upon the wire, the cat in the doorway, the dray horse tugging his weary load, feel the long, keen breaths of winter. It strikes to the heart of all life, animate and inanimate. . . . [How] firmly the chill hand of winter lays upon the heart; how dispiriting are the days during which the sun withholds a portion of our allowance of light and warmth. We are more dependent upon these things than is often thought. We are insects produced by heat, and pass without it. [104]

[Carrie, now Drouet's mistress, and Mrs. Hale, a neighbor, drive along Chicago's Lake Shore Drive.] Lamps were beginning to burn with that mellow radiance which seems almost watery and translucent to the eye. There was a softness in the air which speaks with an infinite delicacy of feeling to the flesh as well as to the soul. . . . As they drove along the smooth pavement an occasional carriage passed. She saw one stop and the footman dismount, opening the door for a gentleman who seemed to be leisurely returning from some afternoon pleasure. Across the broad lawns, now first freshening into green, she saw lamps faintly glowing upon rich interiors. Now it was but a chair, now a table, now an ornate corner, which met her eye, but it appealed

to her as almost nothing else could. Such childish fancies as she had
had of fairy palaces and kingly quarters now came back. She imagined that across these richly carved entrance-ways, where the globed
and crystalled lamps shone upon panelled doors set with stained and
designed panes of glass, was neither care nor unsatisfied desire. She
was perfectly [127] certain that here was happiness. If she could but
stroll up yon broad walk, cross that rich entrance way . . ., and
sweep in grace and luxury to possession and command—oh! how
quickly would sadness flee; how, in an instant, would the heart-ache
end. She gazed and gazed, wondering, delighting, longing, and all
the while the siren voice of the unrestful was whispering in her ear.
. . . [128]

She wanted pleasure, she wanted position, and yet she was confused as to what these things might be. Every hour the kaleidoscope
of human affairs threw a new lustre upon something, and therewith
it became for her the desired—the all. Another shift of the box, and
some other had become the beautiful, the perfect. . . . [159]

[Carrie has become a successful actress. An admirer, Robert Ames,
is talking to her.] "The world is always struggling to express itself,"
he went on. "Most people are not capable of voicing their feelings.
They depend upon others. That is what genius is for. One man ex-
presses their desires for them in music; another one in poetry; another one in a play. Sometimes nature does it in a face—it makes the
face representative of all desire. That's what has happened in your
case." . . . [537]

[At the end of the novel Carrie has risen beyond (and left behind)
both her lovers, Drouet and Hurstwood. She has "attained . . . life's
object"—friends, wealth, fine clothing—and yet she is lonely.] Thus
in life there is ever the intellectual and the emotional nature—the
mind that reasons, and the mind that feels. . . . As harps in the wind,
the latter respond to every breath of fancy, voicing in their moods all
the ebb and flow of the ideal. . . . [555]

Sitting alone, she was now an illustration of the devious ways by
which one who feels, rather than reasons, may be led in the pursuit
of beauty. Though often disillusioned, she was still waiting for that
halcyon day when she should be led forth among dreams become
real . . ., but on and on beyond that, if accomplished, would lie
others for her. It was forever to be the pursuit of that radiance of
delight which tints the distant hilltops of the world. [557]

✌ THEODORE DREISER

The Financier

Theodore Dreiser, *The Financier,* New York, Harper & Brothers, 1912.*

THE BOY FRANK COWPERWOOD has been watching daily the struggle between a lobster and a squid in a tank in a fish-market window. Gradually the lobster has been devouring the squid. As Frank comes up one day:]

"He got him at last," observed one bystander. ". . . The squid was too tired. He wasn't quick enough. . . ."

"That's the way it has to be, I guess," [Cowperwood] commented to himself. "That squid wasn't quick enough. He didn't have anything to feed on." . . . The squid couldn't kill the lobster—he had no weapon. The lobster could kill the squid—he was heavily armed. . . . What was the result to be? What else could it be? "He didn't have a chance," he said, finally, tucking his books under his arm and trotting on.

It made a great impression on him. It answered in a rough way that riddle which had been annoying him so much in the past: "How is life organized?" Things lived on each other—that was it. Lobsters lived on squids [13] and other things. What lived on lobsters? Men, of course! Sure, that was it! And what lived on men? He asked himself. Was it other men? Wild animals lived on men. And there were Indians and cannibals. And some men were killed by storms and accidents. He wasn't so sure about men living on men yet; but men did kill each other. How about wars and street fights and mobs? [14]

[Cowperwood in his teens:] Time and chance happened to all men. Look at the squid he had seen. Was it its fault that it had been put in the tank with the lobster with no chance ultimately of saving its life? Some great curious force was at work here throwing vast masses of people into life; and they could not all succeed. Some had to fail—

* Reprinted with the permission of the World Publishing Co.

many. Only a few could lead. He wondered about himself—whether he was born to lead. He had strength, health, joy in life. . . . [40]

His father talked . . . of business honor, commercial integrity. . . . Frank thought of this a long time at odd moments. What was honor? . . . Honor was almost . . . a figment of the brain. . . . [On the Stock Exchange] men came down to the basic facts of life— the necessity of self care and protection. There was no talk . . . of honor. There were rules of conduct which men observed because they had to. So far as he [102] could see, force governed this world—hard, cold force and quickness of brain. If one had force, plenty of it, quickness of wit and subtlety, there was no need for anything else. Some people might be pretending to be guided by other principles—ethical and religious, for instance . . .—he could not tell. If they were, they were following false or silly standards. In those directions lay failure. To get what you could and hold it fast, without being too cruel, certainly not to individuals—that was the thing to do. . . . [103]

[As Aileen Butler feels herself drifting steadily toward a liaison with Frank Cowperwood, a married man:] It is so easy in this world to divide the sheep and the goats in a superficial way. The slogan of the moralist is that we can all do right if we want to. The answer is that the spirit of man is clothed over with a fleshly envelope which has moods and subtleties of its own. The spirit of man may, as the idealistic metaphysicians have it, be a reflection of a perfect unity which governs the universe, or it may not. It depends on how one conceives the governing spirit of the universe. But of the mold into which this spirit is born, who shall say? There are time moods, and nation moods, and climate moods, and they bring forth great clouds of individuals curiously minded. . . . You might as well have said to a thistle, "Be a grapevine, or we will destroy you," as to have said to Aileen Butler, "Be a calm, placid, virtuous girl, or society will cast you out." Aileen Butler might well have answered, if she could have reasoned so far, "How can I?" Even in the face of the threatening force of society it would have been difficult for her at any time. There were strange, unconventional moods stirring in her, [247] and strange longings. She was seeking some wondrous, peculiar, individual destiny, just as a thistle is unquestionably seeking to perfect a red, thorny blossom. . . . [248]

[Dreiser continues his attack on "immorality":] There is or has been much theorizing . . . concerning the need of following the inward light or leading which all are supposed to possess. That there may be superimposed upon the mass a social conscience which has nothing to do with the normal bent or chemical nature of the individual occurs to few. A Christian ideal had been poured out upon the world like a sea of air, and those who live in it, who are many, draw their convictions as their breath from that. It is not necessarily native to them. Something underneath—the flesh, for instance, and material pleasure—wars against it. . . . Before Christianity was man, and after it he will also be. . . . [250]

[The] large, placid movements of nature outside of man's little organism would indicate that she is not greatly concerned. We see much punishment in the form of jails, diseases, failures, and wrecks; but we also see that the old tendency is not visibly lessened. Is there no law outside of the subtle will and the power to achieve? If not, it is surely high time that we knew it—one and all. We might then agree to do as we do; but there would be no silly illusion as to divine intervention. . . . [254]

Let no one underestimate the need of pity. We live in a stony universe whose hard, brilliant forces rage fiercely. From the prowling hunger of the Hyrean tiger to the concentric grip of Arcturus and Canopus there is this same ruthless, sightless disregard of the individual and the minor thing. Life moves in an ordered heirarchy of forces of which the lesser is as nothing to the greater. Ho, slave! And in the midst of the rip of desperate things—in odd crannies and chance flaws between forces—there [409] spring and bloom these small flowers of sentiment. . . . [410]

[Re Mrs. Cowperwood's plight during her husband's trial:] She was so utterly unhappy. Her fortieth year had come for her, and here she was just passing into the time when a woman ceases to be interesting to men, devoted to her children, feeling innately that life ought naturally to remain grounded on a fixed and solid base, and yet torn bodily from the domestic soil in which she was growing and blooming, and thrown out indifferently in the blistering noonday sun of circumstance to wither. You have seen fish caught ruthlessly in a net and cast indifferently on a sandy shore to die. They have no value save to those sea-feeding buzzards which sit on the shores of some coasts and wait for such food. It is a pitiable spectacle—a gruesome one; but it is life. That is exactly the way life works. [483] [i.e., she knows that Frank has rejected her in favor of Aileen.]

[At end, Frank, out of jail, begins to retrieve his fortune and leaves his old life, old wife, and old reputation as he and Aileen set out for

Chicago:] There is a certain fish whose scientific name is Mycteroperca Bonaci, and whose common name is Black Grouper, [777] which is of considerable value as an afterthought. . . . It is a healthy creature, growing quite regularly to a weight of two hundred and fifty pounds, and living a comfortable, lengthy existence because of its very remarkable ability to adapt itself to conditions. That very subtle thing which we call the creative power, and which we endue with the spirit of the beatitudes, is supposed to build this mortal life in such fashion that only honesty and virtue shall prevail. Witness, then, the significant manner in which it has fashioned the black grouper. One might go far afield and gather less forceful indictments —the horrific spider spinning his trap for the unthinking fly; the lovely Drosera (Sundew) using its crimson calyx for a smothering-pit in which to seal and devour the victim of its beauty; the rainbow-colored jelly-fish that spreads its prismed tentacles like streamers of great beauty, only to sting and torture all that falls within their radiant folds. Man himself is busy digging the pit and fashioning the snare, but he will not believe it. His feet are in the trap of circumstance; his eyes are on an illusion.

Mycteroperca moving in its dark world of green waters is as fine an illustration of the constructive genius of nature, which is not beatific, as any which the mind of man may discover. Its great superiority lies in an almost unbelievable power of simulation, which relates solely to the pigmentation of its skin. . . . You cannot look at it long without feeling that you are witnessing something spectral and unnatural, so brilliant is its power to deceive. From being black it can become instantly white; from being [778] an earth-colored brown it can fade into a delicious water-colored green. . . . One marvels at the variety and subtlety of its power. . . .

What would you say was the intention of the over-ruling, intelligent, constructive force which gives to Mycteroperca this ability? To fit it to be truthful? To permit it to present an unvarying appearance which all honest life-seeking fish may know? Or would you say that subtlety, chicanery, trickery, were here at work? An implement of illusion one might readily suspect it to be, a living lie, a creature whose business it is . . . to get its living by great subtlety, the power of its enemies to forfend against which is little. The indictment is fair.

Would you say in the face of this that a beatific, beneficent creative overruling power never wills that which is either tricky or de-

ceptive? Or would you say that this material seeming in which we
dwell is itself an illusion? If not, whence then the Ten Command-
ments and the illusion of justice? Why were the beatitudes dreamed
and how do they avail? [779]

✿ THEODORE DREISER

The Hand of the Potter

Theodore Dreiser, *The Hand of the Potter: A Tragedy in Four
Acts,* New York, Boni & Liveright, 1918.*

[THE PLAY IS ALMOST OVER. Isadore Berchansky is a young man af-
flicted with a jerking shoulder and an uncontrollable desire to attack
young girls sexually. Before the play opens, he has served a prison
term for one such offense, and during the play he has committed another, this time leading to murder. At the verge of starvation and fear-
ing arrest, he has committed suicide. The newspaper reporters gather
on the scene and speculate about the degree of his guilt.]

QUINN. . . . "The public doesn't understand. . . . I've been reading up on these cases for some time, an' from what I can make out
they're no more guilty than any other person with a disease. [There's]
something they've called *harmones* [*sic*] which the body manufac-
tures an' which is poured into the blood streams of every waan ave
us which excites us to the m'aning ave beauty an' thim things—'sensi-
tizes' is the word they use. Now if a felly is so constituted that he has
more ave that an' less ave somethin' else—somethin' which balances
him a little an' makes him less sensitive to beauty of women or
girls—he's likely to be like that. He can't help it. . . . [193] It's in a
hundred books. Haven't ye ever read Havelock Ellis or Kraft-Ebbing?
They give thousands ave cases—thousands." [194]

[QUINN]: "This felly could no more help bein' what he was than a
fly can help bein' a fly an' naht an elephant, an' that's naht at aal.

* Reprinted by permission of Mr. Harold J. Dies and Mrs. Myrtle Butcher and
with the approval of the Library and Trustees of the University of Pennsylvania.

Nature is deeper an' stronger than anything we know. . . . Don't be
so cocksure in your judgments of who are the good an' who are the
bad in this world. Facts an' proofs are naht aal on the surface, by any
means. . . ." [197]

"Aal men are naht balanced or normal by their own free will an'
say-so, any more than they're free an' aqual in life, an' that's naht at
aal. They're naht aal endowed with [198] the power or the will to do
an' select, aal the rules ave the copybooks to the contrary nahtwith-
standin'. Some are so constituted mentally an' physically that they
can't do otherwise than as they do, an' that's what ye never can get
through the average felly's brain. . . . Most people have a few rules,
a pattern, an' everybody's supposed to be like that. Well, they're naht.
An' naathin' will ever make 'em exactly alike. . . . Nature don't
work that way. An' nature makes people . . . an' she don't aalways
make us right ayther, by a damned sight. . . . Sometimes I think
we're naht unlike those formulae they give ye in a chemical laboratory—if ye're made up right, ye work right; if ye're naht, ye don't, an'
that's aal there is to it—laa or no laa." [199]

𝕏 THEODORE DREISER

Sanctuary

Theodore Dreiser, "Sanctuary," *The Smart Set*, LX (October,
1919).*

I

PRIMARILY, there were the conditions under which she was brought
to fifteen years of age: the crowded, scummy tenements; the narrow
green-painted halls with their dim gas-jets, making the entrance look

* This story appears (with many minor revisions) in a Dreiser collection called
Chains (New York, Boni & Liveright, 1927) and in Bernard J. Duffey (ed.),
Modern American Literature, New York, Rinehart Editions, 1951. It is reprinted
by permission of Mr. Harold J. Dies and Mrs. Myrtle Butcher and with the approval of the Library and Trustees of the University of Pennsylvania.

more like that of a morgue than a dwelling-place; the dirty halls and rooms with their green or blue or brown walls painted to save the cost of paper; the bare wooden floors, long since saturated with very type of grease and filth from oleomargarine and suet leaked from cheap fats or meats, to beer and whiskey and tobacco-juice. A little occasional scrubbing by some would-be hygienic tenant was presumed to keep or make clean some of the chambers and halls wherein they lived.

And then the streets outside—any of the streets by which she had ever been surrounded—block upon block of other red, bare, commonplace tenements crowded to the doors with human life, the space before them sped over by noisy, gassy trucks and vehicles of all kinds, generally carrying filth. Streets stifling in summer, dusty and icy in winter; decorated on occasion by stray cats and dogs, pawing in ashcans, watched over by lordly policemen, and always running with people, people, people—who made their living heaven only knows how, existing in such a manner as their surroundings suggested.

In this atmosphere were always longshoremen, wagon-drivers, sweepers of floors, washers of dishes, waiters, janitors, workers in laundries, factories—mostly in indifferent or decadent or despairing conditions. And all of these people existed, in so far as she ever knew, upon that mysterious, evanescent and fluctuating something known as the weekly wage.

Always about her there had been drunkenness, fighting, complaining, sickness or death; the police coming in, and arresting one and another; the gas man, the rent man, the furniture man, hammering at doors for their due—and not getting it—in due time the undertaker also arriving amid a great clamor, as though lives were the most precious things imaginable.

It is entirely conceivable that in viewing or in meditating upon an atmosphere such as this, one might conclude that no good could come out of it. What! a dung-heap grow a flower? Exactly, and often, a flower—but not to grow to any glorious maturity probably, but nevertheless a flower of the spirit at least might have its beginnings there. And if it shrank or withered in the miasmatic atmosphere—well, conceivably, that might be normal, although in reality all flowers thus embedded in infancy do not so wither. There are flowers and flowers. . . . [35]

What most affected her youth and her life was the internal condition of her family, the poverty and general worthlessness of her parents. They were as poor as their poorest neighbors, and quarrelsome, unhappy and mean-spirited into the bargain.

Her father, for instance, came dimly into her understanding at somewhere near her seventh or eighth year as an undersized, contentious and drunken and wordy man, always more or less out of a job, irritated with her mother and her sister and brother, and always, as her mother seemed to think, a little the worse for drink.

"You're a liar! You're a liar! You're a liar! You're a liar!"—how well she remembered this sing-song echoing reiteration of his, in whatever basement or hole they were living at the time!

Her mother, often partially intoxicated or morose because of her own ills, was only too willing to rejoin in kind. Her elder sister and brother, much more agreeable in their way and as much put upon as herself, were always coming in or running out somewhere and staying while the storm lasted; while she, shy and always a little frightened, seemed to look upon it all as unavoidable, possibly even essential. The world was always so stern, so mysterious, so non-understandable to Madeleine.

Again it might be, and often was, "Here, you, you brat, go an' get me a can o' beer! Gwan, now!" which she did quickly and fearfully enough, running to the nearest wretched corner saloon with the "can" or "growler," her slim little fingers closed tightly over the five-cent piece or dime entrusted to her, her eyes taking in the wonders and joys of the street even as she ran. She was so small at the time that her little arms were unable to reach quite the level of the bar, and she had to accept the aid of the bartender or some drinker. Then she would patiently wait while one of them teased her as to her size or until the beer was handed down.

Once, and once only, three "bad boys," knowing what she was going for and how wretched and shabby was old Kinsella, not able to revenge himself on any one outside his family, had seized her enroute, forced open her hand and run away with the dime, leaving her to return fearsomely to her father, rubbing her eyes, and to be struck and abused soundly and told to fight—"Blank-blank you, what the blank 're you good for if you can't do that?"

Only the vile language and the defensive soberness of her mother at the time saved her from a worse fate. As for the boys who had stolen the money, they only received curses and awful imprecations, which harmed no one.

Wretched variations of this same existence were endured by the

other two members of the family, her brother Frank and her sister
Tina.

The former was a slim and nervous youth, given to fits of savage
temper like his father and not to be ordered and controlled exactly as
his father would have him. . . . [36]

There was something rather admirable and yet disturbing connected dimly with Tina in Madeleine's mind, an atmosphere of rebel-
liousness and courage which she could not have described, lacking as
she did a mind that registered the facts of life clearly. . . . [37]

II

It is not surprising that Madeleine came to her twelfth and thirteenth years without any real understanding of the great world about
her and without any definite knowledge or skill. Her drunken mother
was now more or less dependent upon her, her father having died of
pneumonia and her brother and sister having disappeared to do for
themselves.

Aside from petty beginners' tasks in shops or stores, or assisting
her mother at washing or cleaning, there was little that she could do
at first. Mrs. Kinsella, actually compelled by the need for rent or food
or fuel after a time, would get occasional work in a laundry or kitchen
or at scrubbing or window-cleaning, but not for long. The pleasure
of drink would soon rob her of that.

At these tasks Madeleine helped until she secured work in a candy
factory in her thirteenth year at the wage of three-thirty a week. But
even with this little money paid in regularly there was no assurance
that her mother would add sufficient to it to provide either food or
warmth. Betimes, and when Madeleine was working, her mother
cheered her all too obvious sorrows with the bottle, and at nights or
week-ends rewarded Madeleine with a gabble which was all the more
painful because no material comfort came with it.

The child actually went hungry at times. Usually, after a few
drinks, her mother would begin to weep and recite her past ills: a
process which reduced her timorous and very sympathetic daughter
to complete misery. In sheer desperation the child sought for some
new way in her own mind. A reduction in the working-force of the
candy factory, putting her back in the ranks of the work-seekers once
more, and a neighbor perceiving her wretched state and suggesting
that some extra helpers were wanted in a department store at Christ-

mas time, she applied there, but so wretched were her clothes by now
that she was not even considered.

Then a man who had a restaurant in a nearby street gave her
mother and Madeleine positions as dishwashers, but he was compelled to discharge her mother, although he wished to retain Madeleine. From this last, however, because of the frightening attentions
of the cook, she had to flee, and without obtaining a part of the small
pittance which was due her. Again, and because in times past she had
aided her mother to clean in one place and another, she was able to
get a place as servant in a family. . . .[38]

Daily her mother was growing more inadequate and less given to
restraint or consideration. As "bad" as she was, Madeleine could not
help thinking what a "hard" time she had had. From whatever places
she obtained work in these days (and it was not often any more) she
was soon discharged, and then she would come inquiring after Madeleine, asking to be permitted to see her. Naturally, her shabby dress
and shawl and rag of a hat, as well as her wastrel appearance, were
an affront to any well-ordered household. Once in her presence,
whenever Madeleine was permitted to see her, she would begin either
a cozening or a lachrymose account of her great needs.

"It's out o' oil I am, me dear," or "Wurra, I have no wood" or "bread"
or "meat"—never drink. "Ye won't let yer pore old mother go cold or
hungry, now, will ye? That's the good girl now. Fifty cents now, if ye
have it, me darlin', or a quarter, an' I'll not be troublin' ye soon again.
Even a dime, if ye can spare me no more. God'll reward ye. I'll have
work o' me own tomorra. That's the good girl now—ye won't let me
go away without anything."

Oscillating between shame and sympathy, her daughter would
take from the little she had and give it to her, trembling for fear the
disturbing figure would prove her undoing. Then the old woman
would go out, lurching sometimes in her cups, and disappear, while
an observant fellow servant was probably seeing and reporting to the
mistress, who, of course, did not want her to come there and so told
the girl, or more practical still, discharged her.

Thus from her fourteenth to her sixteenth year she was shunted
from house to house and from shop to shop, always in the vain hope
that this time her mother might let her alone.

And at the very same time, life, sweetened by the harmonies of
youth in the blood, was calling—that exterior life which promised
everything because so far it had given nothing. The little simple

things of existence, the very ordinary necessities of clothing and orna-
ment, with which the heart of youth and the inherent pride of appearance are gratified, had a value entirely disproportionate to their
worth. Yes, already she had turned the age wherein the chemic harmonies in youth begin to sing, thought to thought, color to color,
dream to dream. She was being touched by the promise of life itself.

And then, as was natural, love in the guise of youth, a rather sophisticated gallant somewhat above the world in which she was moving, appeared and paid his all but worthless court to her. He was
physically charming, the son of a grocer of some means in the vicinity
in which she was working, a handsome youth with pink cheeks and
light hair and blue eyes, and vanity enough for ten. Because she was
shy and pretty he became passingly interested in her.

"Oh, I saw you cleaning the windows yesterday," this with a radiant, winning smile; or "You must live down toward Blake Street. I see
you going down that way once in a while."

Madeleine acknowledged rather shamefacedly that it was true:
That so dashing a boy should be interested in her was too marvelous.

In the evenings, or at any time, it was easy for a youth of his skill
and *savoir-faire* to pick her out of the bobbing stream of humanity in
which she occasionally did errands or visited her mother in her
shabby room, and to suggest that he be permitted to call upon her.
Or, failing that, because of her mother's shabby quarters and her
mother herself, that the following Sunday would be ideal for an out-
ing to one [39] of those tawdry, noisy beaches to which he liked to go
with other boys and girls in a car.

A single trip to Wonderland, a single visit to one of its halls where
music sounded to the splash of the waves and where he did his best
to teach her to dance, a single meal in one of its gaudy, noisy restau-
rants, a taste of its whirly pleasures, and a new color and fillip were
given to hope, a new and seemingly realizable dream of happiness
implanted in her young mind. The world was happier than she had
thought, or could be made so; not all people fought and screamed at
each other. There were such things as tenderness, soft words, sweet
words.

But the way of so sophisticated a youth with a maid was brief and
direct. His mind was of that order which finds in the freshness of
womankind a mere passing delight, something to be deflowered and
then put aside. He was a part of a group that secured its happiness in
rifling youth, the youth of those whose lives were so dull and bleak

that a few words of kindness, a little change of scene, the mere proximity of experience and force such as they had never known, were pay ample for anything which they might give or do.

And of these Madeleine was one.

Never having had anything in her own life, the mere thought of a man so vigorous and handsome, one with knowledge enough to show her more of life than she had ever dreamed of, to take her to places of color and light, to assure her that she was fitted for better things even though they were not immediately forthcoming, was sufficient to cause her to place faith where it was least worthy of being placed. To win his way there was even talk of marriage later on, that love should be generous and have faith—and then—

III

Plain-clothesman Amundsen, patrolling like a hawk, the region of Fourteenth and K streets, not so far from Blake, where Madeleine had lived for a time, was becoming interested in and slightly suspicious of a new face.

For several days at odd hours, he had seen a girl half-slinking, half-brazening her way through a region the very atmosphere of which was blemishing to virtue. To be sure, he had not yet seen her speak to any one; nor was there that in her glance or manner which caused him to feel that she might.

Still—with the assurance of his authority and his past skill in trapping many he followed discreetly, seeing where she went, how she lingered for awhile nervously, then returned as she had come. She was very young, not more than seventeen.

He adjusted his tie and collar and decided to attempt his skill.

"Excuse me, Miss. Out for a little stroll? So am I. Mind my walking along with you a little way? Wouldn't like to come and have a drink, would you? I work in an automobile place over here in Grey Street, and I'm just off for the afternoon. Live here in the neighborhood?"

Madeleine surveyed this stranger with troubled eyes. Since the day her youthful lover had deserted her, and after facing every conceivable type of ill, but never being willing to confess or fall back upon her drunken, dreaming mother for aid, she had tested every device. The necessities and expenses incident to a prospective, and to her degrading state, as well as the continued care of her mother, had compelled

her, as she had finally seen it, to come to this—for a time anyhow. A
street girl, finding her wandering and crying had taken her in hand
and shown her, after aiding her for weeks, how to make her way.

Her burden that she feared so much was artificially if ruthlessly
and criminally disposed of. Then she was shown the way of the streets
until she could gain a new foothold in life; only, as she had since
learned, it was difficult for her to accomodate herself to this fell traf-
fic. She was not of it spiritually. She really did not intend [40] to continue in it; it was just a temporary make-shift, born of fear and a
dumb despair. . . .

But neither Detective Amundsen nor the law was ready to believe
that. To the former she seemed as worthless as any—one of those
curious, uncared-for flowers never understood by the dull.

In a nearby café she had listened to his inquiries, the fact that he
had a room in a nearby hotel, or could secure one. Condemning a fate
which drove her to such favors, and fully resolved to leave it soon, to
make something better of her life in the future, she went with him.

Then came the scarring realization that he was an officer of the law,
a cynical, contemptuous hawk smirking over her tears and her explanations. It was absolutely nothing to him that she was so young and
could scarcely have been as hardened as he pretended. She was compelled to walk through the streets with him to the nearest police station, while he nodded to or stopped to explain to passing brothers of
the cloth the nature of his latest conquest. . . .

And so it was that for a period of a year she was turned over to the
care of the Sisterhood of the Good Shepherd.

IV

The gray and bony walls of that institution starkly dominated one
of the barest and most unprepossessing regions of the city. Its northern facade fronted a stoneyard, beyond which were the rocks of the
racing Sound and a lighthouse. To the east, rocks and the river, a gray
expanse in winter picked over by gulls, mourned over by the horns of
endless craft. To the south, bare coal-yards, wagon-yards, tenements.

Twice weekly, sentenced delinquents of various ages—the "children," of whom Madeleine was one; the "girls," ranging from eighteen
to thirty; the "women," ranging from thirty to fifty; and the old people, ranging from fifty until the last years of life—were brought here

in an all but air-tight cage, boxed like a great circus van, and with only small barred air-holes at the top. Inside the van were bare, hard benches, one against either wall. A representative of the probation and control system of the city, a gaunt female of many years, sat within; also an officer of such prodigious proportions that the mere sight of him might well raise the [41] inquiry of why so much unnecessary luggage. For amusement in dull hours he smoothed his broad mouth with the back of his red, hairy hand, and dreamed of bygone days.

The institution itself was operated by a Mother Superior and thirty nuns, all of the order mentioned, all expert in their separate ways in cooking, housekeeping, laundering, buying, lace-making, teaching, and a half dozen other practical or applied arts. . . .

Within the institution were separate wings or sections for each of the four groups before mentioned, sections in which each had its separate working, eating, sleeping and playing rooms. Only one thing was shared in common: the daily, and often twice or thrice daily, religious ceremonies in the great chapel, a lofty, magi-decorated and be-altered and be-candled chamber, whose tall, thin spire surmounted with a cross might easily be seen from many of the chambers in which the different groups worked. There were masses in the mornings, vespers and late prayers in the afternoons, often late prayers at night or on holidays, when additional services of one kind and another were held. To the religious-minded these were of course consoling. To the contrary-minded they became at times a strain.

Always, and over all the work and all the routine relaxations or pleasures of the institution, there hung the grim insistence of the law, its executive arm, upon order, seemliness, and, if not penance, at least a servility of mind which was the equivalent thereof. Let the voices of the nuns be never so soft, their foot-falls light, their manners courteous, their ways gentle, persuasive, sympathetic, their mood tender; back of it all lay the shadow of the force which could forthwith return any or all to the rough hands of the police, the stern and not-to-be-evaded dictum of the courts.

This, much more than any look of disappointment or displeasure, if such were ever necessary, spoke to these delinquents or victims, whatever their mood, and quieted them in their most rebellious hours. Try as they would, they could not but remember that it was the law that had placed them here and now detained them. . . . That there was

peace, order, sweetness and harmony, was well enough, comforting
in cases; only and always it had obviously a two-fold base: one the
power of the law itself, the other in the gentle, appealing, beautiful
suasion of the nuns.

But to so inexperienced and as yet unreasoning a child as Madeleine all of this savored at this time of but one thing: the sharp, crude,
inconsiderate and uninquiring forces of law or life, which seemed
never to stop and inquire how or why, but only to order how, and
that without mercy. Like some frightened animal faced by a terrifying enemy, she had thus far been able to think only of some darksome
corner into which she might slip and hide, a secret place so inconspicuous and minute that the great savage world without would not
trouble or care to follow.

And well enough the majority of the Sisterhood, especially those in
immediate authority over her, understood the probable direction and
ramifications of her present thoughts.

They knew her mood, for had they not during years past dealt with
many such? And stern as was the law, they were not unmindful of her
welfare. So long as she was willing and obedient there was but one
thing more: that somehow her troubled or resentful or congealed and
probably cruelly injured mind should be wooed from its blind belief
in the essential injustice of life, to be made to feel, as they themselves
were ready to believe, that all paths were not closed, all forces not
essentially dark or evil.

For them there was hope of sorts for all, a way out, and many—
even she—might find ways and means of facing life, better possibly
than any she had ever known. [42]

V

Sister St. Agnes, for instance, who controlled the spotlessly clean
but barnlike and bleak room in which were a hundred machines for
the sewing of shirtwaists, was a creature of none too fortunate a
history herself.

Returning at the age of eighteen and at the death of her father
from a convent in which she had been placed by him in order to escape the atmosphere of a home which he himself had found unsatis-
factory, she had found a fashionable mother leading a life of which
she could scarcely conceive, let alone accept. The taint, the subter-

fuge, the self-indulgent waste, had as soon sickened her as had the streets Madeleine.

Disappointed, she felt herself after a time incapable of enduring it and had fled, seeking first to make her way in a world which offered only meagre wages and a barren life to those incapable of enduring its rugged and often shameless devices; later, again wearied of her own trials, she had returned to the convent in which she had been trained and asked to be schooled for service there. Finding the life too simple for a nature grown more rugged, she had asked to be, and had been, transferred to the House of the Good Shepherd, finding there for the first time, in this institution, duties and opportunities which somehow matched her ideals.

And by the same token the Mother Superior of this same institution, Mother St. Bertha, who often came through and inquired into the story of each one, was of a history and of an order of mind which was not unlike that of Sister St. Agnes, only it had even more of genuine pathos and suffering in it. The daughter of a shoe manufacturer, she had seen her father fail, her mother die of consumption, a favorite brother drink and carouse until he finally fell under the blight of disease and died. . . .

The subsequent death of her father, to whom she had devoted her years, and the failing of her own dreams of a personal love, had saddened her, and she sought out and was admitted to this order in the hope that she, too, might still make especial use of a life that promised all too little in the world outside.

Her great comfort was in having some one or something to love, the satisfaction of feeling that lives which otherwise might have come to nothing had by some service of hers been lifted to a better state. And in that thought she worked here daily, going about among those incarcerated in different quarters, seeing to it that their tasks were not too severe, their comforts and hopes, where hope still remained, in nowise betrayed.

But to Madeleine at first the solemn habits of the nuns, as well as the gray gingham apron she had to don, the grayer woolen dress, the severe manner in which she had to dress her hair, her very plain shoes, the fact that she had to rise at six-thirty, attend mass and then breakfast at eight, work from eight-thirty to twelve-thirty, and again from one-thirty to four; lunch regularly at twelve-thirty and sup at six, attend a form of prayer service at four-thirty, play at simple games with

her new companions between five and six and again between seven
and nine, and then promptly retire to a huge sleeping-ward set with
small white iron beds in long rows, and lit, after the retiring bell had
sounded, by small oil cups or candles burning faintly before various
images, all smacked of penance, the more disturbing because it was
strange, a form of personal control which she had not sought and
could not at once accept.

Nor could she help thinking that some severer form of punishment
was yet to be meted out to her, or might ensue by reason of one unavoidable error or another. Life had always been so with her. But,
once here a time, things proved not so bad.

The large workroom with its hundred [43] machines and its tall windows, which afforded a stark view of the coal-pockets to the south,
and the river with its boats and gulls, proved not unpleasing. The
clean, bright windows, polished floors and walls—washed and
cleaned by the inmates themselves, the nuns not disdaining to do
their share—and the habits of the Sisters, their white-fringed hoods,
black robes and clinking beads and their silent tread and low speech,
impressed her greatly.

The fact that there was no severe reproof of any failure to comprehend at first, but only slow and patient explanations of simple things,
not difficult in themselves to do; that aside from the routine duties,
the marching in line with hands crossed over breast and head up, as
well as genuflections at mass, prayers before and after meals, at rising and on retiring, and at the peal of the Angelus, morning, noon
and night, there was no real oppression, finally made her like it.

The girls who were here with her, shy or silent or cold or indifferent
at first, and each with her world of past experiences, contacts, and re-
lationships locked in her heart, were still, placed as they were elbow
to elbow at work, at meals, at prayer, at retiring, incapable of not
achieving some kind of remote fellowship which eventually led to
speech and confidences.

Thus the young girl who sat next at her right in the sewing-room—
Viola Patters by name, a brave, blonde, cheerful little thing—although she had endured much that might be called ill-fortune, was
still intensely interested in life. . . . [44]

And so it was finally that Madeleine was induced to tell her story.
There were other girls here who, once this bond of sympathy was
struck, were keen enough to tell their tales—sad, unfortunate, harried

lives all—and somehow the mere telling of them restored to Madeleine some of her earlier faint confidence or interest in life. It was "bad," but it was vivid. For in spite of their unfortunate beginnings, the slime in which primarily and without any willing of their own they had been embedded and from which nearly all were seeking to crawl upwards, and bravely enough, they had heart for and faith in life.

In all cases, apparently, love was their star as well as their bane. They thought chiefly of the joy that might be had in joining their lives with some man or being out in the free world, working again possibly, at least in touch in some feeble way with the beauty and gayety of life, as beauty and gayety manifested themselves to them.

And so by degrees, the crash of her own original hopes echoing less and less loudly in the distance, the pain of her great shame and rude awakening passed farther and farther from her. The smoothness and regularity of this austere life, indifferent as it seemed at times, consoled her by its very security and remoteness from the world. It was lean and spare, to be sure, but it offered safety and rest to the mind and heart. Now, rising in her dim, silent ward of a morning, repeating her instructed prayers, marching in silence to chapel, to breakfast, to work, hearing only the soft hum of the machines, marching again to chapel, playing each day, but not too noisily, and finally retiring in the same ordered and silent way to her tiny bed, she was soothed and healed.

And yet, or perhaps because of this, she could not help thinking of the clangor and crash of the world without. It had been grim and painful to her, but in its rude, brutal way it had been alive. The lighted streets at night! The cars! That dancing pavilion in which once she had been taught to dance by the great blue sea! The vanished touches of her faithless lover's hands—his kisses—brief, so soon over! Where was he now in the great strange world outside? With whom? What was she like? And would he tire of her as quickly? Treat her as badly? Where was Tina? Frank? Her mother? What had happened to her mother? Not a word had she heard.

To Sister St. Agnes, after a time, sensing her to be generous, faithful, patient, she had confided all concerning herself and her mother, crying on her shoulder, and the Sister had promised to learn what she could. But the investigation proving that her mother had been sent to the workhouse, she deemed it best to say nothing for the present.

Madeleine would find her quickly enough on returning to the world.
Why cloud the new budding life with so shameful a memory?

VI

And then once more, in due time, and with the memory of these
things clinging fast to her, she was sent forth into the world, not quite
as poorly-armed as before, perhaps, but still with the limited equip-
ment which her own innate disposition compelled.

After many serious and presumably wise injunctions as to the
snares and pitfalls of this world, and accompanied by a black-habited
nun, who took her direct to one of those moral and religious families
whose strict adherence to the tenets of this particular faith was held
to provide an ideal example, she was left to her own devices and the
type of work she had previously followed, the nuns themselves being
hard put to it to discover anything above the most menial forms of
employment for their various charges. Theirs was a type of schooling and training which did not rise above a theory of morality [45]
requiring not so much skill as faith and blind obedience.

And again, here, as in the institution itself, the idea of a faith, a
religion, a benign power above that of man and seeking his welfare,
surrounded her as the very air itself or as an aura, although she personally was by no means ready to accept it, never having given it
serious thought.

Everywhere here, as in the institution itself, were little images or
colored pictures of saints, their brows circled by stars or crowns, their
hands holding scepters or lilies, their bodies arrayed in graceful and
soothing robes of white, blue, pink and gold. Their faces were serene,
their eyes benignly contemplative, yet to Madeleine they were still
images only, pretty and graceful, even comforting, but at so great
variance to life as she knew it as to be little more than pretty pictures.

In the great church which they attended, and to which they persuaded her to accompany them, were more of these same candle-lit
pictures of saints, images and altars starred with candles, many or
few, at which she was wont to stare in wonder and awe. The vest-
ments of the priest and the acolytes, the white-and-gold and red-and-
gold of the chasuble and the stole and the cope, the gold and silver
crosses, chalices and winecups, over-awed her inexperienced and
somewhat impressionable mind without convincing it of the imma-

nence of superior forces whose significance or import she could in nowise guess. God, God, God—she heard of Him and the passion and
death of the self-sacrificing Lord Jesus.

And here, as there, the silence, the order, the cleanliness and regularity, as well as simplicity, were the things which most invested her
reason and offered the greatest contrasts to her old life.

She had not known or sensed the significance of these things before. Now, day by day, like the dripping of water, the ticking of time,
they made an impression, however slight. Routine, routine, routine,
and the habit and order and color of a vast and autocratic religion,
made their lasting impression upon her.

And yet, in spite of an occasional supervisory visit on the part of
one or other of the nuns of the probation department, she was not
only permitted but compelled to work out her life as best she might,
and upon such wages as she could command or devise. For all the
prayers and the good-will of the nuns, life was as insistent and driving as ever. It did not appear to be so involved with religion. In spite
of the admonitions of the church, the family for whom she was working saw little more in its religious obligation than that she should be
housed and fed according to her material merits. If she wished to
better herself, as she soon very clearly saw she must, she would have
to develop a skill which she did not now have and which, once developed, would make her of small use here. At the same time, if the
months spent in the institution had conveyed to her the reasonable-
ness of making something better of her life than hitherto she had
been able to do, the world, pleasure, hope, clanged as insistently and
as wooingly as ever before.

But how? How? was the great problem. Hers was no resourceful,
valiant soul, capable of making its own interesting way alone. Think
as she would, and try, love, and love only, the admiration and minis-
tering care of some capable and affectionate man was the only thing
that seemed likely to solve for her the various earthly difficulties
which beset her.

But even as to this, how, in what saving or perfect way, was love
to come to her? She had made one mistake which in the development
of an honest relationship with another would have to be confessed.
And how would it be then? Would love, admiration, forgive? Love,
love, love, and the peace and comfort of that happy routine home life
which she imagined she saw operative in the lives of others—how it
glimmered afar, like a star!

And again there was her mother. [46]

It was not long after she had come from the institution that sheer loneliness, as well as a sense of daughterly responsibility and pity, had urged her to look up her mother, in order that she might restore to herself some little trace of a home, however wretched it might be. She had no one, as she proceeded to argue. At least in her own lonely life her mother provided, or would, an ear and a voice, sympathetic if begging, a place to go.

She had learned on returning to their last living-place on one of her afternoons off, that her mother had been sent away to the "Island," but had come back and since had been sent to the city poor-farm. This last inquiry led eventually to her mother's discovery of her and of her fixing herself upon her once more as a dependent, until her death, somewhat over a year later.

But in the meantime, and after all, life continued to call and call and to drive her on, for she was still full of the hope and fever of youth. . . .

[Her] own life, move about as she might and did after a time from one small position to another, in store or factory, in the hope of bettering herself, held nothing. . . . Day by day as she worked she sensed all the more clearly that the meagre tasks at which she toiled could bring her nothing of permanent value. Her mother was dead now, and she more alone than ever. During a period of several years, in which she worked and dreamed, leading a thin, underpaid life, her mind was ever on love and what it might do for her—the pressure of a seeking hand, the sanctuary of an enveloping heart.

And then, for the second time in her brief life, love came, or seemed to—at least in her own heart if nowhere else.

She had by now, and through her own efforts, attained to a clerkship in one of the great stores at the salary of seven dollars a week, on which she was trying to live. And then, behold, one day among her customers one of those suave and artful masters of the art of living by one's wits, with a fortune of looks, to whom womanhood is a thing to be taken by an upward curl of a pair of mustachios, the vain placement of ringed locks, spotless and conspicuous lines, and clothes and shoes of a newness and lustre all but disturbing to a very work-a-day world. His manners and glances were of a winsomeness which only the feminine heart—and that unschooled in the valuelessness of veneer—fully appreciates.

Yes, the sheer grace of the seeking male, his shallow and heartless courtesy, the lustre of his eye and skin, a certain something of shabby-grand manner, such as she had never known in the particularly narrow world in which [47] she moved, was sufficient to arrest and fix her interest.

He leaned over and examined the stationery and pencils which she sold, commenting on prices, the routine of her work, smiled archly and suggested by his manner entire that she was one in whom he could be deeply interested. At the same time a certain animal magnetism, of the workings of which she was no more conscious than might be any stick or stone, took her in its tow.

Here was one out of many, a handsome beau, who was interested in her and her little life. The oiled and curled hair became the crown of a god; the mustachios and the sharp, cruel nose harmonies of exquisite beauty. Even the muscular, prehensile hands were rhythmic, musical in their movements. She had time only to sense the wonder of his perfect self before he went away. But it was to return another day, with an even more familiar and insinuating grace.

He was interested in her, as he frankly said the next time, and she must be his friend. At lunch-time one day he was waiting to take her to a better restaurant than she would ever have dreamed of entering; on another day it was to dinner that she accompanied him.

According to him, she was beautiful, wonderful. Her flowerlike life was being wasted on so rude a task. She should marry him, and then her difficulties would be solved. He was one who, when fortune was with him, so he said, made much, much money. He might even take her from the city at times to see strange places and interesting scenes.

As for her own stunted life, from most of the details of which she forbore, he seemed in nowise interested. It was not due to any lack on her part in the past that her life had been so ill. . . .

Love, love, love. . . . The old story. In a final burst of admiration and love for his generosity she told him of her one great error, which caused him a few moments of solemn cogitation and was then dismissed as nothing of importance, a pathetic, childish mistake. Then there followed one of those swift and seemingly unguarded unions, a commonplace of the tangled self-preserving underworld of poverty. A clergyman was found whose moral assurances seemed to make the union ideal. Then a room in a commonplace boarding-house, and the newer and better life which eventually was to realize all was begun.

VII

To those familiar with the brazen and relentless methods of a certain type of hawk of the underworld, which picks fledglings from the nest and springlings from the fields and finds life itself only a hunting-ground in which those mentally or physically weaker than itself may be enslaved, this description will seem neither strained nor inadequate. Fagins of sex, creatures who change their women as they would their coats, they make an easy if reprehensible bed of their lives, and such of their victims as have known them well testify that for a while at least in their care or custody they were not unhappy.

So it was with Madeleine and this one. With amused and laughing tolerance toward her natural if witless efforts to build up a home atmosphere about their presumably joint lives, to build for a future in which they should jointly share, he saw in them only something trivial or ridiculous, whereas to her it was as though the heavens had opened and she was surveying a new world. For in his love and care there was to be peace. Latterly, if not now—for already he complained of conditions which made it impossible for him to work—the results of their several labors were to be pooled in order to prepare for that something better which would soon be achieved—a home, an ideally happy state somewhere. Even children were in her mind.

The mere fact that he shortly [48] complained of other temporary reverses which made it necessary for him and her to keep close watch over their resources, and that for the time being, until he "could arrange his affairs," she must find some employment which would pay much better than her old one, gave her no shock.

Indeed, it was an indescribable joy for her to do for her love, for love had come, that great solvent of all other early difficulties, that leveler of all but insurmountable barriers. Even now love was to make her life flower at last. There was an end to loneliness and the oppressive indifference of the great sea of life.

But, as in the first instance, so now the awakening was swift and disconcerting. Realizing the abject adoration in which she held his surface charms and that his thin, tricky soul was the beginning and the end of things for her, it was all the easier to assure her, and soon insist, that the easiest and swiftest way of making money, of which she was unfortunately aware, must be resorted to, for a great necessity had come upon him. The usual tale of a threatening disaster, a sudden loss at cards which might end in imprisonment for him and their enforced separation, was enough.

Swiftly he filled her ears with tales of rescues by women of many of his men friends similarly circumstanced, of the "fools" and "marks" that filled the thoroughfares to be captured and preyed upon by women. Why hesitate? Consider the meagre, beggarly wages she had previously earned, the nothingness of her life before. Why jeopardize their future now? Why be foolish, dull? Plainly it was nothing to love, as he saw it. Should it be so much to her? In this wise she was persuaded.

But now it was not the shame and the fear of arrest that troubled her, but the injury which love had done and was doing to her, that cut and burned and seared and scarred.

Love, as she now began dimly to realize once more, should not be so. More than anything else, if love was what she had always dreamed, should it not protect and save and keep her for itself? And now see. Love was sending her out again to loiter in doorways and before windows and to "make eyes."

It was this that turned like a wheel in her brain and heart. For in spite of the roughness of her emotional experiences thus far, she had faith to believe that love should not be so, should not do so.

Those features which to this hour, and long after, like those features of her first love, seemed so worship-worth, those eyes that had seemed to beam on her with love, the lips that had smiled so graciously and kissed hers, the hands and arms that had petted and held her, should not be part of the compulsion that sent her here.

No, love should be better than that. He himself had told her so at first—that she was worth more than all else to him—and now see!

And then one night, fully a year and a half later, the climax. Being particularly irritated by some money losses and the need of enduring her at all, even though she might still prove of some value as a slave, he turned on her with a savage fury. . . .

He pushed her away, throwing open the door as he did so, and, finding her still pleading and clinging, violently pushed and threw her out with such force that she cut her left eye and the back of her left hand [49] against the jamb of the door.

There was a cry of "Fred! Fred! Please! Please!"—and then the door was slammed and she was left leaning disconsolately and brokenly against the stair-rail outside.

And now, as before, the cruelty and inscrutability of life weighed on her, only now, less than before, had she hope wherewith to buoy herself. It was all so dark, so hopeless. Often in this hour she thought of the swift, icy waters of the river, glistening under a winter moon, and then again of the peace and quiet of the House of the Good Shepherd, its shielding remoteness from life, the only true home or sanctuary she had ever known. And so, brooding and repressing occasional sobs, she made her way toward it, down the long streets, thinking of the pathetically debasing love-life that was now over— the dream of love that never, never could be again, for her.

VIII

The stark red walls of the institution stood as before, only dim and gray and cold under a frosty winter moon. It was three of a chill, cold morning. She had come a long way, drooping, brooding, half-freezing and crying.

"Is Mother St. Bertha here? I was here before. She will know me."

The Sister Secretary surveyed her curiously, sensing more of the endless misery that was ever here, but seeing that she was sick or in despair hastened to call her superior, whose rule it was that all such requests for admission should be referred to her. There was no stir in the room in her absence. Presently pattened feet were heard, and the face of Mother St. Bertha, wrinkled and a-weary, appeared at the square opening. [50]

"What is it, my child?" she asked curiously if softly, wondering at the crumpled presence at this hour.

"Mother," began Madeleine tremulously, looking up and recognizing her, "Don't you remember me? It is Madeleine. I was here four years ago. I was in the girls' ward. I worked in the sewing-room. . . . Can't I just have my old dress and my bed for tonight—that little bed under the lamp?"

"Why, yes, dear, you may have them, of course," said the nun, tactfully sensing a great grief. "And you need not talk now. I think I know how it is. Come with me."

She led the way along bare, dimly lit corridors and up cold solid iron stairs, echoing to the feet, until once more, as in the old days,

the severe but spotless room in which were the baths and the hampers for soiled clothes was reached.

"Now, my child," she said, "you may undress and bathe. I will get
something for your eye."

And so here at last, once more, Madeleine put aside the pathetic if
showy finery that for a time had adorned and shamed her: a twilled
skirt she had only recently bought in the pale hope of interesting *him*,
the commonplace little hat for which she had paid ten dollars, the
striped shirtwaist, once a pleasure to her in the hope that it would
please *him*.

In a kind of dumbness of despair she took off her shoes and stockings and, as the Mother left, entered the warm, clean bath which had
been provided. She stifled a sob as she did so, and others as she
bathed. Then she stepped out and dried her body and covered it with
the clean, simple slip of white which had been laid on a chair, brush-
ing her hair and touching her eye, until the Mother Sister returned
with an unguent wherewith to dress it.

Then she was led along other silent passages, once dreary enough
but now healing in their sense of peace and rest, and so into the great
room set with row upon row of simple white iron beds, covered with
their snowy linen and illuminated only by the minute red lamps or
the small candles burning before their idealistic images here and
there, beneath which so many like herself were sleeping. Over the
bed which she had once occupied, and which by chance was then
vacant, burned the one little lamp which she recognized as of old
—her lamp, as she had always thought of it—a thin and flickering
flame, before an image of the Virgin. At sight of it she repressed a sob.

"You see, my child," said the Mother Superior poetically, "it must
have been waiting for you. Anyhow it is empty. Perhaps it may have
known you were coming."

She spoke softly so that the long rows of sleepers might not be dis-
turbed, then proceeded to turn down the coverlets.

"Oh, Mother," Madeleine suddenly whispered softly as she stood
by the bed, "won't you let me stay always? I never want to go out
any more. I have had such a hard time. I will work so hard for you if
you will let me stay!"

The experienced Sister looked at her curiously. Never before had
she heard such a plea.

"Why, yes, my child," she said. "If you wish to stay I'm sure it can
be arranged. It is not as we usually do, but you are not the only one

who has gone out in the past and come back to us. I am sure God and the Blessed Virgin will hear your prayer for whatever is right. But now go to bed and sleep. You need rest. I can see that. And to-morrow, or any time, or never, as you choose you may tell me what has happened."

She urged her very gently to enter and then tucked the covers about her, laying finally a cool, wrinkled hand on her forehead. For answer Madeleine [51] seized and put it to her lips, holding it so.

"Oh, Mother," she sobbed as the Sister bent over her, "don't ever make me go out in the world again, will you? You won't, will you? I'm so tired! I'm so tired!"

"No dear, no," soothed the Sister, "not unless you wish it. And now rest. You need never go out into the world again unless you wish."

And withdrawing the hand from the kissing lips, she tiptoed silently from the room. [52]

Part III

AIDS AND TOPICS FOR WRITING

A. THEORY

Individual Theorists

➆ MALTHUS

1. *Key Terms*

> Power of population
> Power in the earth
> Ratio
>> geometric
>> arithmetic
>
> Nature's sparsity *vs.* Nature's liberality
> Law of nature: Necessity
> Animate Nature
>> waste, sickness, and death
>> misery and vice
>
> Supreme Being ("infinite power" that is "incomprehensible in idea")
> Providence
> Infinite variety of nature *vs.* undiversified perfection
> Creative process of the world
> Revelation (partial; complete)
> Exertion, activity

2. *Structural Questions*

> *a.* What are the two powers of nature that Malthus points out? Mathematically, what is the relation between them? Physically, what are the setting and process that keep these two powers contending within certain limits?
>
> *b.* What are the steps that lead Malthus in his argument from the starting point ". . . it seems absolutely necessary that we should reason from nature up to nature's God, and not presume to reason from God to nature" to the conclusion "Evil exists in the world, not to create

despair, but activity. We are not patiently to submit to it, but to exert ourselves to avoid it." What are the theological bases as opposed to the empirical bases of his argument? How significant are the concepts "instinct" and "reason" in his argument?

3. Comparative Questions

Concerning man's future, would you say that Malthus is pessimistic, Lyell optimistic? Or is it the other way around? Why? Are Malthus and Lyell both pessimistic (both optimistic?) but for different reasons?

⚛ LYELL

1. Key Terms

> Changing geography and climate
> Law of progressive development
> Special creation
> Modern origin of man
> Physical vs. moral superiority
> Argument from analogy
> Theory of eternal recurrence
> Supremacy of man
> Limitation of human cognition
> Creative intelligence
> Design vs. chance

2. Structural Questions

a. What scientific evidence has convinced Lyell of "a perfect harmony of design and unity of purpose" in the world throughout its existence?

b. What arguments does Lyell use to counter the objection that man's appearance on this earth is an exception to the law of progressive development; that once this law has been violated in the past, it can be expected to be violated in the future?

c. In general does this scientific treatise contain much, little, or no evidence that (1) man is justified in thinking of himself as an order above and apart from other mammals; (2) a correspondingly different destiny determines his actions on earth and state after death?

3. Comparative Questions

a. Relate Lyell's assertion that "we stand in a relation to contemporary species of animals and plants widely different from that which other irrational animals can ever be supposed to have held to each other" to Huxley's view on this distinction. Is the distinction that Lyell insists on an important one, philosophically speaking?

b. Show how, on the one hand, Malthus in his remarks tries to reconcile a Supreme Being which is at the same time a Providence with the misery and vice that man suffers under the powers of nature; and how, on the other hand, Lyell in his remarks tries to reconcile nature's uniformity with novelty in nature.

✎ MARX

1. Key Terms

Economic determinism
Proletariat
Bourgeoisie
Class exploitation
Social antagonisms
Capitalism
Phenomena
Primitive accumulation
Feudalism

2. Structural Questions

a. What degree of responsibility for his actions does Marx allow to man as an individual? For what reason?

b. To what extent does Force (in the form of economic evolution) determine the course of human events?

c. Formulate briefly Marx's theory of the evolution of society.

d. Does Marx consider the course of social evolution ontologically? That is, does it ever occur to him to explain—whether to justify or condemn—the definite laws he takes for granted in the evolution of societies? In short, is he ever philosopher as well as theorist and analyst?

3. *Comparative Questions*

a. Indicate the comparative complexity of Marx's theory of economic determinism as opposed to Malthus's. Do they both begin with the same premise?

b. In what sense is Marx's view of man scientific? Would it be accurate to say that in terms of "progressive development," he begins where Lyell leaves off? If so, show how.

c. Is Marx actually condemning Malthusian thinking in his sneer at "The Secret of Primitive Accumulation"?

☍ DARWIN

1. *Key Terms*

Variations from species

Natural selection (Survival of the Fittest)

Artificial selection

Co-adaptation

Interdependence

Growth with reproduction

Omniscient Creator

Predestination

Disuse of parts

Homology

2. *Structural Questions*

a. If variations (evidently resulting from the agency of nature) tend to favor an individual of a species, what does Darwin leave us to assume is the corresponding importance of individual effort (assuming that man is subject to the same laws as lower species)?

b. What far-reaching philosophical conclusion underlies Darwin's declarations that "Natural Selection includes no necessary and universal law of advancement or development" and that species have not undergone variation along necessarily beneficial lines?

c. Can you reconcile Darwin's later (1861, 1868) conclusions with his original pious wonder at the grandeur of creation, his worship of the "most beautiful and most wonderful" forms of life being evolved?

   d. What distinction does Darwin make between the social instincts of the lower animals and those of man?

   e. What is Darwin's 1874 stand on Design *vs.* Chance in the origin of species?

   f. By "survival of the fittest" does Darwin always mean of the *physically* fittest? Would you agree with Samuel Butler that he "banished mind from the universe"?

   g. Darwin found cause for both pride and concern at the realization that man had risen "to the very summit of the organic scale" *not through his own efforts.* To what extent were piety and scientific fact at war here, when Darwin was trying to find an analogy that would leave room for future improvement in the human condition?

3. *Comparative Questions*

   a. List characteristically Malthusian phraseology.

   b. Compare Darwin's view of the agency of Change with Malthus's.

   c. Compare Darwin's theory of the stages of evolution of animal species with Marx's theory of the evolution of society from economic causes. (Recall that Engels himself pointed out the analogy.)

❷ SPENCER

1. *Key Terms*

   Evolution

   Dissolution

   Persistence of force

   Unknown Reality

   Progressive adaptation

2. *Structural Questions*

   a. In interpreting all phenomena in terms of "Matter, Motion, and Force," what agency or agencies may Spencer be omitting?

   b. Why should Spencer have felt it necessary or advisable to defend himself against the charges of omniscience and materialism?

   c. The "closing words" of *First Principles* are possibly the most memorable ones in nineteenth-century philosophy (judging from the number of well-known thinkers who have testified from their own experience). Can you conjecture what it was about them that influenced people's thinking?

d. In Spencer's *Sociology* a kind of millenium awaits mankind in the form of a gradual debrutalization. Examine his grounds for this belief. Then defend or attack them. Are they consistent with his earlier conclusion (in *First Principles*)?

3. *Comparative Questions*

a. Show, first, how Spencer's explanation and defense of the evolution hypothesis is a combination of Malthusian piety and Darwinian biology; then, the degree of variation from—or actual contradiction of —both of these theorists.

b. What is the basic difference between Marx's theory of social evolution and Spencer's?

ಢ HUXLEY

1. *Key Terms*

Segmentation of egg

Structural affinity

a priori considerations

Divine intervention

2. *Structural Questions*

a. Trace the steps in Huxley's theory of the "great progression" in Nature.

b. What irony does Huxley see in the triumphs of man's intelligence? What paradox in man's relationship to lower forms of life?

c. What important traditional explanation of the cause of various events in the earth's history does Huxley refuse to allow?

3. *Comparative Questions*

a. Compare Huxley's early optimism with regard to the future of the human race with Spencer's and Darwin's.

b. Compare Huxley's later philosophical despair with Marx's scientific explanation of man's degradation.

🕸 TAINE

1. *Key Terms*

Primitive disposition
Primordial forces:
Race (*race*)
Surroundings (*milieu*)
Epoch (*moment*)

2. *Structural Questions*

a. Point out the basic scientific premise of Taine's theory of art.

b. Put the chain of causes leading to Protestant religious music in its proper chronological sequence.

c. List the various analogies from science in Taine's explanations of human behavior. What color does this accumulation give to Taine's over-all speculations?

d. List the various kinds of surroundings which influence human behavior.

e. Do the three Primordial Forces exhaust "the whole of the possible causes of motion," as Taine claims?

3. *Comparative Questions*

Does Taine's theory completely disregard or subsume the *differences* that the biologists (Darwin, Huxley) were pointing out between man and the lower forms of life (as well as the similarities)?

🕸 ZOLA

1. *Key Terms*

Science as observation
Science as experimentation
Natural phenomena
Determinism *vs.* Fatalism
Vitalism
Physiology

Heredity

Environment

2. *Structural Questions*

a. In one place Zola claims to be employed in the "noble work"—sociologically speaking—of regulating society, *etc.;* in another, he insists on being thought of as an experimentalist, rather than practitioner. Is there an inconsistency here?

b. Does Bernard (*i.e.,* Zola) attempt to disprove the arguments of the Vitalists methodically, or by mere disclaimer?

c. Follow through Bernard's analogy of "the science of life." Show how it—as well as the other Zola remarks—incline toward a belief on his part of a basic piety, or righteousness, of his profession as a novelist.

3. *Comparative Questions*

a. Relate Zola's basic concept of human conduct to Marx's; to Taine's.

b. Relate his ontological attitude toward life to Darwin's.

c. Can the distinction of determinism (as opposed to fatalism) be made to include Malthus's philosophy?

❦ SCHOPENHAUER

1. *Key Terms*

Propagation of the species

Sex

Will to live

Passionate *vs.* rational choice

?. *Structural Questions*

a. In what sense is Schopenhauer's concept of sexual determinism depressing to the spirit? In what sense, ideal?

b. Nietzsche later said of Schopenhauer that this part of his philosophy, (the book's emphasis on the erotic), written when he was young, betrayed his youthfulness. From what you can observe, is mere youth speaking or are the facts speaking, scientifically arrived at?

3. Comparative Questions

a. There is a strikingly similar absolutism about Schopenhauer's explanation of human conduct and the essentially unrelated explanation of Marx's. Elaborate this similarity.

b. Compare Schopenhauer's scientific analogy between chemistry and human conduct with Taine's. Have these men been led to their conclusions from scientific observation?

c. Compare Schopenhauer and Darwin on the question of similarity of human behavior with brute behavior.

GENERAL

From the source materials presented in Part I try to arrive at an extended definition of Naturalism, making room for variations and possible inconsistencies, and considering the possible influence of one point of view on another. In order to pursue this aim thoroughly, it will be valuable to compare the views on man and his place in nature in this philosophy with those expounded in such contrasting writings as:

a. Shakespeare   *Hamlet*
b. Alexander Pope   *Essay on Man*
c. Alfred Tennyson   "Locksley Hall"
                                    "The Higher Pantheism"
                                    "To an Evolutionist"
d. Robert Browning   "Rabbi Ben Ezra"
                                    "Caliban Upon Setebos"
e. R. W. Emerson   "Nature"
                                    "Ode Inscribed to W. H. Channing"
                                    "The Over-Soul"
f. R. L. Stevenson   "Pulvis et Umbra"

B. PRACTICE

Individual Authors

❧ MELVILLE

1. *Short Papers*

    a. May Melville be considered a naturalist?

    b. Is it at all possible that in this chapter Melville was approaching a concept of *Super*naturalism (occasionally defined as the *opposite* of Naturalism)?

    c. What purpose, if any, is served by offering the views in this chapter in the form of questions?

2. *Long Papers*

Read the whole of *Moby-Dick*. Is the book as a whole naturalistic? Try to identify the point of view as you go, noting whether it is Ishmael's, Ahab's, or Melville's. Does a consistent attitude toward nature emerge?

❧ GARLAND

1. *Short Papers*

    a. Would you call Garland a naturalist? (You should know that not only is the case for Naturalism in the early Garland a disputed one, but that in later years Garland wrote extremely "romantic" fiction.) Keep in mind not only the protagonist's final fate and his earlier history but those of all the other characters in the story.

    b. Is "Under the Lion's Paw" drama or melodrama? (Here again are terms that require careful use.)

2. *Long Papers*

"The Economic Man": Consider "Under the Lion's Paw," Norris's "A Deal in Wheat," and Dreiser's *The Financier* as a group of stories illustrating the condition of man in society as it is determined by economic forces. Does he appear as victim or victor? Are the forces complex or simple? Arbitrary or inevitable?

ஐ CRANE

1. *Short Papers*

a. Would you call Crane's work naturalistic in the sense of the Zola formula? Does Zola provide for situations such as those in "The Open Boat" and "God Is Cold"?

b. *Maggie* is about a slum family; "The Open Boat," about some men in a boat. What do they have in common as regards Crane's attitude toward them, and the reasons for that attitude? Together what force do they have as a philosophical indictment?

2. *Long Papers*

"Naturalism in *Maggie*": Read all of *Maggie*. To what extent do the other sections of this novel support the impression created by Chapters III–V? Are *all* the descriptive details and characterization employed for the purpose of supporting that impression?

ஐ LONDON

1. *Short Papers*

a. What kind of Naturalism does London subscribe to?

b. Compare London's concept of Whiteness with Melville's.

ஐ NORRIS

1. *Short Papers*

a. To what extent is Norris a naturalist?

b. Compare these selections from *The Octopus* with its "Conclusion." What total picture of man in nature do they give?

c. Compare the importance of man as seen here with that in "Under the Lion's Paw."

    d. Compare the McTeague-Trina relationship with the Drouet-Carrie relationship in Dreiser's *Sister Carrie.*

2. *Long Papers*

    a. "Doctrine and Practice in *The Octopus*": Read the rest of *The Octopus.* You will find in it actual references to some of the doctrines in Part I of this volume. What *use* is actually made of these doctrines in the novel?

    b. "Taine, Zola, and *McTeague*": Read the rest of *The Octopus.* Is there any apparent kinship between the concept of human personality here and in Taine and Zola?

ॐ DREISER

1. *Short Papers*

    a. Give a definition of man as Dreiser sees him. Is it a naturalistic one? What corollary definition of morality emerges?

    b. Is Berchansky less responsible for his actions than Madeleine?

    c. Is there anything in Madeleine's characterization that was lacking in Carrie's?

    d. Illustrate Zola's and Taine's theories from "Sanctuary."

    e. Compare Dreiser's final ("harp in the wind") reflections in *Sister Carrie* with the following of Schopenhauer:

    "Now the nature of man consists in this, that his will strives, is satisfied and strives anew, and so on for ever. Indeed, his happiness and well-being consist simply in the quick transition from wish to satisfaction, and from satisfaction to a new wish. For the absence of satisfaction is suffering, the empty longing for a new wish, languor, *ennui.*"

2. *Long Papers*

    a. "Sister Carrie: The Vocation of Desire." Read all of *Sister Carrie.* What is the psychological mechanism that Dreiser uses to propel Carrie Meeber on her quest for "happiness," and how do you see this mechanism at work in Carrie's relations with Drouet, Hurstwood, and Ames, as well as with Mrs. Hale and Mrs. Vance? Why is Carrie doomed in Dreiser's view to fail in her quest at the very moments she appears to have succeeded? Whose portrait is more memorable for you, Carrie's or Hurstwood's? Why?

b. "George W. Hurstwood: The Way of the Beaten." Read all of *Sister Carrie*. What is the psychological mechanism at work in George W. Hurstwood, the "liberal, opulent manager" of Fitzgerald and Moy's, which leads him to become a nameless suicide in a Bowery flophouse? Account carefully for the causes that force Hurstwood down each step of the "ladder." Whose portrait is more memorable for you, Carrie's or Hurstwood's? Why?

GENERAL

1. In III, A GENERAL (p. 189) you were asked to consider Naturalism as a *philosophy*. Now try to determine the extent to which Naturalism utilizes or requires a *technique* of composition. In order for your findings to have weight, they will have to take into consideration all of the selections in Part II. (Incidentally, you may find it useful here to read Edmund Wilson's analysis of Symbolism in *Axel's Castle*, as well as Malcolm Cowley's commentary on this analysis in *Exile's Return*—both books now available in paperback reprint.)

2. "The Male in Naturalistic Fiction": Is it possible to generalize about the naturalists' philosophy from their treatment of the various males included in the selections in this volume?

3. "Woman in Naturalistic Fiction": Study the treatment of Maggie, Trina, Carrie, and Madeleine. Is there any consistency in their characterization and fate, suggesting a philosophical kinship among their creators?

Part IV

TOPICS FOR FURTHER WRITING

A. THEORY

Individual Theorists

❀ MALTHUS

Compare Malthus's view of the function of nature with Jeremy Bentham, *Introduction to the Principles of Morals and Legislation* (1789), *e.g.*, Ch. I.

❀ LYELL

Write a brief account on the extent to which Lyell's findings are related to Bishop William Colenso, *The Pentateuch and Book of Joshua Critically Examined* (1863).

❀ MARX

1. Compare Marx's interpretation of the outcome of the free private enterprise system with that of:

   a. Adam Smith, *Inquiry into the Nature and Causes of the Wealth of Nations* (1776), *e.g.*, Bks. I, III.

   b. David Ricardo, *Principles of Political Economy and Taxation* (1817), *e.g.*, Ch. V.

2. Compare Marx's "Genesis of the Industrialist Capitalist" with Gletkin's lecture to Rubashov in Arthur Koestler, *Darkness at Noon*.

❀ DARWIN

Write an essay on Darwin and W. Somerset Maugham's *Of Human Bondage*.

❧ SPENCER

1. In "Books That Changed the World," Professor Eric F. Goldman gives prominent mention to Spencer. If Spencer's generation had derived its concept of man from Scripture, what might it have considered most striking in his theories? In answering this question, you should consult representative passages from Scripture, such as Isaiah, 40, 42, 55; I Corinthians, 15.

2. Compare Spencer and John Stuart Mill, "Nature," (in *Three Essays on Religion*, 1874).

3. Discuss briefly the connection between Spencer and Sidney Lanier, *The English Novel*.

❧ HUXLEY

Compare "Agnosticism" and Henry Adams, *The Education of Henry Adams*.

❧ TAINE

In the epigraph for his novel *A Mummer's Wife* (1885), the writer George Moore declared: "Change the surroundings in which man lives, and in two or three generations, you will have changed his physical constitution, his habits of life, and a goodly number of his ideas." To what extent does this theory match Taine's? What bearing does it have on *A Mummer's Wife* itself?

❧ ZOLA

1. Zola's *L'Assommoir* is usually looked upon as the literary application of the theories expressed in *The Experimental Novel*. Investigate this relationship. Why might Chapter Six have been termed a "classic document of Naturalism"?

2. Zola's *Germinal* invites comparison with both Darwin and Marx. In an extended essay, advance your own opinion of their relationship.

3. Try to determine why Guy de Maupassant's preface to his *Pierre et Jean* ("Le Roman," 1885) has been linked recently with Zola's *Experimental Novel* as "the two classic statements of Naturalism."

✷ SCHOPENHAUER

Compare Schopenhauer's concept of man's individual importance with Tennyson, *In Memoriam* (Sections 54–56) and "The Passing of Arthur."

OTHER THEORISTS

Below is a partial list of prominent philosophers of recent years whose thinking shows varying degrees of conformity with the philosophy of Naturalism or of opposition to it. Take any one of these men for further study and write an essay establishing his position with regard to Naturalism.

a.	John Dewey	*Experience and Nature*
		Human Nature and Conduct
		The Quest for Certainty
b.	W. G. Sumner	*The Challenge of Facts*
		Science of Society
		What Social Classes Owe to Each Other
c.	Bertrand Russell	*A Free Man's Worship*
d.	Lester Ward	*The Psychic Factors of Civilization*
e.	F. J. E. Woodbridge	*An Essay on Nature*

B. PRACTICE

Individual Authors

✷ MELVILLE

1. Read Melville's verse, especially *Clarel*. Is this the same Melville, philosophically speaking?
2. Compare Melville's concept of nature with James Fenimore Cooper's in *The Pathfinder*, or any other of the Leatherstocking series.

3. From a reading of Thoreau's "Spring" (in *Walden*) and Melville's "The Funeral" (in *Moby-Dick*), write an essay on "The Vulture and Naturalism."

4. Compare Melville's "Whiteness" with Thomas Mann's in *The Magic Mountain* (Chapter VI).

5. Compare Melville's "Whiteness" with Edgar Allan Poe's in *Narrative of Arthur Gordon Pym* (Chapter XXV).

6. Compare Melville's "Whiteness" with Robert Frost's in "Desert Places" and "Onset."

❦ GARLAND

1. Read the other stories in *Main-Travelled Roads;* some of Garland's literary criticism, in *Crumbling Idols* (called a "manifesto" of American Naturalism); and part of his autobiography, in *A Son of the Middle Border*. What was Garland trying to do in fiction, and how well did he succeed?

2. Compare man's condition in *Main-Travelled Roads* with that in
   a. Erskine Caldwell   *Tobacco Road*
   b. John Steinbeck   *The Grapes of Wrath.*

❦ CRANE

1. Compare *Maggie* as Naturalism with George Moore, *Esther Waters*. Which of the characterizations is more convincing? Which of the endings is more satisfactory?

2. Compare "The Open Boat" as Naturalism with other Crane stories:
   a. "The Blue Hotel"
   b. "A Man—and Some Others"
   c. "An Experiment in Misery"

3. Read three or four classic nineteenth-century poetic statements about nature and man's place in nature, such as:
   a. Wordsworth   "The Tables Turned"
                        "The Tintern Abbey Ode"
   b. Coleridge   "Dejection: An Ode"
   c. Fitzgerald   "The Rubaiyat"
   d. Tennyson   "The Song of the Brook"
                        "Flower in the Crannied Wall."

Add Crane's verse to theirs. What consistency or variety of moods and attitudes towards nature emerges from this random group of poems?

❧ LONDON

1. Read Charmian London, *The Book of Jack London* (especially Volume I). Then read *Martin Eden,* London's fictional autobiography (recently reissued by Rinehart & Co.). What do these sources add to the concept of nature presented in "The White Silence"?

2. Compare "The White Silence" with other London stories such as:
    a. "To Build a Fire"
    b. "When God Laughs"

❧ NORRIS

1. Confirm or qualify the opinion you have formed of Norris as a naturalist by reading his *Vandover and the Brute* and *Moran of the Lady Letty.*

2. Relate Norris's "The Novel with a Purpose" (in *The Responsibilities of the Novelist*) to the theories of human personality expressed in *McTeague.*

3. Professor Richard Chase has pointed out the opposite effects of the endings of *Moby-Dick* and *The Octopus.* From a reading of both novels, determine the difference between these two authors' fundamental beliefs in the comparative importance of man and nature.

❧ DREISER

1. What opinion of man does Dreiser express in
    a. *A History of Myself* (*Dawn; Newspaper Days*)
    b. *Hey Rub-a-dub-dub*

and how does it compare with his opinion expressed in the passages included in Part II here? Compare Dreiser's position, as expressed in Part II and in the references above, with that of the theorists in Part I.

2. Compare Carrie Meeber's moral responsibility with that of
    a. Isabel Archer in Henry James, *Portrait of a Lady*
    b. Tess Durbeyfield in Thomas Hardy, *Tess of the Durbervilles.*

3. Compare Cowperwood's reflections on life as a teenager with those of the young Lieutenant Frederick Henry in Ernest Hemingway, *A Farewell to Arms*. Show in detail how Lt. Henry's reflections in Chapter XXXIV ("That night at the hotel . . .") are related most closely to the structure of events in *A Farewell to Arms*.

4. Compare Dreiser's sentiments about individual responsibility in *The Financier* with those expressed in its sequel, *The Titan*.

OTHER AUTHORS

Below is a partial list of foreign and native writers whose fiction (or verse) has been considered naturalistic. Take any one for further study and write an essay determining the extent to which this judgment is just. (Since several of them were, or are, prolific writers, you will want to be guided by your instructor's advice in limiting the scope of your research.)

Nelson Algren	E. M. Forster
Benjamin Appel	Harold Frederic
Matthew Arnold	Thomas Hardy
Erskine Caldwell	Ernest Hemingway
Robert Cantwell	Edgar W. Howe
Joseph Conrad	Aldous Huxley
Edward Dahlberg	Robinson Jeffers
John Dos Passos	John O'Hara
James T. Farrell	John Steinbeck
William Faulkner	Mark Twain (S. L. Clemens)

Richard Wright

BIBLIOGRAPHY

Ahnebrink, Lars, *The Beginnings of Naturalism in American Fiction*, Uppsala, Lundequistska Bokhandeln, and Cambridge, Harvard University Press, 1950.

Allen, Walter, *The English Novel*, New York, E. P. Dutton & Co., Inc., 1957.

Becker, George J., "Realism: An Essay in Definition," *Modern Language Quarterly*, X (June, 1949).

Cargill, Oscar, *Intellectual America*, New York, The Macmillan Company, 1941.

Chase, Richard, *The American Novel and its Tradition*, New York, Doubleday & Co., Inc., 1957.

Commager, Henry S., *The American Mind*, New Haven, Yale University Press, 1950.

Cowley, Malcolm, "'Not Men': A Natural History of American Naturalism," *Kenyon Review*, IX (Summer, 1947).

Curti, Merle, *The Growth of American Thought*, New York, Harper & Bros., 1943.

Farrell, James T., *Reflections at Fifty*, New York, Vanguard Press, 1954.

Gosse, Edmund, *Father and Son*, New York, Charles Scribner's Sons, 1908.

Hartwick, Harry, *The Foreground of American Fiction*, New York, American Book Co., 1934.

Hofstadter, Richard, *Social Darwinism in American Thought*, Philadelphia, University of Pennsylvania Press, 1944.

Horton, Rod W. and Herbert W. Edwards, *Backgrounds of American Literary Thought*, New York, Appleton-Century-Crofts, Inc., 1952.

Jones, A. E., Jr., "Darwinism and . . . American Fiction, 1860–1890," *Drew University Bulletin*, XXXVIII (December, 1950).

Josephson, Matthew, *Zola and His Times*, New York, The Macaulay Co., 1928.

Kazin, Alfred, *On Native Grounds*, New York, Reynal & Hitchcock, 1942.

Kennedy, Gail (ed.), *Evolution and Religion*, Boston, D. C. Heath & Co., 1957.

Loewenberg, Bert J., "Darwinism Comes to America, 1859–1900," *Mississippi Valley Historical Review*, XXVIII (December, 1941).

Meyer, George W., "The Original Social Purpose of the Naturalistic Novel," *Sewanee Review,* L (October, 1942).

Miller, Perry, *American Thought,* New York, Rinehart & Co., Inc., 1954.

Parrington, Vernon L., *Main Currents in American Thought,* New York, Harcourt, Brace and Company, 1930; Vol. III.

Persons, Stow (ed.), *Evolutionary Thought in America,* New Haven, Yale University Press, 1950.

Rahv, Philip, *Image and Idea,* New York, New Directions Press, 1949.

Smith, L. W., "The Drift toward Naturalism," *South Atlantic Quarterly,* XXII (October, 1923).

Spiller, Robert E., *et al.* (eds.), *Literary History of the United States,* New York, The Macmillan Company, 1948; Vols. II, III.

Walcutt, Charles C., *American Literary Naturalism, A Divided Stream,* Minneapolis, University of Minnesota Press, 1956.